# Gaslighting, the Double Whammy, Interrogation, and Other Methods of Covert Control in Psychotherapy and Analysis

# Gaslighting, the Double Whammy, Interrogation, and Other Methods of Covert Control in Psychotherapy and Analysis

THEO. L. DORPAT, M.D.

JASON ARONSON INC.
*Northvale, New Jersey*
*London*

This book was set in 11 pt. Berkeley Book by Alpha Graphics of Pittsfield, New Hampshire, and printed and bound by Book-mart of North Bergen, New Jersey.

**Library of Congress Cataloging-in-Publication Data**

Dorpat, Theodore L.
  Gaslighting, the double whammy, interrogation, and other methods of covert control in psychotherapy and analysis / Theo. L. Dorpat.
    p.  cm.
  Includes bibliographical references and index.
  ISBN 1-56821-828-1 (alk. paper)
  1. Psychoanalysis—Moral and ethical aspects.  2. Control (Psychology)  3. Psychotherapist and patient—Moral and ethical aspects.  4. Mental suggestion—Moral and ethical aspects.
  5. Brainwashing.  6. Manipulative behavior.  I. Title.
  [DNLM:  1. Power (Psychology)  2. Psychotherapy.
  3. Psychoanalysis—methods.  WM 420 D715i 1996]
  RC506.D668  1996
  616.89'14—dc20
  DNLM/DLC
  for Library of Congress                                    96-14098

Manufactured in the United States of America. Jason Aronson Inc. offers books and cassettes. For information and catalog write to Jason Aronson Inc., 230 Livingston Street, Northvale, New Jersey 07647.

*To my wife, Doris,*
*and my daughter, Joanne Halverson,*
*gratefully.*

For those who stubbornly seek freedom, there can be no more urgent task than to come to understand the mechanisms and practices of indoctrination. These are easy to perceive in the totalitarian societies, much less so in the system of "brainwashing under freedom" to which we are subjected and which all too often we serve as willing or unwitting instruments.

Noam Chomsky, 1987

# Contents

**Part III**
**Remedies and Correctives**

# Acknowledgments

I would like to express my appreciation and gratitude to the following colleagues who provided me with valuable criticisms and recommendations for the preparation of this manuscript: Dr. Maxine Anderson, Dr. Katalina Bartok, Dr. Robert Bergman, Dr. Austin Case, Dr. Margaret Crastnopol, Dr. Raelene Gold, Dr. Mel Knight, Dr. Robert Langs, Dr. Stanley S. Mandell, Dr. Karol Marshall, Dr. Paul Ornstein, Dr. James Raney, Dr. David Rowlett, Dr. Robert Stolorow, Dr. Max Sucharov, and above all, Dr. Michael Miller, who carefully checked the entire manuscript.

I am especially grateful to Ms. Jean Keating for editing and preparing the manuscript.

# Introduction and Overview

My overall aim in this book is to write about a widespread and serious malady in the way many clinicians conduct psychotherapy. I believe this unrecognized disorder has been present throughout this century and that it is widely prevalent in this country and elsewhere. There are two chief symptoms or manifestations of this disorder and they are (1) the clinician frequently uses methods of indoctrination for the purpose of controlling and directing the patient, and (2) the clinician is unaware because of ignorance and/or denial of the fact that he or she uses such indoctrination methods and their short-term and long-term effects on patients. More often than not, patients are also not aware of the use of these methods or of their effects on themselves.

My purposes are to describe and discuss this hidden disorder as well as its multiple manifestations, signs, and symptoms, and I shall illustrate my arguments with vignettes and case studies. Also, I present some hypotheses and speculations about its different causes.

A major part of this book is taken up with a study of eleven psychoanalytic and psychotherapy treatment cases in which the use of indoctrination methods either caused treatment failure or greatly impaired the therapeutic process. Psychotherapy or psychoanalytic cases that have failed are seldom talked about or written about. The fields of psychotherapy and psychoanalysis have something immensely important to learn from the examination of cases that have failed, or in which the process and progress of the patient have been adversely affected by the use of indoctrination methods. A recent panel (Nuetzel 1993) at a meeting of the American Psychoanalytic Association concluded that case reports of failed treatment could teach us at least as much as reports of successful treatment.

The sexual seduction and overt abuse of patients by some practitioners is only the visible tip of the iceberg of the widely prevalent abuse of power by mental health professionals. The more gross kinds of patient abuse, such as financial or overtly sexual exploitation, are expressly forbidden by rules and bylaws in medical, psychotherapy, and psychoanalytic organizations. Both in Freud's time and in our own time, however, there are few laws or regulations set down to discourage the more subtle and covert forms of interpersonal control, exploitation, and abuse. The use of more covert methods of interpersonal control and other indoctrination methods is not even considered abnormal or exploitative by many clinicians.

Occasions when practitioners are *overtly* cruel, abusive, demeaning, or in other ways directly hurtful to patients are most uncommon and such actions among mental health professionals are universally proscribed and condemned.

This is not so with the less obvious kinds of controlling, directive, and *covertly* abusive communications by clinicians which I aim to describe and discuss in this book. Though (unlike some other types of psychotherapy) psychoanalysis specifically proscribes the use of directive and controlling methods and the varied forms of indoctrination, their use is nevertheless widespread in psychoanalytic treatment. For the purposes of this book, I use the term *psychoanalytic treatment* to refer both to psychoanalytic psychotherapy and psychoanalysis.

From Freud on to the present time, psychoanalytic treatment has often been compromised by a set of controlling attitudes and indoctrination methods contrary to its avowed values and technical precepts. My studies suggest there exists among many, perhaps most, practitioners a complex of disavowed aims, strategies, and actions carried out for the most part unconsciously in the interests of directing and dominating their patients.

Because these actions are basically the same as the ways individuals in nontreatment situations control and indoctrinate others, I have used the general term *indoctrination methods* to refer to all of the ways clinicians control, direct, and manipulate patients.

For the purposes of this study, I have coined the term *covert methods of interpersonal control* to refer to a subclass of indoctrination methods. The tactics and methods of covert interpersonal control include different types of projective identification wherein individuals, through various kinds of interpersonal manipulation, exert control over the cognitions, affects, and overt behaviors of others. My definition of covert methods of interpersonal control specifically excludes overt and explicit communications or concrete actions of control and abuse such as threats of violence, rage, tantrums, denunciations, and other openly hostile actions taken by individuals to dominate and/or shame other persons.

The use of covert methods of interpersonal control, and other indirect as well as direct methods of indoctrination, is far more common in nonpsychoanalytic therapies than it is in the psychoanalytic therapies where it is explicitly proscribed. Many schools of psychotherapy are avowedly directive. Behavior therapy, for example, employs rewards and punishments for controlling and shaping patients' behaviors. Except for the few older surviving followers of the non-directive methods of Carl Rogers, the majority of mental health practitioners in private practice today deliberately employ directive and manipulative methods to shape and control the behaviors and cognitions of their patients. Mental health practitioners in the United States are increasingly becoming engineers of the soul, what with the impressive and powerful array of biological, social, and psychological modalities they have available for manipulating the minds as well as the brains of their patients.

Where do these indoctrination methods come from and where do mental health professionals learn them? In part, they learn them in their professional training programs, in their psychiatric residencies, and in psychoanalytic institutions mainly through identifying with the practitioners who educate, supervise, and treat them. Today, the trend toward the use of indoctrination methods has been amplified by the markedly diminished time in psychiatric training specifically set aside for learning psychoanalytic psychotherapy. The increasing emphasis placed on the use of manipulative, short-term, and directive methods in the training institutions for mental health professionals (psychiatry, psychology, nursing, social work) has contributed toward the increased employment of indoctrination methods among mental health practitioners.

In my opinion, some of the most important causes for the use of indoctrination methods in psychotherapy and psychoanalytic treatment are social and cultural. Practitioners, like nearly everyone else in Western cultures, learn these ways of communicating and relating early in life in their families, schools, and other social groups and more often than not they continue to do so throughout their lives with their patients as well as others.

My first clinical studies on the use of covert methods of interpersonal control in psychotherapy and psychoanalysis were concerned with the effects of the clinician's use of questioning on the patient and the treatment process (Dorpat 1984, 1991a). My clinical investigation led me to conclude that questioning was frequently prompted by unconscious countertransference problems and was often used in behalf of directing and controlling patients. More often than not, questioning has a stultifying and inhibitive effect on the treatment process.

Later, my clinical observations on the use of indoctrination methods derived from the following sources: (1) a critical review of Freud's classic case studies, including especially Dora and the

Wolf Man, as well as the extensive literature about them, (2) an investigation of other published analytic case studies such as, for example, Kohut's "The two analyses of Mr. Z.", (3) psychotherapy and psychoanalytic cases whose treatment I supervised, and (4) patients I treated in psychoanalysis or psychoanalytic psychotherapy, whose previous therapists had used indoctrination methods. The formulations and conclusions I have reached about the use of indoctrination methods came mainly from my studies of these four types of clinical data.

I have been supervising and teaching psychoanalytic and psychotherapy treatment for over 35 years, and each year in my individual and group supervision sessions, I hear about approximately 100 patients in some kind of psychotherapy or psychoanalysis. I am completely confident of my opinion that the use of covert methods of interpersonal control and other indoctrination methods is (1) widely prevalent among clincans, and (2) most practitioners, and especially those who use such approaches, are unaware of their significance or their effects. In the approximately 100 cases I hear about each year, I estimate that in 40 percent there is the mild and occasional use of indoctrination methods, and in another 40 percent there is a moderate employment of such methods. In a third group of around 10–20 percent, there is a very serious and destructive use of such methods. Three of the eleven cases presented in this volume are in this latter serious category, and the patients involved suffered from chronic and severe mental and emotional impairments caused by the destructive treatment they received.

## STEREOTYPED VERSUS HEURISTIC APPROACHES TO PSYCHOANALYSIS

For his enlightened concepts about the psychoanalytic process, I am deeply indebted to Peterfreund (1983), whose book writes about how *stereotyped* approaches and strategies bring about a process of indoctrination rather than a truly psychoanalytic process of discovery and personal growth for the patient. The over-riding goal of stereotyped approaches is to fit the case into the clinical theory that forms the basis for the analyst's initial formulation about the patients. In contrast to stereotyped approaches, the fundamental aim in what Peterfreund (1983) calls *heuristic* approaches is to initiate and foster a process whereby patient and therapist work together to understand as much as possible about the patient and his or her interactions with others. Some of the stereotyped approaches he mentions include "the psychoanalytic process is viewed as an attempt to get the patient to understand the [analyst's] initial formulation," "the patient's failure to understand the analyst or to accept what he says is viewed as resistance," "the issue of evidence is of little importance" and several more. (The entire list of Nine Stereotyped Approaches described by Peterfreund (1983) may be found in Chapter 11.)

This investigation strongly supports what Peterfreund said about the relationship between the use of stereotyped approaches and an indoctrination process. All of the ten clinicians who used indoctrination methods and whose treatment of their cases is described in Part II of this book also employed the stereotyped approaches and strategies described first by Peterfreund (1983).

Though the use of indoctrination methods and the use of stereotyped approaches are both important causes of failure of psychotherapy and psychoanalytic treatment and the formation of a process of indoctrination, this book's primary focus is on indoctrination methods and especially on covert methods of interpersonal control.

For nearly two decades, I have become increasingly alarmed both by the widespread prevalence of the use of indoctrination methods by psychoanalysts and by psychotherapists, as well as by the unawareness on the part of both clinicians and patients about these methods and their harmful effects. Because (except for Peterfreund's [1983] contributions) I could not find much about this problem in the psychoanalytic and psychotherapy literature, I turned to the literature in several other fields, including linguistics, feminist studies, and the Marxist literature. For more knowledge about indoctrination methods, I also reviewed the scientific literature on the use of mind-control, indoctrination methods, and brainwashing methods used in totalitarian countries and in cults.

The review of this literature on this subject yielded a rich harvest of facts and theories which proved helpful to me in formulating my ideas. In this book I have cited and summarized these studies to further illuminate the psychosocial dynamics regarding the use of indoctrination methods in psychotherapy and psychoanalytic treatment situations as well as in everyday life. Two important conclusions coming from my readings of the literature on mind-control and indoctrination methods are similar to the ones I mentioned above about the occurrence of methods of indoctrination in psychoanalytic treatment.

First, the employment of covert methods of interpersonal control and other subtle methods for abusing, controlling, and intimidating other persons is common in everyday life and such methods are used intensively and extensively in special situations such as in cults. Secondly, in everyday life more often than not both victims and victimizers are unaware of the nature and psychic effects of these directive and abusive methods of communicating and relating. This is not so in cults or in totalitarian societies where the same or similar methods are used, but because the victimizers employ them deliberately and systematically, they have much more powerful and devastating psychiatric effects on the victims.

I want to clearly mark and emphasize the boundaries of my investigation. With few exceptions, my purpose is to examine and discuss the use of *covert not overt* methods of interpersonal control. I propose to describe, and in some ways to explain, the subtle and indirect ways clinicians communicate demeaning, directive, and abusive messages to their patients. I also aim to examine the interactional dynamics and unconscious communications occurring in psychotherapy and psychoanalytic dyads where these methods are used, as well as the short- and long-term psychic effects on patients.

## FROM OVERT AUTHORITY TO COVERT METHODS OF INTERPERSONAL CONTROL

The ways individuals in Western cultures typically attempt to control and dominate others has changed in the past several centuries. With the rise of the democracies and the dethronement and disempowering of previously powerful groups such as the military, the nobility, and the like, there has been a gradual shift from the conscious and explicit use of direct methods of interpersonal and social control to ones that are more indirect, subtle, and covert.

During the eighteenth century in Western societies, the ideals of freedom, democracy, and self-determination were extolled both by philosophers as well as the uneducated masses. One basic change in the institutions of Western societies arising out of this was the replacement of overt authority by some measure of freedom from external oppression.

Except in totalitarian dictatorships, authoritarianism, whether in government, in schools, in medicine, or wherever is no longer a conscious ideal among most people. However, the tendency of many humans to seek power and control over others did not disappear when authoritarianism was rejected or at least modified in many social institutions, including the family and the profession of psychotherapy.

What happened was that in many areas of our communal life, in families as well as in education, medicine, and elsewhere, the frank use of overt authority (except for a few situations such as law enforcement, the penal system, and the military) disappeared and was replaced by covert methods of interpersonal control.

Overt authority is carried out directly and explicitly, and it uses force or threats of force and punishment for interpersonal and social control. In contrast, communications containing covert methods of interpersonal control are indirect. Commonly, both the subject as well as the object of such indirect and subtle coercive messages are unaware of the controlling and directive quality of their communications, or its psychic effects on the recipients.

Fromm (1960) has described the shift from overt to covert authority in this way:

> It is not that authority has disappeared, nor even that it has lost in strength, but that it has been transformed from the overt authority of force to the anonymous authority of persuasion and suggestion . . . in order to be adaptable, modern man is obliged to nourish the illusion that everything is done with his consent, even though such consent be extracted from him by subtle manipulation [p. xi].

Freud and the psychoanalytic movement made an important contribution to psychiatry and psychotherapy in the transition from overt authority to covert authority. What happened in the general culture in Western societies also occurred in the development of psychoanalysis and other forms of psychotherapy. Values of personal freedom and self-determination were important to Freud personally and in his work with patients (Dorpat 1987a). Through his example and his writings, psychoanalysis took a long step away from the *overt* authoritarian attitudes previously embedded in practices of psychiatry and psychotherapy.

Freud's encouragement of the patient's capacity for self-determination in the face of the authoritarian rigidity of nineteenth-century psychiatry has disguised the more covert and subtle control he, and later many other psychoanalysts, have exercised over their patients.

Though the ideals and principles of freedom and self-determination were ones Freud repeatedly espoused for himself and others, my investigations on the ways he related to his patients (particularly Dora and the Wolf Man) demonstrate his continued use of covert methods of interpersonal control as well as other indoctrination tactics.

In Freud, I surmise, as with many other analysts following him, there developed a vertical split in the ego in which one complex of conscious attitudes upholding values of freedom, autonomy, and self-determination was separated by the defense of disavowal from a largely unconscious complex of controlling and authoritarian attitudes contradictory to his consciously avowed values.

As I shall later discuss in Chapters 6 and 7, Freud's need for power and control over his patients, and to some extent also his followers, was sufficiently strong that it prevailed irrespective of what he said in his discussion of technique and theory. Perhaps this is an instance of what Freud himself referred to as a "return of the repressed."

As shown in the following passage, Freud (1937a) apparently was unaware of his use of suggestion when he wrote:

> The danger of our leading a patient astray by suggestions, by persuading him to accept things which we ourselves believe, but he should not accept, has certainly been greatly exaggerated. The analyst would have behaved very incorrectly if such a misfortune had happened to him: above all, he would have to blame himself for not allowing the patient to have his say. *I can assert without boasting that such an abuse of suggestion has never occurred in my practice* [p. 262, italics added].

By means of a close examination of Freud's writings, the French psychoanalyst Roustang (1983) shows that Freud did, in fact, rely on the power of suggestion, but he was exceedingly adept at concealing this fact from himself and his readers.

As I indicate in Chapters 6 and 7 on the Dora and Wolf Man cases, Freud made repeated and extensive use of covert methods of interpersonal control in cases he analyzed before the end of World War I. There is some evidence from an investigation made by Linn (1994) that Freud often was directive with his patients from the beginning to the end of his career. By an examination of a variety of different records, letters, and books written by Freud as well as by his patients, Linn was able to elucidate how Freud conducted the analyses of forty-two patients. In 83 percent of forty-two patients, Freud was often directive. The actual percent is probably higher because Linn was unable to obtain information about this variable in the other 17 percent. In his report, Linn emphasizes that Freud was often self-revealing, expressive, and directive with his patients in ways that were clearly contrary to the recommendations he had made in his writings.

## AN OVERVIEW OF THE BOOK

The book is divided into three parts. Part I is titled Covert Methods of Interpersonal Control and Other Indoctrination Methods and is concerned with the description and phenomenology of the various types of covert methods of interpersonal control. Part II is called Studies of Psychotherapy and Psychoanalytic Treatment Cases Subjected to Indoctrination Methods, and it is mainly devoted to a study of eleven cases. Using an interactional perspective, I describe the conscious and unconscious communicative interactions between the clinicians and patients occurring in these treatments, as well as the short-term and long-term effects on the patients. Part III is entitled Remedies and Correctives, and it presents some basic principles derived mainly from contemporary schools of psychoanalysis which have been found helpful for facilitating a non-directive, egalitarian ambience and attitude in psychotherapy and psychoanalytic treatment.

Chapter 1 describes and illustrates with vignettes the various kinds of covert methods of interpersonal control used in psychotherapy and psychoanalytic treatment.

In Chapter 2, I describe and discuss different forms of gaslighting used in therapy as well as in everyday life. With a few exceptions, such as in cults, gaslighting techniques in psychotherapy and psychoanalytic contexts, as well as in everyday life, are carried out unconsciously by the perpetrators. Gaslighting, broadly defined, is one of the most important approaches used in cults and totalitarian societies for what has been called thought-reform, mind-control, or brainwashing.

Chapter 3 is devoted to my clinical investigations on the use of questioning as a type of covert method of interpersonal control. Questioning is probably the most common kind of intervention used in psychoanalytic treatment for purposes of directing and controlling patients.

Chapter 4 concerns a microanalytic study of selected parts of one analytic hour in which the analyst used various covert methods of interpersonal control. A major purpose of this chapter was to illustrate the methods of analytic listening and validation I use both in my clinical practice as well as in the studies summarized in this book. In brief, the method of validation I advance evaluates the effectiveness and therapeutic value of all of the clinician's interventions by examining the responses of the patient to the intervention. Particular attention is given to the patient's primary process derivatives and to changes in the patient's mode of communication in response to the analyst's interventions.

Chapter 5 provides six case studies of patients in psychoanalysis or psychotherapy where therapists made extensive use of indoctrination methods. These case studies also describe some of the unconscious interactions occurring involving the patient and clinician as well as an account of the effects these interactions had on the patient.

Chapter 6 describes how Freud's use of covert methods of interpersonal control converted his analysis of the compliant Wolf Man into a process of indoctrination.

Using an interactional perspective in Chapter 7, I review Freud's analysis of Dora, and I tell about his use of gaslighting, shaming, and other covert methods of interpersonal control as well as their effect on Dora.

Heinz Kohut's (1979) paper on the Two Analyses of Mr. Z. is examined in Chapter 8, where I conclude that the poor results in the first analysis were brought about by Kohut's use of indoctrination methods. The excellent therapeutic results in the second analysis came about because of Kohut's changed attitude and technique.

In Chapter 9, I make a comparative analysis of cults and the eleven patients described in earlier chapters who were treated with indoctrination methods. This chapter discusses the kinds of mind-control and thought-reform methods used in cults and the nature of the interactions between cult leaders and cult followers.

Chapter 10 is a study of the long-term treatment of two schizophrenic patients; one was treated with non-directive psycho-analytic methods and the other treated by directive and management approaches. Though the patient treated psychoanalytically attained to a marked degree the traditional goals of psychoanalytic treatment, the one who was treated by directive and management approaches obtained only temporary and symptomatic benefits. The principal difference between the two approaches is that the management approach uses manipulative methods whereas the psychoanalytic approach uses nonmanipulative methods that facilitate insight and psychic development.

Chapter 11 presents six basic principles regarding psycho-analytic technique that are needed for creating an egalitarian and non-directive ambience in the psychoanalytic treatment situation. The tactics and treatment methods stemming from these principles are useful for preventing and correcting the use of indoctrination methods and other antianalytic interventions. These principles assist the analyst in constructing heuristics and tactics to substitute for stereotyped approaches and indoctrination methods.

# *Part I*

---

# Covert Methods of Interpersonal Control and Other Indoctrination Methods

# Covert Methods of
# Interpersonal Control

It has been said that fish don't know they swim in water until they are out of the water. Similarly, most people do not know about the subtle and covert types of interpersonal control, domination, and abuse they are exposed to all of their lives in their families, at their schools, or in their work place. Not until they have experienced relationships that are more caring, respectful, and nonmanipulative are they able to recognize how much they have been covertly manipulated, controlled, and abused by others. In what follows, my purpose is to describe and discuss the widespread use and significance of different methods of covert interpersonal control in everyday life and in psychoanalytic treatment.

The covert methods of interpersonal control include gaslighting and a variety of other types of projective identifications wherein individuals, through different kinds of manipulation, exert control over other persons. Two defining characteristics of covert methods of interpersonal control are (1) the action, manipulation, or practice is one in which an individual attempts to exert control over the feelings, thoughts, or activities of another individual, and (2) the action or practice is carried out covertly. By covertly I mean that these actions are not carried out in an overt or direct way. My definition of covert methods of interpersonal control specifically excludes *overt* methods of control and verbal abuse such as threats of violence, explicit expressions of rage and anger, as well as tantrums, denunciations, hostile name-calling, or other openly hostile actions which may be taken by individuals to dominate, control, or abuse other persons.

This chapter focuses on convert methods of interpersonal control and other indoctrination methods, their effects on interpersonal relations including the analytic interactions, and the reasons why so many individuals are unaware of their existence or their importance both in everyday life and in psychoanalytic treatment.

Any kind of intervention, including interpretations, questions, confrontations, clarifications and the like, can be used for purposes of interpersonal control and domination. Though I claim that some methods such as questioning and confrontation are often used by clinicians as covert methods of interpersonal control, I recognize that sometimes they are not. Only by a study of the context in which some intervention occurs can an investigator make reasonable inferences and judgments about whether a particular intervention was intended to be controlling, directive, or intimidating.

An appreciation of interactional dynamics requires us to recognize the surprising extent to which presumably therapeutic interventions can be used for controlling, harassing, manipulating, demeaning, patronizing, humiliating, intimidating, and gaslighting patients.

In what follows, I shall list, explain, and illustrate with vignettes various ways in which practitioners use covert methods of interpersonal control (usually unconsciously) and discuss the implications of these practices for their effects on their patients and the treatment process.

## PROJECTIVE IDENTIFICATION AND COVERT METHODS OF INTERPERSONAL CONTROL

Nearly all of the tactics and methods of interpersonal control I shall discuss may be considered to be different species of projective identification. The widespread ignorance and/or denial on the employment of indoctrination methods in psychoanalytic treatment also obtains for the prevailing conceptions about projective identification. One group of psychoanalytic writers would limit it to include a mode of primitive defense found only in psychotic or other seriously disturbed patients. I believe the use of projective identification is far more widespread among both the general population and among mental health professionals than is generally recognized. Far from being rare, projective identification is one of the most common modes of communicating and relating in groups of two or more. (For similar views, see Bion 1959a and Langs 1978a.)

The most effective communications containing projective identifications are ones in which the victim does not know that he or she has been manipulated. One of the most destructive effects of projective identification occurs when the victim identifies with what has been projected onto herself or himself. The harmful effects of projective identification are nullified when the victim is capable of disbelieving the negative and pathologic ideas attributed to him and when he can disidentify with whatever negative introjects result from the projective identification (Dorpat 1985).

Ogden's (1982) view of projective identification as having three aspects [i.e., (1) a type of defense, (2) a mode of communication, and (3) a primitive symbiotic kind of object relation] has gained wide acceptance.

The therapist's use of covert methods of interpersonal control tends to create a pathological symbiotic mode of interacting characterized by mutual projective identification; in the therapeutic context this mode of interaction has been called a Type B field by Langs (1978a). In the Type B field, both the therapist and the patient extensively employ projective identification and use the other member of the dyad as a container for disruptive projective identifications. My clinical and supervisory experiences with psychotherapy trainees in various mental health professions and with psychoanalytic candidates indicates that a Type B field is a common one in both psychiatric and psychoanalytic practice and that psychotherapists and analysts often unconsciously either initiate or maintain this pathological mode of relatedness. Langs's (1976a,

1978a, 1979a, 1980a, 1981) psychotherapy seminars for psychiatric residents suggest the alarming prevalence of the Type B field in the practice of psychoanalytic psychotherapy.

The basic interactional mechanism in projective identification and in many of the different methods of covert interpersonal control is one in which one individual manipulates another individual in such a way as to evoke disturbing ideas and affects (such as shame, guilt, and anxiety) in the other person. Through the manipulation and its effects on the victim's thoughts and feelings, the perpetrator gains some control over the victim. In projective identification, the subject first unconsciously projects unwanted aspects of themselves onto another person and pressures the object to contain, as it were, the subject's disavowed affects and other contents.

The induction of emotions such as fear, shame, and guilt are powerful methods used in families as well as larger groups and institutions (government, schools, churches, the military, and the like) for controlling and regulating the cognitions and behaviors of individuals.

## COVERT METHODS OF INTERPERSONAL CONTROL IN THE THERAPEUTIC SITUATION

### Gaslighting

Gaslighting is a type of projective identification in which an individual (or group of individuals) attempt to influence the mental functioning of a second individual by causing the latter to doubt the validity of his or her judgments, perceptions, and/or reality testing in order that the victim will more readily submit his will and person to the victimizer. (See Chapter 2 for a more comprehensive discussion of gaslighting.)

Gaslighting is a common and powerful interpersonal dynamic in a variety of different tactics and techniques both individuals and groups have used for attaining interpersonal and social control over the psychic functioning of other individuals and groups. Gaslighting is an important aspect in many of the brainwashing and indoctrination techniques employed by cults and by totalitarian fascist and communist regimes in their coercive management and oppression of political prisoners and prisoners of war.

The various types of gaslighting have in common two defining features. The first is an attempt to impair or destroy an individual's confidence in his or her psychic abilities. After this first aim has been achieved, the second aim is to attain control over the feelings, thoughts, and behaviors of the victim.

By making another person feel fearful, guilty, or ashamed, the manipulator is in a position to gain control over the other individual's affects, thoughts, and behaviors by substituting his own beliefs. This is the basic mechanism of gaslighting whether used in everyday life, in psychotherapy situations, or in the thought-reform and mind-control manipulations of cult leaders. Some advertising and many social interactions in which one person attempts to gain control over another are based on this principle.

## Questioning

Questioning, especially if it is repetitive and directive, is a method by which clinicians can and often do gain control over their patients' mental functions and communications. (See Chapter 3 for a comprehensive study on the use of questioning as a method of interpersonal control.) As I indicated in previous publications, questioning tends to promote in the patient a mode of thinking and communication opposed to the methods and goals of psychoanalysis (Dorpat 1984, 1991c). Frequently, questioning shifts the patient's communication away from the Type A mode[1] of communication (also called derivative or symbolic communication) toward the Type C mode (communication that is literal, superficial, impersonal, and affectless).

---

1. Langs (1978a) describes three communicative modes, the Types A, B, and C. The Type A mode is characterized by symbolic imagery and authentic affects, and it is the optimal mode for both therapist and patient. Projective identification is the defining feature of the Type B mode. The defining property of

In inexperienced and/or anxious psychotherapists, one can note a common interactional pattern connected with the use of questions. Sometimes, when such therapists are unable or unwilling to tolerate frustrations such as silence, they attempt to control the situation by questioning the patient. Patients typically respond to such questions by defensively adopting a Type C mode of communicating.

## Defense Interpretation

Lomas (1987) presents a convincing argument that many classical analysts have given too much weight to the masculine qualities of disciplined reticence, toughness, and control—qualities that are often considered valuable in the interpretation of defenses. In preserving their sexual identity, such tough analysts not only seek to distinguish their mode of being from that of women but also attempt to define the latter's realm as inferior.

Lomas correctly, in my view, believes there is an excessive need on the part of some psychotherapists to make defense interpretations. Such zealous assaults by the therapists on their patients' defenses often constitute the enactment of hidden agendas for the control and domination of the patient. In my supervisory experience I have found that the excessive and inappropriate use of interpretations of unconscious defense is often done for purposes of controlling the patient. Compliant and/or Type C responses are the most common types of ways patients react to these forceful attacks and confrontations on their defenses and such responses are illustrated in the following vignette.

-------

the Type C mode is the absence of primary process derivatives. In a previous publication, I labeled as the Type D mode of communication a specific type of interactional defense consisting of inauthentic communication, and I described it as a defining property of what Winnicott (1960) called the False Self (Dorpat 1994a). The significance of shifts in the patient's modes of communication is also discussed in Chapter 10.

A repetitive but unconscious sadomasochistic interaction between therapist and patient occurred in which the therapist repetitively and unempathically confronted the patient with his defenses of intellectualization and isolation of affect.

The patient was a socially isolated middle-aged scientist with severe narcissistic problems who suffered from deep feelings of inferiority and shame. On the manifest level, the patient responded to these defense interpretations by compliance, withdrawal, and Type C communications. The therapist aggressively made interventions such as the following: "What's happened to your feelings today?," "Your voice sounds flat and devoid of all emotion," "Your talk is very intellectualized. Can't you bring out more feelings?" At a conscious level, the patient responded compliantly and without protest to the therapist's impatient and repetitive confrontations and interpretations about his affectless and intellectualized mode of communication.

An examination of his primary process derivatives (e.g., affects, imagery, metaphors, narratives, and nonverbal communications) following the therapist's interventions about his defenses revealed that he unconsciously had evaluated the therapist's interventions as attacking and humiliating. My efforts as a supervisor consisted of using the patient's primary process derivatives to show the therapist how the patient had experienced her defense interventions as harsh and humiliating.

One day, for example, the patient began a session by telling in a somewhat halting and reserved manner some insights he had attained after his last session with the therapist. In his characteristically distant and cautious way, he told about his new understanding into why he had become "addicted" to watching Clint Eastwood movies. He described how he came to understand his fascination for identifying with Clint Eastwood as a compensation for his feelings of shame and inferiority.

At this point, the therapist interjected, "You sound like a boy whistling in the dark." At first, the patient was startled by the therapist's inopportune and tactless remark so lacking in attunement with his state of mind and with the suppressed pride he felt for his new insights. Then, he became depressed and in the following session he spoke of quitting the therapy. Fortunately, the therapist, with the supervisor's assistance, was able to understand how her poorly timed defense interpretation about "whistling in the dark" had disrupted the mirror transference and precipitated a depressive response. When the therapist was then able to acknowledge to the patient her own contribution to the patient's depressive response, the selfobject transference and the therapeutic alliance were restored.

## Confrontations

The technique of confrontation is made to order for serving purposes of controlling, directing, humiliating, or dominating. Though some of the older texts on psychoanalytic technique describe confrontations as an acceptable and useful technique, my own experience in doing, teaching, and supervising psychoanalytic treatment has witnessed few occasions in which confrontations have facilitated the therapeutic process. Often confrontations are antitherapeutic projective identifications in which therapists consciously, or more often unconsciously, attempt to intimidate or at least influence and control patients by engendering painful emotions such as fear, guilt, shame, or anxiety. (For similar views on confrontation see Langs 1982a.)

## Interrupting or Overlapping?

Interrupting another person who is talking, especially if it is done in a loud and commanding tone of voice, is another way individuals may assert their dominance and need to control others in interpersonal situations.

However, the fact that one speaker begins talking to another person while the other person is already talking should not always be interpreted as controlling or abusive. The person who begins speaking while another person is talking and who does so in a way that is affectively and thematically attuned to the first speaker may be doing what professor of linguistics Tannen (1990) calls "overlapping." In her view, overlapping speech is not destructive, not intended to exercise dominance and violate others' rights. Instead, it is cooperative, a means of showing involvement, participation, and connection. In short, simultaneous talk can be supportive. Tannen (1990) describes regional differences in speech patterns. Individuals from the West Coast may often (as I did until twenty years ago) mistakenly consider the custom of some individuals on the East Coast to participate in overlapping speech as evidence of Easterners' need to rudely dominate the conversation.

### Abrupt Change of Topic

A therapist's abrupt change of topic in psychotherapy situations can be emotionally disruptive, fragmenting, and disorganizing to the patient. Such unexpected and disturbing kinds of interventions most often stem from the therapist's unresolved countertransference problems. Though the need to intimidate and control the other person is often an unconscious aspect of this technique, I do not think it is always present. Sudden changes in the topic derail the psychoanalytic dialogue, and they are disturbing because they are unempathic and not attuned to the patient's state of mind. Frequently this kind of intervention leads to the patient becoming emotionally disturbed and/or disorganized. In response to such disruptive interventions, many patients may withdraw and shift to a Type C mode of communication and defense.

## FRAGMENTING THE PATIENT'S EXPERIENCE

Interventions such as questions or interpretations that focus on details that are not relevant to the patient's concerns and current state of mind tend to derail the patient, to fragment the patient's experience, and to disrupt the selfobject transference. They may bring about at least temporary affective turmoil and disorganization. The fragmenting influence of this type of intervention is illustrated in the story of the centipede who became disorganized and unable to walk after he was asked, "What's wrong with your 34th left foot?"

In the following vignette,[2] a patient became disturbed and withdrew into a compliant Type C communication when the analyst fragmented her experience by directing her attention to a detail in a reported dream.

> A 32-year-old married woman in analysis for anxiety attacks and disturbed relations with men dreamt about being in a bedroom. She described the bedroom as a sunny room with a beautiful view of nearby snowcapped mountains. Sunlight was streaming through the window near the bed. A revolver was lying on a dresser. After a few minutes of anxiously discussing her associations to the dream and a recent quarrel with her husband, the analyst interrupted her with a question, "What comes to your mind about the gun?"
>
> The patient replied in a matter-of-fact way, "A penis comes to my mind. I believe a gun is a symbol of a penis— oh—I guess that the gun in the dream has to do with my penis envy." The patient proceeded in a monotonous tone of voice in which her associations were impersonal and vague. All emotion drained from her speech and for the remainder of the hour her mode of communication was predominantly a Type C mode.
>
> The analyst's unempathic question was disruptive to the patient's psychic equilibrium, and it did not reflect adequate attunement with the patient's anxiety. Furthermore, his intervention was premature and intrusive because she had not associated to this detail of the manifest dream.

---

2. I am indebted to Dr. Joseph Lichtenberg for this vignette.

In response to the analyst's disruptive intervention, the patient experienced a momentary threat of self-fragmentation. To allay this fragmentation and to prevent further cognitive and affective dyscontrol, she switched to using a Type C communication as a mode of defending herself and distancing herself from the analyst. Her affectless response about the gun being a symbol for the penis was a compliant response in which she unconsciously told the analyst what she thought he expected her to think.

In her discussion of the different modes of overt and covert verbal abuse, Evans (1992) lists the following types of covert verbal abuse: "withholding," "countering," "discounting," "verbal abuse disguised as jokes," "blocking and diverting," "trivializing," and "undermining."

## COVERT METHODS OF INTERPERSONAL CONTROL IN EVERYDAY LIFE

Gaslighting and other covert methods of interpersonal control are common modes of relating in our culture, and most people, including mental health professionals, are unaware of their existence or they consider them normal (Carter 1989, Elgin 1980, Evans 1992, Tannen 1990). Covert methods of control are *some of the time* embedded in the ways nearly all individuals in Western societies talk and relate to each other. In some people, these methods are used *most of the time* in communicating with others.

For the purposes of this chapter, I use the terms covert methods of interpersonal control and covert verbal abuse as synonyms because in my view the various covert types of interpersonal control with few if any exceptions are abusive.

The findings and conclusions I have reached from clinical studies on the use of covert methods of interpersonal control and other methods of indoctrination are similar in two ways to the findings and conclusions of investigators in cognate fields such as studies of verbal abuse and investigations on the mind-control methods employed by cult leaders (Langone 1993a, Singer 1995). First, my repeated clinical observations while doing individual and group supervision plus the examination of hundreds of hours of process notes of psychotherapy and psychoanalytic hours has revealed the widespread use of these methods of indoctrination. Though there are important differences in the frequency, style, and tactics used for covert interpersonal control by clinicians, their use is alarmingly prevalent and widespread. Secondly, I found that most often both clinicians and their patients were not consciously aware of the abusive and controlling quality of covert methods of interpersonal control.

Another finding in my informal clinical studies and the investigations of others in cognate fields is the presence of a universal property in both overt and covert verbal abuse: the aim of controlling, dominating, and exercising power over others. Anger, contempt, hatred, envy, and a host of other affects and aims may or may not be expressed in both covert and overtly abusive communications, but the wish to control the other is always present.

My major findings and conclusions are supported by investigations carried out in three different disciplines: feminist studies, linguistics, and Marxist studies (Chodorow 1989, Flax 1990). Many studies in the above three disciplines support the conclusion that there is a widespread pattern of relationships in Western societies in which certain individuals and groups exert control and dominance over other individuals. Feminist studies emphasize, document, and attempt to explain male domination of women and studies by Tannen (1990) and Elgin (1980) demonstrate that men tend to commit more verbal abuse than women. Marxist scholars emphasize the domination in capitalist countries of the have-nots by those who have money, power, and status.

The conclusions I have reached both about extensiveness of methods of covert interpersonal control and about the unawareness of it are supported, as I mentioned, by extensive investigations of speech patterns of individuals in the United States. Professor of linguistics Tannen (1990) investigated gender differences in communication and she concludes that men live in a hierarchical social order in which they are either one-up or one-down. She states, "In this world conversations are negotiations in which people try to achieve and maintain the upper hand if they can, and protect themselves from others' attempts to put them down and push them around. Life then is a contest, a struggle to preserve independence and avoid failure" (p. 25).

In her book *The Verbally Abusive Relationship*, Evans (1992) notes that "verbal abuse is an issue of control, a means of holding power over another" (p. 13). Later she writes, "all verbal abuse is dominating and controlling" (p. 40). Carter (1989) in his volume about verbal abuse emphasizes that the major dynamic in verbal abuse is the need to control the victim, and he writes about Hitler as a prime example of someone who was exceedingly abusive and who did so out of a persistent, deep need for dominating and controlling other persons.

## THE CONTRIBUTIONS OF ELGIN

Professor of linguistics Suzette Elgin (1980) has described a common type of covert verbal abuse that, to the best of my knowledge, has not been noted in the psychiatric or psychoanalytic literature. Though many persons in our American culture are both perpetrators as well as victims of this kind of projective identification, few are aware of its existence or its significance in everyday life or in psychotherapy. This kind of mental abuse is more common, according to Elgin (1980), in men than it is in women.

In this type of projective identification, emotionally disturbing messages are hidden away or concealed, as it were, as a *presupposition* of the subject's communication. Using psychoanalytic terms, one could say that the benign manifest content of the message covers a latent content consisting of an abusive message.

In the following examples, all but the final one are taken from Elgin's (1980) book. The explicit communication in these examples is given first, followed by the unspoken presupposition. I have added the last item (i.e., "affects evoked") because in my opinion the affective responses of the victim are important interactional effects of this type of covert verbal abuse. The evoked affects and the cognitions linked with the painful affects are what makes these communications abusive and disturbing.

*Example 1*
    "If you *really* loved me, you wouldn't go bowling."
*Presupposition*
    "You don't really love me."
*Affects Evoked*
    Guilt, shame.

*Example 2*
    "Don't you *care* about your children?"
*Presuppositions*
    "You don't care about your children."
    "You should care about your children; it's wrong of you
        not to."
*Affects Evoked*
    Guilt, shame, depressive affect.

*Example 3*
    "Even an *elderly* person should be able to understand this
        rule."
*Presuppositions*
    "There's something wrong with being an elderly person."
    "It doesn't take much intelligence or ability to understand this
        rule."
*Affects Evoked*
    Guilt, shame, depressive affect.

*Example 4*
    "*Some* husbands would object to having their wives going
        back to school when the kids are still just babies."
*Presuppositions*
    "It's wrong for you to go back to school."

"I'm not like other husbands—I am unique and superior to them because I'm not objecting to your going back to school."

*Affects Evoked*
Anxiety, fear, guilt, shame.

*Example 5*
To a patient who had been in psychotherapy for many years his therapist asked, "Are you still worried about whether people like you or not?"

*Presuppositions*
"You are childish to still worry about whether people like you."
"There is something wrong with you for continuing to worry about whether people like you."

*Affects Evoked*
Shame, anxiety, anger.

As Elgin explains, victims of covert verbal abuse may be unaware of the abusiveness of such communications because they have not been taught to watch out for presuppositions, or to pay attention to them instead of the words that form the surface (i.e., manifest) sequence. Consequently, they feel hurt or insulted in response to something that sounds on the surface level like a benign and reasonable thing to say. Victimizers, as well as victims of this kind of verbal abuse, according to Elgin, are most often unaware of the abusive character of their communications. As a protection against this type of verbal abuse, Elgin (1980) recommends watching out for and identifying the hurtful presuppositions contained in the victimizer's communication.

As a second line of protection she recommends that the victim or potential victim adopt what she calls the "computer mode" of communication, which consists of speaking in generalities and abstractions and reducing to a minimum any body movement or emotional expression. The mode of communication she recommends is identical with what Langs (1978a) calls Type C communication. (See Dorpat 1993d, for more on the "computer mode" and Type C Communication.)

## THE IDEALIZATION OF "POWER AND MASTERY OVER PEOPLE"

Controlling, abusive, and coercive modes of communicating and relating are embedded in many speech patterns of Western societies because power over people is idealized and sought for in the Western world (Gruen 1988). A disturbing and vulgar illustration of this passion for power over people is the popularity of books by Van Fleet and others of his ilk. Van Fleet (1983) makes his living conducting seminars and writing books on techniques for gaining power and control over individuals.

In his popular book, *25 Steps to Power and Mastery Over People*, Van Fleet claims that by reading his books and following his recommendations the reader "can gain power, influence, and control over others and *attain complete mastery over people*" (p. 7, italics added).

Van Fleet understands, as few people do, the interpersonal power accruing to individuals who know how to evoke strong emotions of fear and desire in others. He explains in detail effective methods for covertly gaining control and how these methods require some knowledge of human emotions and motivation. He recommends motivating a person to do something like buying a car he does not need by arousing his desire. If you can't control a person by arousing his desire, then he suggests trying to make him feel fearful. Van Fleet said, "If you can't move a person to action by arousing his desire, then turn the coin over and move him to action by arousing his fear" (p. 131).

Another of his recommended strategies for obtaining interpersonal control is attacking a person's weak and vulnerable points. With no trace of conscious guilt, he suggests, "Always go for a weak one where she cannot protect herself" (p. 141). Van

Fleet accurately describes his coercive and abusive methods as "verbal brainwashing."

Unconsciously, Van Fleet, I surmise, at some level has some questions about the unethical and grossly immoral quality of his recommendations. I infer the above from his extravagant and defensive claims about his techniques being legitimate and morally correct:

> It is *certainly not illegal or immoral* for you to use brainwashing as a powerful but fully *legitimate* technique for persuasion to convert a person to your way of thinking so he will do what you want him to do [p. 217, italics added].

Van Fleet cites John Wesley's extraordinary charismatic abilities in the seventeenth century to convert thousands to Christianity as an example of how to use brainwashing to "Change Behavior Patterns." Van Fleet is unusually perceptive for understanding the similarity between the methods evangelists such as Wesley use for bringing about conversion with the methods totalitarian political regimes use for brainwashing. In political, psychotherapy, and religious cults, the authorities in charge are able to gain control over their hapless victims after they have first managed to convince them of their actual or imagined failings and inadequacies, be they moral, cognitive, or psychiatric. (See Chapter 9 in this book for more about the use of brainwashing methods in political, religious, and psychotherapy cults.)

Van Fleet's recommendation ("constant repetition is the key to success in brainwashing") explains the efficacy of repetitive defense interpretations in attaining control over patients. (For a case example of this, see my commentary on the repeated interpretations of defense made by the analyst Silverman in the case report in Chapter 4.)

My initial reaction to reading Van Fleet's book was one of moral outrage over his recommended techniques and disbelief about his claims for how the reader could attain financial success and power over people by following his strategies and techniques. Further reflection and study led me reluctantly to conclude Van Fleet was correct in concluding that brainwashing methods could win "Power and Mastery Over People" as well as achieve professional and financial success.

The use of both overt as well as covert methods of interpersonal control is a common and popular pathway to success in business and some professions, such as law. Attorneys who command the highest hourly fees and who have a reputation for success are too often the ones who are the meanest, most unscrupulous, and harshly dominating individuals one could imagine living outside the walls of penal institutions. They are the "hired guns" of America in the twentieth century.

My experience in doing forensic psychiatry supports the appraisal of the attorney Benson (1991) about the legal system in the United States. Today's adversarial system creates a warlike atmosphere for attorneys in which they are pressured by their clients to win at any cost and by any means available. Lawyers who act ethically often put themselves at a competitive disadvantage. Benson concludes, "We have created a profession in this country that by its very nature encourages being disagreeable, pushy and sometimes even dishonest to be successful" (p. 10).

## INDOCTRINATION TECHNIQUES USED BY INSTITUTIONS

The covert methods of interpersonal control used mainly unconsciously by some mental health professionals are similar in some ways to the indoctrination, brainwashing, and social control methods used by various institutions (e.g., governmental, educational, religious, etc.). A major difference is that these institutions for the most part consciously and deliberately use overt as well as covert methods for interpersonal and social control, whereas clinicians use only covert methods and these are carried out for the most part unconsciously. (See Chapter 9 for a discussion of the use of overt and covert methods of interpersonal control and brainwashing methods in cults.)

Many types of psychiatric treatment and psychotherapy are deliberately organized to systematically carry out methods for shaping, controlling, and/or directing the behaviors of patients. The widespread support of directive techniques is illustrated in the recent writings and seminars of psychotherapist Jay Haley. About thirty years ago, he wrote a satirical polemic against psychoanalysts for using controlling and directive methods (Haley 1969). In his attack on psychoanalysts, he accused them of practicing "one-upmanship" with their patients, and he criticized them for being masters of the art of putting their patients "one-down." He appears to have changed his attitude toward "directive" methods because he now conducts summer conferences on Cape Cod for instructing therapists on how to conduct "directive" therapy.

Some of the damaging effects of using covert or overt methods of interpersonal control in psychoanalytic treatment stem from the fact that their use is contradictory to the avowed purposes, methods, and traditions of psychoanalysis. In situations where patients receive contradictory messages about the nature and purpose of the therapist's communications, the patients may be placed in what Bateson (1972) and others call a double-bind. The therapist's implicit or explicit message, "What I say is not directive or prescriptive. My purpose is to enlighten you, not to control you," is contradicted by messages and communications of the therapist which are directive, controlling, and/or manipulative.

## BEHAVIOR MODIFICATION THERAPY

The explicit aim of behavior modification therapy is the control of patients' behavior through the use of rewards and punishments. Though Skinner claims his findings and theories about operant conditioning are science, he has not discovered anything *new* nor has he enlightened us about anything *old*. Humans and certain other mammals (for example, mother bears) have used reward and punishment as effective means of training and attaining social control over others, especially their offspring, for millions of years. Though Skinner did not, in my opinion, make an important contribution to knowledge or science, he did develop an efficient technology and an effective methodology for shaping and controlling the behaviors of animals (including man) through the systematic application of rewards and punishments.

## PSYCHOLOGIC EFFECTS OF BEHAVIOR MODIFICATION THERAPY

The following vignette illustrates how behavior modification can support the formation and consolidation of a false self personality organization and inauthentic communication. (See Chapter 4 for a clinical case study of a patient with false self psychopathology.)

> A 32-year-old single man was admitted to the psychiatric service of a hospital for treatment of depression and an attempted suicide.[3] The hospital staff treated him with behavior modification treatment which consisted of attempts to control and modify his behavior through rewarding behaviors the staff deemed acceptable and ignoring or punishing behaviors they considered "sick" or in other ways unacceptable. He became deeply disappointed when the psychiatric staff did not want to listen to him or to understand him. In fact, at most times they ignored him except on occasions when they would unaccountably praise him for "behaviors" he did not care about.
>
> He came to the realistic judgment that the staff were not interested in what he felt or what he thought. They were, however, sometimes very much concerned about "behaviors" he considered to be among the more unimportant and superficial things about himself. They praised and "rewarded" him for his good manners, for "socializing" with other patients,

---

3. I am indebted to Dr. Robert Bergman for this vignette.

for keeping his room tidy, and for dressing in ways pleasing to the staff.

To protect himself from being disappointed over not being understood in an empathic way and not having his experience validated in any way, he became more vigilant about what the staff wanted from him and he gradually learned what would win staff approval and eventual discharge from the psychiatric ward. Above all, he should at all times *act* normal. Moreover, he should not express his genuine feelings or bother the staff by talking to them about his problems.

What I have just described is, of course, a formula or recipe for the reinforcement and maintenance of inauthentic ways of relating. The psychiatric ward's behavior modification program succeeded all too well in getting the patient to suppress his symptoms, to conceal his spontaneous feelings and thoughts, and most importantly, to shape and support his inauthentic ways of relating to others. In short, behavior modification therapy suppressed his true self and supported and partly shaped his false self. Partly because of such dehumanizing and affectively damaging experiences on the psychiatric service many months of psychotherapy were necessary before he could trust his therapist to not attempt to stifle his individuality or to control his "behavior."

## GROUP DENIAL

Other investigators who have noted the fact that both victimizers as well as victims are often unaware of the existence and/or of the significance of covert methods of interpersonal control and abuse include Carter (1989), Elgin (1980), Evans (1992), Lakoff and Coyne (1993), and Tannen (1990).

Carter (1989) notes that only 1 percent of persons are intentionally verbally abusive. In his view, "Twenty percent do it semiconsciously as a defense mechanism. The rest of us do it only occasionally, usually unconsciously and unintentionally" (p. 9).

Elgin (1980) discusses the widespread unawareness, especially among men, of the controlling and abusive aspects of their verbal communication. She concludes, "Take as a given that men are brought up to be verbally abusive, *usually without conscious awareness* of that fact" (p. 286, italics added).

Individuals who have been systematically subjected to covert methods of interpersonal control and who have been followers of religious, political, or psychotherapy cults most often do not understand the traumatizing ways they have been manipulated and exploited by their oppressors (Singer 1995). Patients I have treated or examined who have been subjected to these covert kinds of interpersonal control and abuse by their families, by cults, or by their previous therapists have, for the most part, denied either the fact or the meaning of these oppressive practices until they, like the victims of childhood sexual and physical abuse, are able to work through the denial defending against the awareness of their cumulative trauma and then begin to understand the significance of their traumatic experiences.

How do we account for the prevailing and widespread unawareness of the various methods of covert interpersonal control and abuse not only among mental health professionals but also among the general population? Though there are, of course, individual differences in both the degree and quality of unawareness, I believe there is a collective denial among many persons in Western societies of various aspects of these practices. I suspect but cannot prove that this collective denial accounts for a substantial part of the prevailing unawareness of the existence as well as effects of covert verbal abuse.

The covertness of covert methods of interpersonal control partly serves to conceal the abusive and controlling nature of the communication. In my professional experience, many therapists who use covert methods of interpersonal control rationalize the use of such methods and deny the controlling oppressive aspect of their communication. Dewald (1972), for example, rationalizes what others, including myself, consider his oppressive and controlling use of questions by stating questions are required to get the patient to follow the basic rule and to prevent silences.

The highly prevalent unawareness of victims of verbal abuse that they are being controlled and abused has also been demonstrated by investigators who have studied this in cults. Cult experts Langone (1993b) and Singer (1995) report that cult members are rarely aware of the subtle techniques and mind-control methods used for shaping their behavior, thoughts, and feelings. Cults are able to operate successfully because at any given time most followers are either not yet aware that they are being controlled, abused, and exploited or, less commonly, they cannot express such awareness because of uncertainty, shame, or fear of doing so.

Here is a brief, familiar example of a group denial involving medical and surgical residents. In a previous publication I reported that residents in training and graduates of residency training programs tended to deny certain emotionally disturbing aspects of their physically and psychologically abusive and harmful training programs (Dorpat 1989a). I refer here particularly to the excessively long hours—often exceeding 100 hours a week—of work required of residents, as well as the concomitant fatigue and sleep loss. Their denial of the traumas and stress they had sustained for many months was organized and shaped by their relationships to their peers and to their teachers. The unconscious message they received from others at their training institutions was to minimize and discount their work stress and its harmful effects on their physical and mental health. In fact, many residents rationalized their situation by patently false assertions about how much their arduous work schedule added to their personal and professional development.

In a group as with the self, schemas[4] shape the flow of information. In any group, the relevant schemas are those that are

---

4. Schemata are memory structures that organize the mind and serve as its contents. A schema functions as a template for organizing and interpreting lived experience. A schema is not a carbon copy of the event it represents; rather, a schema is an abstraction representing the regularities in a particular type of person-event interaction.

shared by members, the subset of schemas that are the "we." Groups, whether large or small, are as vulnerable as individuals to denial and self-deception. In the groups of residents the group schema used to deny the stress and its effects could be put into words in this way: "Don't complain! The long hours of work, the loss of sleep, and the fatigue are good for you." According to Bion (1959a), a most crucial aspect of a group mentality are those basic assumptions about how to handle anxiety-evoking information. This includes an unconscious collusion by the group members about what to deny.

Persons in groups come to share a large number of schemas, most of which are communicated without being spoken of directly (Reiss 1981). Foremost among those shared, yet unspoken, schemas are what group members are tacitly enjoined to deny. When the persons in a group have made the tacit or unconscious choice about what they will deny, they have established a shared defense. (See also Dorpat and Miller 1992 for more discussion about shared defenses.)

## GROUP DENIAL AMONG PSYCHOANALYSTS

I believe the group denial (and/or ignorance) in the general population concerning covert methods of interpersonal control also applies to American psychoanalysts and psychoanalytic psychotherapists. As evidence of this I cite the responses of a group of analysts to the presentation of a case in which there was flagrant and repeated use of different covert methods of interpersonal control.

The treating analyst, Dr. Martin Silverman (1987), provided uncensored process notes of four successive analytic hours. A total of thirteen different eminent analysts provided discussion papers of Silverman's process notes. Only one, Merton Gill, noted and discussed what I, along with Gill, consider to be the central interactional dynamic of the four analytic sessions—namely, the analyst and the analysand are engaged in a continuing sadomasochistic interaction. Neither the patient nor the analyst explicitly addresses this ongoing pathological interaction. Their sadomasochistic interaction and the analyst's repeated employment of gaslighting tactics, as well as other methods of covert interpersonal control, provide a unifying frame of reference for understanding what is occurring in the analysis and for explaining the prolonged stalemate in the analysis. One discussant, Dr. Charles Brenner, who explicitly shares the same classical theoretical orientation as the treating analyst, Silverman, found nothing to criticize in Silverman's conduct of the analysis.

## DENIAL LEADS TO IGNORANCE AND DYSCONTROL OVER WHAT IS DENIED

In this and later chapters of this book when I discuss the unawareness of persons who use covert methods of interpersonal control, I often ascribe it to two possible factors, denial and/or ignorance. Although I have no hard evidence, my clinical experience and self-analysis leads me to believe that the most common causes for the wide prevalence of covert abuse and covert methods of interpersonal control is the defense of denial and that the lack of knowledge (i.e., ignorance) about the existence and various meanings (such as its harmfulness) of covert abuse and covert methods of interpersonal control is secondary to the denial.

The ignorance or defect in knowledge secondary to denial responses I explained in previous publications in this way (Dorpat 1985, 1987b). In denial reactions, a subject shifts his focal attention from whatever is disturbing or experienced as potentially disturbing to something and this shift away from the disturbing object I call *cognitive arrest*. This cognitive arrest in clinical reactions prevents the subject from fully and accurately symbolizing in words whatever it is that he or she has defensively disavowed. Denial thus prevents the formation of secondary process products (i.e., verbal representatives) about whatever is disavowed.

Though I shall in this book frequently discuss the damaging psychic effects of covert methods of interpersonal control, I believe we should exercise some restraint in criticizing mental health professionals and other persons who use these directive methods. Most often they do not consciously intend to injure others, and most often because of the group denial they are unaware of *what* they are doing and of the psychic *effects* of what they are doing.

An important consequence of denial is the avoidance of responsibility and the rejection of authority or "ownership" over what is denied. The one who denies is not irresponsible; he or she is *aresponsible* (the prefix has the same meaning as does the "a" in words like *amoral*). Denial, then, is marked by an unconscious rejection of personal responsibility for some action, rather than a conscious shirking of responsibility. The denier does not intend to act in an immoral or irresponsible way but, rather, cuts short self-reflection regarding his actions before even knowing what he is doing.

Another consequence of denial is dyscontrol, the subject's loss of control over whatever he has denied. The denier's failure to avow and to assume responsibility over what he denies (disavows) leads to a loss of direct, conscious control over what is denied. The widespread, excessive, and damaging effects of covert methods of interpersonal control among mental health professionals is then a type of dyscontrol.

In sum, denial leads to ignorance about and dyscontrol over what is denied.


## CONCLUDING COMMENT

I have little doubt that the various covert methods of interpersonal control are used more extensively by nonpsychoanalytic therapists than by psychoanalysts and psychoanalytically oriented psychotherapists. In psychoanalysis, however, the use of such methods of indoctrination are opposed to both the values and traditions of psychoanalysis from Freud on. Respect for the patient's autonomy, the rule of neutrality, and the value placed on being non-directive are just three traditional psychoanalytic principles standing in opposition to using methods of indoctrination.

It is not my aim to have therapists eliminate any type of unconscious influence or suggestion because it would not be either possible or desirable to so do. However, the influence exerted by the covert methods of interpersonal control is harmful to human well-being and normal development. One of the major ways such methods work is through the evocation of human misery in the myriad forms of shame, guilt, and anxiety.

My hope is that this study will help persons doing psychoanalytic therapy to work through and identify their unawareness and/or denial of covert methods of interpersonal control. In this way, psychoanalytic therapy can bring about truly permanent changes produced by constructive forces within the patient rather than by the temporary changes made in compliance to the therapist's use of methods of indoctrination.

In psychoanalytic treatment there exists a prevalent error of putting an excessive faith in the certainty of doctrine at the expense of an open-ended exploration between patient and psychotherapist. When psychoanalytic practitioners overvalue their theory and method and assume the right to control the conditions and content of the dialogue, they are making the same kind of destructive error as the unethical politician or the shady used-car salesman.

The ideas and methods of Freud and his heirs can be and have been used for dominating rather than healing by far too many psychotherapists. They do this by undermining people's respect for their conscious perceptions and judgments (as for example in gaslighting) and by degrading ordinary caring in favor of techniques that fly in the face of common sense.

The abuse of power in psychotherapy is linked with an idealization of technique in human relations (Lomas 1987). A mode of behavior is advocated or required on the basis of a theory that either claims or implies a right to supersede the ordinary caring and respect that people have a right to expect from others.

# On Gaslighting:
# How to Dominate Others without
# Their Knowledge or Consent

The purpose of this chapter is to describe and discuss the use and significance of different methods of gaslighting in everyday life and in psychoanalytic treatment. Gaslighting is probably the most commonly used and effective type of verbal communication individuals have for manipulating and controlling other persons.

Gaslighting can be carried out consciously or unconsciously. The two defining characteristics of gaslighting and other covert methods of interpersonal control are (1) the manipulation is one in which an individual attempts to exert control over the feelings, thoughts, or activities of another individual, and (2) the practice is carried out covertly, and it is not explicitly or directly hostile, abusive, coercive, or intimidating.

## AN OVERVIEW OF THE LITERATURE
## ON GASLIGHTING

The concept of gaslighting was derived first from Hamilton's (1939) play *Angel Street* and later from the 1944 movie *Gaslight* starring

Charles Boyer and Ingrid Bergman. In both the play and the movie, the victim's husband manipulated the gaslight in a way that made his wife's complaint about it seem as if she were going insane. The husband's aim was to have her committed to a mental hospital so that he could gain her property for himself. Several British authors employ the terms *gaslighting* or *gas light phenomenon* to describe those situations in which one individual attempts to make others feel that a second individual is insane so that the latter will be taken to a mental hospital. Later studies in England and the United States considerably broadened the boundary of the gaslighting concept.

Though previous reports have highlighted the consciously malicious intent of the exploiter (Barton and Whitehead 1960, Gass and Nichols, 1988, Lund and Gardiner 1977), one report by Cawthra (1987) describes a case of imposed illness in which the intent of the inducer was not primarily malicious.

Other investigations, including Bateson and colleagues (1956), Searles (1959), and Laing (1961) have written about abusive techniques either similar to or the same as what I call gaslighting. Searles (1959) identified a form of transference enactment in which the schizophrenic patient creates in actuality a struggle in which either he or the analyst, or both, attempt to drive the other crazy. His article, "The Effort to Drive the Other Person Crazy," lists six modes of driving the other person crazy. Each of these techniques tends to undermine the other person's confidence in his affective reactions and his own perception of reality.

Laing (1961) has discussed some of the ways in which individuals, in speech and deed, attempt to destroy the life in others. He claims that this is done through interpersonal actions which tend to *confuse* or *mystify*, actions which make it difficult for the one person to know "who" he is, "who" the other is, and what is the situation they are "in."

Bateson and colleagues (1956) described a pattern known as the *double-bind* situation wherein the victim is caught in a tangle of paradoxical injunctions in which he cannot do the right thing.

An example they cite is the mother who says to her schizophrenic son, "Don't you want to kiss your mummy," at the same time that her cold and stiff nonverbal communication is, "Stay away!"

Covert verbal abuse has been described by Bach and Goldberg (1974) as "crazymaking," and they describe it as "a form of interpersonal interaction that results from the repression of intense aggression and which seriously impairs its victims' capacity to recognize and deal with the interpersonal reality" (p. 251).

Using a psychoanalytic perspective, Calef and Weinshel (1981) argue persuasively that gaslighting phenomena are both ubiquitous and inevitable. They play a significant role in human relationships, exert an important influence in the marriage relationship, and exercise a sometimes overlooked impact on the course of psychotherapy. They describe situations in which either the therapist or the patient may attempt to gaslight the other.

Like Calef and Weinshel, I have adopted a broad definition of gaslighting, one that includes a wider range of victims in addition to those who have become psychotic (Dorpat 1985, Dorpat and Miller 1992). In my usage, the term gaslighting includes a variety of brainwashing techniques. Brainwashers are trying to undermine their victim's belief system and to replace it with another. They are not, for the most part, trying to drive their victims crazy.

## INTERACTIONAL DYNAMICS

Gaslighting involves one person (or sometimes a group of persons), the victimizer (who tries to impose his or her judgment on a second person, a victim), and a second person, the victim. This imposition is carried out by the "transfer," via projective identification, of disturbing unconscious contents from the victimizer to the victim. Gaslighting often evokes disturbing emotions, low self-esteem, and cognitive dyscontrol by causing the individual to question his own abilities for thinking, perceiving, and reality testing. Along with the emergence of self-doubt and diminished self-esteem there also may develop confusion, anxiety, depression, and in a few cases, psychosis.

As a form of projective identification, gaslighting serves a defensive function. The defenses of denial and projection occur first, and they are followed by some interpersonal manipulation that is an enactment of the subject's wish to control the other person. Some psychic content which is denied as belonging to the self is projected on to another person. The victimizer's wish to control the object is first actualized when he or she is able to manipulate the object in such a way (as, for example, by shaming him) that the object begins to doubt his own judgment. After the victim loses confidence in his mental capacities, he becomes an easy prey for the victimizer's need to direct the victim's cognition, feeling state, and overt behavior.

In my view, gaslighting is the common denominator of a variety of different psychological techniques and manipulations both individuals and groups have used unconsciously as well as consciously for attaining control and domination over other individuals' psychic functioning. Gaslighting is a major element in many of the brainwashing and indoctrination techniques employed by totalitarian fascist and communist regimes in their management of both political prisoners and prisoners of war. The psychological and physical methods used for brainwashing or indoctrination have as their goal the impairment or destruction of certain mental functions and beliefs of the individual so that the victim will submit to his or her persecutors.

To win converts and followers, fundamentalist religious groups, cults, encounter groups, and large-group awareness training make extensive use of gaslighting and other brainwashing techniques (Singer 1995).

Techniques used for controlling and disrupting another person's mental functioning should be distinguished from techniques used for controlling and shaping another person's outward behavior. For example, some authoritarian governments try to control, through a variety of methods, what their citizens *do*. Their aim is to proscribe certain kinds of overt actions, and they do not attempt to systematically compel their citizens to think or feel in any prescribed way. In contrast, totalitarian regimes (such as Germany during Hitler's regime and Russia headed by Stalin) try to rigorously direct and control what their citizens feel and think, as well as what they do.

Psychological methods such as gaslighting used by totalitarian regimes may be supplemented and enhanced by physical means such as sleep deprivation, torture, psychotropic drugs, sensory isolation, and solitary confinement.

Studies of individuals and groups subjected to brainwashing show how the victims are first led to doubt or even reject their own judgments at the same time that they are pressured to follow and believe what their victimizer wants them to believe.

As I hope to demonstrate in the following vignettes, the unconscious gaslighting carried out by psychoanalytic therapists and others is a part of a complex interpersonal manipulative interaction in which the gaslighter tries to cause the victim to doubt his perceptions and judgments at the same time that he or she attempts to have the patient accept the therapist's judgments.

## A Case of Suicidal Depression Brought on by a Therapist's Gaslighting

Bill was a 35-year-old married teacher who consulted a psychiatrist (Dr. T.) for himself and his wife, who had recently arrived at the understanding of being sexually molested by her father when she was a child. The psychiatrist began seeing each of them in individual therapy on a two or three times a week basis and continued to see them for a period of over four years. After two years of therapy, the wife, Lorna, became increasingly involved, socially at first and later sexually, with a group of persons who were followers or relatives of Dr. T. Her intense involvement in these relationships was a marked change from her previous life and her two teenage sons as well

as her husband, Bill, were increasingly troubled by her repeated absences from her home.

Dr. T. developed what Temerlin and Temerlin (1982) call a
*psychotherapy cult* in which he functioned as the charismatic leader
with his patients, ex-patients and associates who were his followers. As my account of Bill indicates, in such cults there is a breakdown of major boundaries between the cult leader and his followers. (For more about psychotherapy cults and other types of cults,
see Chapter 9.)

Dr. T. sponsored parties which included Bill's wife, Lorna, a
lay psychotherapist (Ms. A.) who worked in Dr. T.'s office,
and sometimes Bill. In the third year of her psychotherapy,
Lorna began a sexual affair with the lay therapist, Ms. A. Later,
Lorna and Dr. T. shared sexual intimacies just short of intercourse. Bill became increasingly depressed as his wife seemed
to become more estranged from him. Dr. T. placed him on
antidepressant medication. When Bill discussed his marital
problems or concerns about his wife with Dr. T., he was subjected to a repeated and highly destructive gaslighting.

When he spoke of his worries about his wife being ab-
sent for most of the time and engaged in questionable activities with Dr. T.'s followers, he was told by Dr. T. that he was
"distorting reality." Dr. T.'s attacks on Bill's judgments and
perceptions were backed up by appeals to accept Dr. T.'s views
about the therapeutic nature of Lorna's relationships with him
and his other followers.

At the same time that Dr. T. was attempting to get Bill to
accept his explanations of what was happening to Lorna, he
was also repeatedly and successfully attempting to disqualify
and discredit Bill's judgments and perceptions.

Bill's initial reaction to these attacks on his judgments
and perceptions was to feel confused and bewildered. Gradually he felt more and more helpless and hopeless. His self-
esteem fell as his confidence in his reality-testing and mental
functions was markedly lowered. He became severely de-

pressed to the point of seriously contemplating and planning suicide. One day he set off in his car with the aim of driving off a steep cliff. When, however, he thought of how hurtful this would be to his two children, he turned back.

When several women patients sued Dr. T. for sexual abuse, Lorna began to realize how badly she had been treated by him. She then broke off her treatment with Dr. T., sued him for malpractice, and won a sizeable award. Dr. T. finally confessed to these crimes and sexual intimacies with Lorna and other patients. Bill's gradual improvement began when both Dr. T. and Lorna revealed the truth about what had taken place. Bill's recovery from depression began then because, as he said, "Somebody turned the light on."

Bill's recovery from the depression and the other destructive effects of his treatment with Dr. T. depended on regaining confidence in his own judgments and his abilities for reality testing. He brought a malpractice suit against Dr. T., and one of the allegations was Dr. T.'s repeated gaslighting. The case was settled out of court a few hours before a trial was scheduled to begin.

In this case, as well as others where the victimizer's manipulation is successful, the gaslighting contains a self-fulfilling prophecy. Dr. T.'s repeated interpretations that Bill was distorting reality and that there was something wrong with his thinking came true. Not only did Bill lose confidence in his mental capacities as a result of Dr. T.'s gaslighting, he also developed a depressive illness in which his cognitive capacities were temporarily impaired.

## Gaslighting in the Analytic Situation

In an analysis reported by Dewald (1972), the analyst used a number of techniques of covert interpersonal control including repetitive, directive questioning and gaslighting. In this section we shall examine two of many episodes of gaslighting.

The following vignette is taken from Session 3 in Dewald's (1972) book in which he presents process notes of an entire analysis. A repeated examination of his process notes revealed that many of his questions had a directive and controlling quality.

> In session 3, the patient arrived five minutes late. In response the analyst asked, "What comes to your mind about the trouble getting started today?"
>
> The patient responded to the question by telling Dewald that she felt hostile toward him. He rejoined with, "What's the detail?" She continued to protest, saying that he was the coldest man she had ever met. Several more brief exchanges follow, each one involving a directive type of question. Several times she spoke of her discomfort elicited by the analyst's impatience and directiveness. She paused a minute after the analyst's question, "What are your associations?" and then said,
>
>> I think of the time that my father told me how to drive the car. He told me to put on the brake and somehow I couldn't do it. He got furious and screamed at me, "Get out of my car!" . . . I have such hostility, but I've never shown it. I think about my terrible temper when I was little. Mother had such pride that she was able to squelch it [p. 198].
>
> The patient's memories about her father's impatience and rejection of her while teaching her how to drive may be viewed as derivatives of her unconscious meaning analysis of her interactions with the analyst. Dewald's impatience and directiveness are represented in her memory about her father's fury at her while trying to teach her to drive.
>
> The analyst responded, "So we can see how hard it is for you to accept this basic idea of analysis. You expect me to react either as your father did and tell you to get out, or else as your mother did and try to squelch you if you show your feelings" (p. 198).

From the traditional perspective some would evaluate this intervention as a transference interpretation in which the analyst has interpreted the patient's complaints and protests as distortions of reality. In my opinion the analyst's intervention was a gaslighting manipulation unconsciously designed to discredit the patient's judgments. His interpretation served to deny the valid aspects of the patient's complaints about the analyst's directive behaviors. Through this and later similar gaslighting interventions, the analyst unconsciously attempted to intimidate the patient and to direct her communications.

> After a brief silence the patient replied, "I really think that you do feel this way. I think that it's in your tone of voice. It's as if you're saying, 'Be perfect or else forget it.'" In this spirited response to Dewald's gaslighting intervention, the patient showed unusual ego strength in maintaining her evaluations of what was occurring in her transactions with the analyst and in withstanding his pressures to relinquish her judgments in favor of his.
>
> The analyst responded, "Your feeling is that I expect you to be perfect here. What comes to your mind?" After a minute's pause, the patient replied, "You expect me to be perfect and I'm not. I never will be. . . . You can't control my mind and I want to express myself. It's just your tough luck!"
>
> The analyst responded, "I wonder if this thought doesn't really reflect your own fear about your feeling and your thoughts and your ideas about your fear of the whole process of analysis?"

Again in the foregoing intervention Dewald used a gaslighting technique to reassert his control over the patient, to displace her protests away from himself, and to discredit her negative judgments about him.

> The patient stoutly maintains her evaluations about what is going on in her interactions with Dewald by stating, "What happens if I can't accept my imperfections? I could do that if my parents only had. I feel as if you are detouring me and you are making me direct my hostility against myself."

Note how perceptive and accurate were the patient's statements about the analyst's communications to her. Clearly, as she states, his interventions in this session were aimed at getting her to "detour" (displace) to others her disturbing concerns about the ways he was relating to her. Also, as she indicated, he probably was, for defensive purposes, attempting to induce her to direct her anger against herself and away from him.

More clinical examples of gaslighting may be found in chapters 4, 5, 6, and 7.

## THE DOUBLE WHAMMY

In this section, my aim is to describe and illustrate a specific gaslighting technique I have called the double whammy. It is a tactic many individuals consciously or unconsciously employ in everyday life and psychotherapy contexts to shame, disorganize, humiliate, and above all to control other persons.

I call this tactic the double whammy because it consists of two projective identifications made by the victimizer separated by one communication made by the victim in response to the victimizer's initial projective identification. The first projective identification is one in which the victim is verbally attacked, insulted, or disparaged. Then after the victim has protested, the victimizer, in the second projective identification, again verbally abuses the victim by discrediting and invalidating the judgments made by the victim in his responses to the initial verbal assault. In what follows, I present three vignettes from everyday life and a final one describing the use of the double whammy in psychoanalytic treatment.

### Vignette #1

In the following example, an older woman speaks to her daughter who has had economic problems trying to start a new business.

*Mother:* Everything you do turns to shit!
*Daughter:* Ouch! That's mean! I wish you wouldn't say that.
*Mother:* You have no sense of humor. I was only kidding.

The second projective identification in the above vignette was more abusive than the first because, in addition to being insulting, it invalidated the daughter's abilities for interpersonal perception. The daughter accurately observed and responded to the hostile quality of her mother's first utterance. The second verbal attack is the gaslighting communication designed not only to shame the daughter, but also to impair her confidence in her abilities for perception, judgment, and reality testing.

In the foregoing vignette, the mother claims she was only kidding. How does one person ordinarily convey to another person the message that one is trying to be funny, to tease, to make a joke, rather than being serious or "straight"? Most often this is done nonverbally by what are called *metacommunications*. A slight smile, a raised eyebrow, a gesture, a tone of irony or exaggerated dramatization, and the like, are metacommunications used to convey a message such as, "I'm only teasing," "This is a joke," or "Don't take me seriously."

The expert in the double whammy technique makes a point of expressing his first disparaging message either in a "straight" way without the accompanying metacommunications noted above or in an ambiguous way in order to engender doubt and confusion in his victim.

The double whammy, as well as other forms of gaslighting, is a potent tactic individuals have for controlling others. The double whammy is an informal method of *behavior modification* employed widely in everyday life as a method for controlling others through causing emotional distress and impairing, at least temporarily, their cognitive functions. The most common ways individuals control others are by the induction of painful affects such as guilt, shame, fear, and anxiety. When the double whammy is done repeatedly, the psychic damage may be more serious and lasting and include psychosis.

The double whammy is analogous to the one-two punch in boxing, wherein a quick left jab or upper cut is followed immediately by a powerful haymaker to the head of one's opponent. Like the one-two punch, the double whammy is an effective two-phase type of abuse for silencing and conquering one's opponent. The initial insulting projective identification sets up the patient for the even more powerful and destructive gaslighting intervention.

### Vignette #2

The following account of a marital interaction describes how the double whammy may be used to induce mental confusion. Gass and Nichols (1988) write about certain destructive male behaviors during and after their extramarital affairs and the impact of those actions on their wives.

> Harry, for example, had an affair and his wife, Jane, found out about it. Harry then lied to his wife, stating he was not having an affair. To this the wife responded, "The worst part, Harry, is the lying." In response, Harry replied, "I'm not lying; you're just imagining things."

Gass and Nichols conclude, "The gaslighting behaviors of the husband provide a recipe for a so-called 'nervous breakdown' for some women, for collapse or suicide in some of the worst case situations" (p. 14). My studies on the traumatizing effects of the double whammy and other kinds of gaslighting agree with the conclusions of Gass and Nichols; gaslighting methods can precipitate a wide range of psychiatric disorders, up to and including psychosis and suicidal acting out on the part of victims.

## SHAME INDUCTION AND THE DOUBLE WHAMMY

### Vignette #3

As shown in the following vignette, the double whammy is a powerful method of attaining interpersonal control through shame induction.

A businessman, Mr. B., unconsciously had identified with his mother's propensity for publicly shaming others, and he frequently used this method on his wife in social situations. In this way he unconsciously attempted to enlist others as witnesses and validators of his superiority and domination over her.

One evening Mr. and Mrs. B. had the following interchange in front of some friends while saying goodbye at the front door of their friends' home.

Mr. B.: Why are we leaving so early? You are being antisocial! (Though he talks in a joking way there is an angry and contemptuous edge to his voice.)

Mrs. B.: It's getting late, and we have to get up early tomorrow.

Mr. B.: It's not so late! You are a party pooper! (said contemptuously.)

As a result of Mr. B.'s two insulting communications, the wife first felt acutely embarrassed and within an hour this turned into a depressive state.

## Vignette #4

This vignette illustrates the abusive effects of the double whammy in psychoanalytic interventions.

Dr. A.: You reacted to my last statement as if I were criticizing you. Actually what I said was an interpretation.

Patient: Well—ahh—it certainly sounded to me like you were criticizing me.

Dr. A.: You are distorting reality. Your unconscious memories of your critical father keep you from seeing me objectively.

Out of a feeling state of defeat, helplessness, and shame over his alleged distortion of reality, the patient complies with the analyst's view of what is going on.

Clinicians like Dr. A., who have interpreted defenses and transferences as distortions of reality, have often been unwittingly practicing a form of gaslighting. At the same time that they set themselves up as arbiters of what is real and undistorted, they undermine their patients' mental capacities and self-esteem by labeling their patients' perceptions and judgments as distorted and unrealistic.

## DISCUSSION

Gaslighting and other covert methods of interpersonal control are frequently used by many people in Western societies.[1] Most individuals have little understanding or awareness of covert types of interpersonal control, domination, and abuse they are exposed to all of their lives in their families, their schools, and their workplaces. They are not able to understand how much they have been subjected to such covert methods of manipulations and abuse until they have experienced relationships in everyday life or in psychoanalytic treatment that are more caring, more respectful, and non-manipulative.

My conclusions about both the frequency and the prevalent ignorance (and/or denial) of these covert methods of interpersonal control are supported by studies carried out in three other disciplines: feminist studies, linguistics, and Marxist studies. In her summary of research on speech patterns of Americans, professor of linguistics Elgin (1980) stated, "Take as a given that men are brought up to be verbally abusive, usually without conscious awareness of that fact" (p. 286).

---

1. My sentence on the frequent use of gaslighting and other covert methods of interpersonal control should not be interpreted to mean such methods are not used in non-Western societies. I do not have any information about how frequently such methods or other methods of indoctrination are used in non-Western countries.

Gaslighting and other covert methods of interpersonal control are widely used by mental health professionals as well as other people in everyday life because they are effective means for shaping and controlling the behavior of other individuals. Brainwashing methods work—but so does torture!

Gaslighting and other methods of covert interpersonal control are opposed to the values and precepts of psychoanalysis from Freud on to the present time. Respect for the patient's autonomy, the rule of neutrality, the value placed on being interpretive rather than directive, are just three of the principles proscribing use of gaslighting and other methods of covert interpersonal control.

Though psychoanalysis explicitly opposes gaslighting and similar methods of indoctrination, there are several important features of the classical clinical theory that support and facilitate the use of gaslighting. Classical Freudian and Kleinian psychoanalysis views the patient's manifest behaviors, dreams, communications, and transferences as the distorting transformations of unconscious fantasies. Traditionally, the task of the analyst is to unearth both the underlying unconscious fantasy as well as the way in which it has been distorted by defenses. The analyst's interpretations are supposed to include not only what are the actual unconscious fantasies and percepts but also how and why the patient has been unconsciously distorting these unconscious contents. Note that what I have been describing in a schematic way about the psychoanalytic theory of technique closely approximates the essence of gaslighting. In order to be effective, gaslighting depends on first convincing the victim that his thinking is distorted and secondly persuading him that the victimizer's ideas are the correct and true ones.

## CONCLUDING REMARKS

Though an unconscious or covert kind of gaslighting is used by many mental health professionals, few of them realize its damaging effects on patients. My hope is that this study will assist therapists in first recognizing and then eliminating gaslighting and other indoctrination techniques. In this way, psychoanalytic treatment can bring about therapeutic and permanent structural changes rather than the temporary and cosmetic changes made by patients in unconscious compliance with their therapists' gaslighting.

# On Questioning Used as a Covert Method of Interpersonal Control

The aim of this chapter is to examine and discuss the technique of questioning in psychoanalysis and psychoanalytic psychotherapy. Following a review of the relevant literature, I shall present some clinical studies on questioning. In previous publications on questioning, I concluded that most questioning done by clinicians was a countertransference based covert method of interpersonal control (Dorpat 1984, 1991c). Aside from articles by Boesky (1989), Olinick (1954, 1957, 1980), and some brief comments by Eissler (1953), Greenson (1967), Paul (1989), and others, few analysts have studied or written about the use of questions in psychoanalysis. In the field of psychoanalytic psychotherapy, Langs (1979a, 1980a) is one of the few who has performed clinical studies on questioning.

With few exceptions, most writings on questions repeat what earlier authors have said and few provide clinical evidence to support their conclusions and recommendations regarding questioning in psychoanalytic treatment. The reader of the literature on this subject gains the unmistakable impression that contemporary writers have merely passed on to the present generation what they learned from past generations of analysts about this subject.

Eissler (1953) considered the question to be a basic and indispensable tool of analysis, and one that is essentially different from interpretation. Greenson (1967) recommended the use of questions in psychoanalysis, but he provided little comment on the indications or contraindications for their use. He subscribed to the traditional view that all analytic techniques are subordinate to interpretation, and he included questions along with clarifications and confrontation as acceptable techniques preparatory to interpretation. In a section on the pursuit of the transference trigger, he gave examples of questioning such as, "If a patient tells me I am disgusting, I ask what is disgusting about me" (p. 308). Other examples of questions include "What occurs to you if you let your thoughts drift with these feelings and impulses?" (p. 311); and "Towards whom did you feel this way in the past?" (p. 313).

Glover (1955) sent a questionnaire on psychoanalytic technique to twenty-nine practicing analysts in England, and he received replies from twenty-four. One item in the questionnaire was, "Do you ask direct questions (a) about matters of fact, e.g., family history; (b) about matters of phantasy; (c) about emotional reactions?" A majority of the respondents said they asked questions freely, others occasionally. Some said they never ask questions in the early stages of analysis.

Glover commented that it seems quite natural to ask questions about matters of fact concerning which one is in doubt. Some patients are put at ease by being asked questions. Many family situations, he opined, would be grasped much more quickly by the analyst if he did not hesitate to ask about some detail instead of waiting. He warned against any use of "history taking" procedure since it tends to stultify free association.

In their book on psychoanalytic technique, Menninger and Holtzman (1973) have only one paragraph on questions. According to them, it is often important in the early stages of analysis to ask questions about details or other matters of fact and to inquire as to the patient's feelings about something or other. Standard questions in their view include, "What occurs to you about that?", "What associations do you have to that?", "What do you think?"

What Olinick (1954) said in 1954 still holds true today. "Of the behavioral interventions available to the psychoanalyst, perhaps none has been more taken for granted and less subjected to careful scrutiny than has questioning" (p. 57). He claimed that the use of questions by the analyst is more frequent in the early phase of treatment. Olinick (1954) argued that the discrepancies, misinformation, and omissions of the patient reflect a need on the part of the patient for a guideline, an orienting pattern to which the analyst by tactful questions may give a "nudge" to the patient. He noted that the act of questioning may be predicated on the reluctance or the passivity of the person questioned or on the impatience or curiosity of the questioner. He recommended questioning when instances of interpretation require for preinterpretive validation an inquiry into external and internal circumstances.

Olinick (1954) listed the conditions, such as anxiety or resistance of the patient, that must be obtained before a question is asked. Other conditions included are special situations such as inarticulate, borderline, or psychotic patients. His guidelines and indications for questioning are too general; they cast too large a net to serve as suitable and specific guides for questioning. Except for a brief clinical vignette, Olinick did not provide clinical evidence to support his claims for the conditions for questioning. His vignette did not give sufficient data to enable the reader to draw his own inferences or to make his own conclusions about the merits or demerits of the questioning used with the case presented.

Olinick (1954) warned about the misuse of questions, and he cautioned that questions may become an intrusion into the patient's freedom of choice. He differed from Eissler's (1953) view that questions are part of the basic model of analytic technique, and he considered questioning to be a parameter, a deviation from the basic model of technique. He claimed that questions should be self-eliminating, but he did not say how they can be self-eliminating. He recommended that analysts should look to their countertransference to determine that questioning is not used in an antitherapeutic manner such as, for example, to enforce a sadomasochistic relationship.

Another article by Olinick (1957) concerned the psychology of the question generally and was not concerned specifically with the use of questioning as it pertains to psychoanalytic technique. He was the first to describe questioning as a device for the expression of aggression and active mastery, and he made an important contribution in emphasizing the intrusive, acquisitive, and aggressive aspects of questioning.

Paul (1989) recognizes the directiveness of questioning in psychoanalytic treatment and discourages its use. He writes:

> But a true question—namely, one that asks for more information—is more likely than an interpretation to command, if not also deflect, attention, and rarely can it be ignored the way an interpretation can. A direct question virtually demands a direct response [pp. 40–41].

Hollender (1965) discussed the reasons for asking questions in psychoanalytic psychotherapy, including (1) to clarify a point (he does not state whether or not the clarification is made for the patient's sake or for the therapist's), (2) to elicit additional information "which might be helpful in substantiating or excluding one or another hypothesis being considered as the basis for an interpretation" (p. 87), and (3) "to encourage the patient to explore a subject mentioned in passing. . . ." (p. 87). He proscribed questions designed to satisfy the therapist's personal curiosity.

There are no systematic studies on the frequency with which questioning is used in psychoanalytic treatment. My impression from reading the relevant literature and from my work as a supervisor is that questioning is the most common mode of intervention used in both psychoanalysis and psychoanalytic psychotherapy. In the type of psychoanalytically oriented therapy called "sector therapy" by Deutsch and Murphy (1955), questions make up the preponderance of the therapist's interventions. My study of Dewald's report (1972) of an entire analysis revealed that questioning was the most frequent type of intervention. Dewald used questions on an average of 8.7 times per session, and questions comprised 70.5% of all of his interventions.

Langs (1976a, 1978a, 1980a) considers questioning anti-therapeutic and recommends discontinuing its use. In his view, questioning moves the patient toward the surface of his thoughts, stresses manifest content, and is inimical to Type A communication. Langs (1979a) said, "Active questioning can shift a patient capable of symbolic communication toward projective identification or intense defensiveness" (p. 213). In his books which report on seminars where residents presented psychotherapy patients, he demonstrated that questions tend to generate resistances and defensive activity (1976a, 1979a, 1980a).

Instead of the overt questioning of the patient, Langs (1979a) recommends the use of "silent questions" that arise in the mind of the therapist as he listens to the patient. Such silent questions can be used to construct hypotheses that the therapist can validate by the patient's response to the therapist's interventions.

The following vignette of Langs (1979a) illustrates the defensive and countertransference aspects of questions. A male patient remarked, "By the way, I met a woman that you know." The therapist responded, "Who is she?" According to Langs, the question reflected considerable anxiety on the part of the therapist, and the intervention was a type of projective identification. The question reflected the therapist's difficulty in managing his own curiosity, and it placed into the patient the therapist's sense of anxiety: his poor controls and his defensiveness. The therapist's presentation of what happened after this incident confirmed Langs' prediction that the patient would unconsciously introject the therapist's lack of a sense of patience and management.

Langs offered the following formulation about the persistent questioning of the therapist mentioned above. The therapist's active inquiries were unconsciously designed to restrict the patient's communications in the area connected with his patient dating an acquaintance of the therapist. The questioning interventions constricted the communicative field and protected the therapist from the communication of unconscious derivatives related to the patient's date with the therapist's acquaintance. While the conscious communication was "tell me more," the unconscious communication was "tell me nothing more."

In Langs's more recent writings, various commonly used interventions were studied from a communicative perspective in which the unconscious qualities and functions of such interventions became the subject of extensive investigation. Langs (1978a) recommended discarding questions and other previously employed interventions such as clarification and confrontation. His position was based on repeated tests of the unconscious functions, communications, and meanings conveyed in the actual interaction between the patient and therapist or analyst by each of the interventions mentioned above (1978a). Each instance of the use of such interventions was taken as an adaptive context, and the patient's responses were studied in terms of primary process derivatives and as commentaries in terms of both meanings and validity.

Langs (1978a) claimed that questions and clarifications are used largely because of confusion as to the nature of neurotic communications and the best means of obtaining derivatives from patients. Rather than recognizing that silence and a secure frame offer conditions that best facilitate the patient's expressing himself in the form of analyzable primary process derivatives, some analysts mistakenly believe that pertinent questions and confrontations foster their expression. We can end this review of the literature with the conclusion that there has been little systematic study on the use of questioning. With the exception of the papers by Dorpat, Olinick, and Langs, the subject of questions has been unexamined and unquestioned!

## CLINICAL INVESTIGATIONS OF QUESTIONING

We turn now to the author's clinical studies on the use of questioning in psychoanalysis and psychoanalytic psychotherapy. My findings and conclusions apply equally to both types of treatment. I have examined the unconscious meanings, functions, and interactions occurring when clinicians ask questions, and I have been especially attentive to the effects of questioning on the patients' communications. With the exception of the first section, the clinical data is taken from supervisory work with analysts, psychotherapists, and individuals in various kinds of training programs.

## COUNTERTRANSFERENCE AND QUESTIONING

As part of this study on questioning, I reviewed some process notes taken during the analysis of a case reported previously (Dorpat 1978–1979). Process notes were taken during the second year of a seven-year successful analysis of a 32-year-old woman who began treatment with symptoms of depression and fears of her suicidal impulses.

One of the principal concerns in this period of her analysis was her unstable capacity for object constancy. When she could maintain an image of the analyst outside of analytic hours, her symptoms disappeared. When she could not remember my "presence" (her word) or recall my talking and listening to her, she would relapse and her symptoms would reappear. My initial explanatory formulations about the above changes followed classical dynamic concepts about unconscious conflicts over aggression. In brief, at first I thought that the patient's anxiety over unconscious angry feelings toward the analyst prevented her from recalling the image of the analyst. Later I found that my questioning was a more important proximal cause of her inability to recall my presence than were her conflicts over aggression.

Repeated study of the process notes of sixty sessions revealed a consistent interactional pattern. Active questioning was regularly followed by her communication of feeling distant and detached from the analyst and sometimes by the recrudescence of her depressive symptoms. In one session she said, "I had a dream last night. In the dream I am with you. We were talking together. It was very nice. You left. I was all alone. I felt lost. I could not find you." After a moment's pause she went on in a sarcastic tone, "I suppose you will ask me, 'How does the dream apply to your life?' I don't know and I guess I don't care." Her sarcastic remark referred to my questioning the previous day, and the question ("How do you think your dream applies to your life?") I had asked her the day before after she had told me about a dream. Her dream about my leaving her replicated and symbolized the effects of my intrusive and intellectualizing questions.

In one session I made an interpretation that she had a need to prevent herself from maintaining an image of me because of her fear that she would feel angry toward me. At the onset of the next session she said, "I was so pleased to find I could be angry and still have an encounter with someone. I would not have to withdraw when I became angry. I was so pleased—but I tried to hide it—like a squirrel who finds a nut and then tries to hide it."

"What was the need to hide your pleasure?" I asked. She answered in an anguished voice, "I don't know." After a few moments' silence she went on talking about going on a trip with her family the previous weekend. While on the trip she tried to think of me. She explained that when she is anxious she tries to imagine my listening to her. "If you are there, I don't feel so afraid. But sometimes I can't find you. I know why now. It's because I misunderstood trusting you. I never realized that trust was an emotional thing. It's not intellectual! You have to feel it!" In this interaction she again became depressed following my questioning. Her remarks about trust being an "emotional" and not an "intellectual" matter unconsciously refer to the analyst's intellectualizing questions.

Unconsciously the patient's comments meant something like the following. "Don't worry about not immediately knowing something about me. Your questions are pushing me away!" Her statements about not being able "to find" the analyst unconsciously refer to the interpersonal distance and disrupted communication brought about by my questioning. As is typical with depressive patients, she took full responsibility for what occurred between us, and she tended to absolve the analyst for any disruptions in the relationship. She perceived herself as the sole cause of difficulties she had in experiencing or recalling the "presence" of the therapist. My systematic review of the process notes convinced me that my frequent questioning played a significant contributing role in her problems with being able to experience, both within and outside of analytic hours, the "presence" of the analyst.

In the next hour, she told of feeling angry at me since the previous hour. She said, "I can relate to nature, to trees, animals and to the desert but not to people." She seemed about ready to cry, and she spoke with a tone of dread and despair about the "faceless people." People she had been with lately had seemed "faceless" to her. I asked her what "faceless people" meant. With considerable anger she replied, "Oh, so you don't know! That's just too bad. You mean, I'm supposed to tell you so you can know?" Her statements and her question constituted a confrontation and unconscious quasi-interpretation about my countertransference-based questioning. Translated, her communication contained the meaning, "Your intrusive questions are part of your problem. You are not asking them to help me to understand me, but to satisfy your own compulsion to know."

She entered one session feeling depressed, and she spoke about wanting to stop the analysis. Then she told of growing tired of "looking," "hearing," and asking "Why?"; and she described having a fantasy of a vulture perched on her shoulder waiting to eat someone. While she was associating to the vulture fantasy in a somewhat depressed way, I too began thinking about what it could mean. At first I thought of her mother who had been so possessive and demanding and who had, in a sense, attempted to "eat" her daughter.

I rejected my impulse to interpret the vulture symbol as a representation of her mother because such an extraanalytic interpretation would go against a rule of thumb I had developed in the analysis with this patient. The rule was to look first at disruptions in the patient-analyst relationship to account for any disturbances in the patient. Since any return of her symptoms usually came because of some rupture in a selfobject transference, I had gradually learned to first attend to events of the analytic hour in my search for the meaning of her regressive lapses. Then I recalled that I had felt impatient with her during the previous hour and that I had asked several questions. I made the interpretation, "You fear that the image you have of me asking 'Why?' will envelop you until there is nothing left of you. The vulture stands for your fear of being enveloped."

She replied, saying that she recalled feeling tense in the previous hour and being withdrawn after my questioning. Her further remarks had to do with fears of being close to the analyst and of her anxiety over being "swallowed up" by the analyst as she had felt in her relationship with her mother.

My interpretation implicitly acknowledged that my questions had disturbed her, and this led to the restoration of the therapeutic alliance and to alleviating her depressive symptoms. The vulture symbol in her fantasy correctly identified the unconscious aggressive wishes in my questioning and my voracious need to know. The realization that the vulture symbol revealed a countertransference problem shocked me, and eventually (along with other efforts toward self-analysis) induced me to question my previous attitude toward questioning. Where before I had taken pride in being able to construct searching questions, I now became dismayed at them, not only because repeated observations in this case and with other patients had shown me their detrimental effects, but also because I began to become aware of the aggressive need to control patients that had previously energized my questioning technique. Recall in this connection what I noted earlier about Olinick's (1957) emphasis on unconscious aggressive and acquisitive wishes expressed in questioning.

The above vignettes are only a few of the many instances in which questioning evoked in the patient a shift from a Type A mode of communication to a Type B or C mode. A review of process notes of sixty sessions revealed at least forty instances where questioning had this negative effect, and I did not find a single instance where questioning facilitated the analytic process.

Repeated and emotionally painful times of self-analysis revealed other unconscious sources of the countertransference-based questions. Some countertransference elements were similar to those described by Kohut (1971) as typical responses to the idealizing transference. The patient's idealizations led me to sometimes feel uncomfortable with the grandiose contents projected onto me. Initially what was most threatening to me was the patient's regressive and temporary dissolution of self and object boundaries, and the concomitant fusion and confusion over who was doing what and to whom in the analytic relationship. Months of the analysis went by before I could gradually understand the therapeutic necessity of the patient's regression to early symbiotic modes of relating. Questioning the patient was an unconscious device for attaining affective control of myself and the patient and for reversing the therapeutic regression taking place within the patient and (through temporary, trial identifications with the patient) within myself. Through questioning, I unconsciously tried to block the patient's disturbing mode of communication and attempted to substitute for both of us a more rational mode of discourse that would support my defenses and provide emotional equilibrium.

## INTERACTIONAL ASPECTS OF QUESTIONING

The question and answer pattern of communication is a mode of interaction in which both partners contribute and participate. This perspective is akin to that of the bipersonal field concept (Baranger and Baranger 1966, Langs 1976a) and the intersubjective field concept of Stolorow and colleagues (1987, 1994) by which it is postulated that every interaction between the two parties to the analytic situation, and every experience within either, is a product of the field and, as such, receives contributions from both its members.

In question and answer transactions, each participant partially shapes the responses of the other person. Many patients unconsciously evoke questions on the part of the therapist, and the therapist's questioning tends to contribute to the nature and content of the patient's answers. The transactions in question and answer interactions may be studied from the point of view of interactional processes such as introjection and projection. Some of the more common contents introjected and projected in question and answer interactions include the following polarities: independence–dependence, power–helplessness, sadism–masochism. In these interactions the questioner assumes the role of the active agent for both parties and projects onto the person he/she questions what the questioner feels to be the less desired quality—for example, dependence, helplessness, masochism. Then the patient introjects the role of the one acted upon and projects the more active role onto the therapist. What we are describing are pathological symbiotic kinds of relations in which emotionally important contents and functions of the more passive partner are projected onto the therapist who, in turn, introjects these contents and functions and acts upon them in questioning.

In the following vignette the question and answer mode of interaction involved primarily the independence-dependence polarity.

A resident in supervision with the author saw a married graduate student in twice-a-week psychotherapy. She was accompanied to her initial interviews by her overprotective husband, and her presenting symptoms were those of feeling depressed and of being phobic about social situations. In the first interview and decreasingly thereafter, she related to the resident in a helpless and dependent fashion. She was often silent, and she communicated both consciously and unconsciously her wish for the psychiatrist to be directive and to lead the interviews. Over the nine months of supervision, I attempted with some success to assist him in understanding and inhibiting his need to direct and to question the patient. Gradually, he decreased his questioning, and he was able to understand and to interpret the unconscious defensive and transferential meanings of the patient's behavior.

As the therapist increasingly adopted an interpretive rather than a directive approach, the patient improved. Since the resident's duties required him to leave town, it was necessary for him to terminate both the treatment and the supervision. He was troubled by the patient's apparent unresponsiveness to the impending termination, since she had said nothing about it during the several sessions prior to the last one. During the last therapy hour, she seemed to regress back toward the dependent and passively quiet attitude she had shown at the onset of treatment. Feeling frustrated, the therapist reverted to his defensive need for questions by asking, "What are your feelings over the termination?" Her answer was flat and conforming. Still frustrated, he asked another question, "What do you want to work on when you continue your treatment with another resident?"

Again the patient responded in a compliant and matter-of-fact manner. Then she added in a more lively way, "I'm sorry I don't have any strong emotion for you. But I have made headway on my problems of treating people as stereotypes." She went on to explain how the treatment had helped her to be more flexible and free with other people. The short remaining time in the therapy hour went well, and the resident told the supervisor that both the patient and he had said goodbye with tears in their eyes.

In the supervisory hour the resident, with some assistance from the supervisor, learned how and why both he and the patient had temporarily reverted to the sterile question and answer pattern of interaction. He understood that his regression in this regard had been triggered by his anxieties over terminating both the treatment with the patient and his supervision with the author. Also, the resident appreciated how kind the patient had been toward him in reassuring him that she had benefitted from the therapy. She had probably unconsciously perceived that anxiety had prompted his need to question her. This was my last supervisory hour with the resident and when he left he thanked me by saying, "You taught me how to shut up and listen."

The following case vignette from supervision describes how the question and answer form of interaction unconsciously acted out the patient's childhood traumatic relationship with her father.

She was a 41-year-old married nurse who had been in analysis for five months and who, from about age 11 to 14, was sexually abused by her father. The patient began a session by telling about having, during the previous evening, one of her repetitive "box" dreams. In these dreams she anxiously viewed herself as being alone in a box or a room. The analyst became impatient with the vague and hesitant manner in which the patient was talking about the dream and he pressured her with questions about the details of the dream.

In response to his questions, the patient described the dream as one in which the moving walls seemed as if they were about ready to collapse. She awoke frightened, and she had the premonition that something bad was about to happen to her father. She described anxiously calling her father on the telephone in the middle of the night and finding out that he was all right. She told the analyst about a picture book her father had put together about her when she had her first date and attended a prom at age 13. Again, she was vague and circumstantial and again the analyst "took the bait" (as he later said about himself). He impatiently confronted the patient with her vagueness, and he again asked for details about the picture book.

Prompted by the analyst's questioning, the patient with much embarrassment told the analyst of how her father took pictures of her preparations for the prom. He took photos of her taking off her panties, of her stepping into the shower, and of her dressing. The patient continued with other accounts of her father's seductiveness and intrusiveness. Often he "leered" at the patient, and he would touch her in ways and places that were acutely disturbing to her. She exclaimed that many times she felt like telling her father, "Keep your flabby hands off of me!"

At this point in the supervisory hour, I became aware that *both* the patient and the analyst were unconsciously repeating the sexual trauma she sustained in the relationship with her sadistic father. I explained to the supervisee that the patient's angry warning, "Keep your flabby hands off of me!" referred to the analyst as well as to the father. Her statement was an unconscious commentary on the analyst's persistent questioning and probing. The analyst's questioning unconsciously acted out the role of the intrusive father. He was dismayed by my confrontation of what he was doing, and he recalled that his questioning had also been prompted by his anxiety that the patient was forming an oedipal transference neurosis "too soon."

The crucial issue, as the patient's dreams of moving and collapsing walls suggested, had to do both with the patient's personal boundaries between herself and others and the boundaries of the patient-analyst relationship. Her incestuous relations with her father had compromised the patient's boundaries, and the analyst's impatient and intrusive questioning constituted a symbolic and unconscious reenactment of the trauma.

My recommendation to the supervisee was to cease his questioning and probing and to explore ways in which he could restore and maintain the psychoanalytic frame. The integrity of the patient—analyst boundaries was a necessary condition for the patient to work through in the analysis traumas and unconscious conflicts stemming from her experiences with her father. I predicted that an important adaptive context for the next hour would be the analyst's active questioning and that the patient would unconsciously continue to struggle with the issue of boundaries. This prediction was confirmed when at the beginning of the next session the patient told of being angry at a pharmacist who was acting like a doctor in countermanding her work as a nurse and who pushed his unsolicited advice on a patient of hers. Her remarks about the pharmacist may be viewed as a disguised and unconscious commentary on the analyst's tendency in previous hours to overstep the boundaries of their relationship by his impatient and intrusive questioning.

In the above case example, the patient evoked active questioning behaviors in the therapist by her hesitant and vague way of talking. Her attitude of helplessness served as a defense against unconscious rage against both the analyst and her father. In behaving helplessly in relation to the analyst, the patient was unconsciously projecting onto the analyst the role of one who would lead and direct her. The analyst introjected what had been projected onto him and he, in turn, assumed an active role in his questions that guided and directed what she attended to and talked about. In so doing, he was also, of course, projecting onto the patient the passive and helpless parts of himself. Direct questioning of patients about their feelings is usually useless and it may strengthen their resistances to free association and to communicating in the Type A mode. A similar point was made by the author and interviewer Studs Terkel (1967) in his discussion of his interviewing method. In his view, one gets only clichés from people in response to direct questions about their feelings. It is necessary instead, he says, to talk to them and let them talk to you.

Therapists should as a rule respond to but not answer their patients' questions. An acceptable response to a patient's question is to explain tactfully reasons for not answering questions. Most clinicians understand or intuit that answering questions usually derails the therapeutic dialogue and inhibits the abilities of both parties to associate and communicate freely. Frequently patients ask questions as an unconscious means for avoiding free association and as a means for directing and controlling the analyst as well as the analytic situation.

These and other important reasons why therapists should usually not answer their patients' questions also apply to why therapists should not ask their patients questions. Whether initiated by the therapist or by the patient, the question and answer type of communication usually presents a formidable resistance to the therapeutic process.

## QUESTIONING AND
## UNCONSCIOUS COMMUNICATION

Questioning tends to evoke in the patient a mode of thinking and communication opposed to the methods and goals of analysis. As Langs (1978b) noted, questioning usually has the consequence of shifting the patient's communication away from derivative communication (i.e., Type A mode communication) toward communication which is more literal, superficial, and lacking in affect or derivatives (i.e., Type C mode communication).

The supervision of a psychiatrist's psychotherapy cases showed how the use of questioning blocks symbolic or derivative communication (i.e., the Type A mode). In my supervision of this psychiatrist's therapy of four women patients, I noted a common interactional pattern connected with his use of questions. Therapy with these patients started out well, and the patients reported improvement. Then the treatments stalemated, and I observed that his active and repeated questioning played a role in the therapeutic stalemates. When he felt frustrated over what was happening in the therapy, he would typically try to take control of the situation by questioning. His patients responded to his questioning by becoming more literal, defensively compliant, and matter-of-fact. Their associations became reality-oriented and symbolic or derivative communication dropped off sharply. The type of communication for both participants shifted toward what Langs (1979a) called the Type C mode.

The therapist was unaware of the unconscious sadism and need for control which was being acted out in his repetitive questioning. Over time I was able to demonstrate to him how his questioning was evoking passive compliant behavior on the part of his patients and how the questions tended to stultify communication.

Partly as a result of these confrontations and explanations, he was able to gain some insights into his own unconscious conflicts regarding aggression toward women and to seek psychoanalysis for himself.

Hollender (1965) provided a clinical vignette in which questioning was unconsciously used to attack and to demean the patient.

> The patient arrived seven minutes late and after apologizing for being late, she was silent for eight minutes. Breaking the silence, the therapist asked, "I wonder why you are silent today?" The patient replied that she didn't know why she was late. "I've been silent before, you know. . . . My mind is just a blank." Then the therapist remarked that he wondered if her mind being blank had anything to do with her being late. With a trace of petulance, the patient responded, "Well, I got up on time today. I dressed slower than usual. I was too involved, I guess, and the next thing I knew, the clock said ten of nine, and I realized I was going to be late. (A silence of ten minutes ensued.) I was just thinking about an upsetting incident at work the other day. My boss is really something. He is so full of nervous energy—he's gotta know what's going on all the time, interested in everybody's affairs, expects everybody to be perfect." She went on to tell how her boss assumes everybody is dishonest, and she told of a quarrel between the boss and another woman employee.
>
> Then the therapist asked her why she went into accounting. First she discussed her conscious reasons for entering the accounting field and then said, "I've often thought, in this field the women do the dirty work and the men get the gravy." The therapist responded with still another question containing an unconscious accusatory and critical message, "Are you saying, in a way, it's sort of a man's field?"

In this vignette questions were unconsciously used to criticize and to control the patient and to displace the patient's unconscious commentaries on his sadistic behavior onto other less-charged topics. The patient displaced her anger about his initial questions to her discussion about the intrusive and accusatory boss who harassed women. Her statements about the boss were an unconscious commentary on the therapist's dominance toward the patient and his intrusive and attacking questions. Unconsciously the therapist perceived the patient's communication about the therapist's destructiveness contained in her remarks about the intrusive boss. He unconsciously retaliated with another question asking her why she went into accounting. This question was, I believe, unconsciously prompted by his defensive need to change the topic and to lead the patient. She, in turn, responded with another unconscious commentary about his sadistic behavior when she said that "women do the dirty work and the men get the gravy." He returned with an attacking and demeaning question about her entering a man's field.

Clearly the therapist-patient relationship was marked by an ongoing struggle, one in which both persons appeared to view the man–woman relationship as a struggle for dominance. Although Hollender (1965) noted the therapist's need to dominate the patient in this and previous sessions, the interpretations about unconscious communications in the foregoing vignette are my own.

The unconsciously attacking and critical questions of the therapist may be evaluated both in terms of their aggressive and defensive functions and meanings. He unconsciously responded to the patient's hurt feelings and resentment toward himself by his hostile questions, and at the same time he defended himself from hearing what she was saying about him by displacing the manifest content of his questions to matters outside the patient–therapist relationship. The manifest content of all four of his questions contained no mention of the patient–therapist relationship. Although his attacking questions indicated that he was unconsciously responsive to the patient's resentment toward men, the manifest content of his questions showed that he was not consciously hearing or responding to the disturbing feelings his questions had engendered in the patient. In other words, from the point of view of consciousness, he did not hear her or respond to her.

Unconsciously, he did perceive her resentment, and he responded with attacks upon her, camouflaged as questions.

In another psychotherapy case a psychotherapist, through his questions, unconsciously communicated to the patient his wish for her to surrender her autonomy, to fuse herself with him, and to follow his direction.

The patient was a 30-year-old single nurse who was being seen in twice a week psychotherapy. The therapist complained to the supervisor about the patient's tendency to fall asleep during therapy sessions, and he described his fruitless efforts to deal with her resistance by interpretations. In one session she came late, apologized for sleeping in previous sessions, and said that she was considering terminating her therapy. The therapist made lengthy interpretation about the sleepiness stemming from the patient's need to defend herself against her conflicts over anger at her sister, whereupon the patient responded by saying that she could not remember anything about getting angry. Then the therapist interjected, "Don't you remember about how angry you got at your sister and how you would work it out on a punching bag?"

Immediately following his question she fell asleep. Several minutes later when she awoke, the therapist told her that her falling asleep was a kind of communication to him that she still wanted therapy. The patient replied, "Okay, I guess I must be angry at my sister." She went on, telling how much difficulty she had in remembering her anger. Then the therapist said, "Some of the anger you have about your sister is displaced from your mother, and you really feel angry with your mother." Again the patient fell asleep for about five minutes. When she awoke, the therapist asked her what had happened. The patient said she did not remember. After the therapist said, "We were talking about your anger toward your mother," the patient promptly fell asleep again.

Interactions in which the patient fell asleep were repeated five more times. Each time the patient woke up the therapist attempted by means of questions and other interventions to induce the patient to talk about her anger toward her mother.

Throughout the session the therapist attempted to lead and to control the patient with his questions and interpretations. Nearly all of his interventions, including his questions, were covert methods of interpersonal control in which he told the patient what she should think and talk about. In so doing, he was enacting the role transferred onto him of the powerful, dominating mother. His directive interventions discounted or ignored what she was doing and saying and what he said to her was not responsive to what she was trying to communicate to him. His questions could also be viewed as projective identifications, unconscious attempts to evoke in the patient his repudiated feeling of anger, frustration, and helplessness. The patient responded to his directive and controlling behavior by falling asleep. Evidently going to sleep was the only autonomous activity that she could initiate and use to escape both from her internal conflicts and the therapist's coercive control.

Her sleeping during the hour also represented an enactment of her introjection of the therapist's projection onto her as being a person who could not initiate or contribute to the communicative interaction. His interventions persistently ignored on a manifest level what she was communicating and attempted to pressure her to follow his lead and agree with his perspective of what was happening to her. His interpretations and questions communicated the implicit message, "Follow me because you are not capable of thinking for yourself or regulating your own life." Her sleeping in the session symbolized and expressed both her introjection of this demeaning view of herself and her passive-aggressive defiance of it.

By emphasizing the therapist's unconscious communications and their critical role in the psychogenesis of the patient's sleeping, I do not mean to imply that there were not also symbolized in the patient's symptom of sleeping important unconscious transference components involving conflicts over anger toward her sister and mother. However, the therapist's transference interpretations in this regard were counterproductive and to no avail because he was actively, though unconsciously, involved in interactions with the patient that repeated what she had experienced with her dominating mother.

## UNCONSCIOUS COMMUNICATIONS CONTAINED IN QUESTIONING IN EVERYDAY LIFE

A major reason why the use of questions in psychoanalytic treatment is so widespread and why the value of questioning has not been challenged or investigated is because clinicians tend to consider only the manifest and conscious meanings in questioning. Questioning, like other interventions, always carries with it unconscious meanings and messages in addition to its manifest content. The following examples from everyday life are used to illustrate the unconscious meanings and messages conveyed in questions. Often questions are used as projective identification, as efforts to coerce another individual to think, feel, or act in a certain way. Some examples are:

Why must you *always* embarrass me?

Why don't you think logically?

Why do you *always* act that way?

Whose side are you on, anyway?

Some questions provoke answers that either feed the questioner's anxieties or provoke an argument:

Do you think I'm getting old . . . fat . . . bald?

Do you think I'm stubborn . . . bossy . . . sloppy?

Do you think so-and-so is attractive?

Are you having an affair?

Some questions are masked criticisms and/or covert types of verbal abuse. The question "Are you angry *again*?" is a kind of masked criticism because it contains the presupposition that the other individual is frequently angry. What follows are examples of questions containing demeaning presuppositions.

Why don't we talk anymore?

Why don't you ever tell me how you feel?

Why don't you ever ask me what I want?

The following kinds of questions are often typical of sado-masochistic marital and other dyads where one of the partners attempts to assert power and control over the other.

> Why can't you learn to be more responsible and balance the checkbook?
>
> Who taught you to do *that*?
>
> Why are you acting just like your mother?
>
> Isn't it your turn to take out the garbage?
>
> Why can't you do anything right?

## DISCUSSION

A skeptical reader might object that this chapter only uses examples of the misuse or abuse of questions by therapists whose question-ing actions toward their patients were strongly and adversely influenced by such factors as countertransference, inexperience, and inadequate training. Someone could argue that the author has left out the positive and constructive communications and effects of questioning. My rebuttal to this line of argument is that in nearly two decades of studying the use of questions, I have found very few instances in which the validity and value of questioning could be validated by the patient's responses to the questioning.

Hollender (1965) held that the wording of a question deter-mined whether a question either opens up or closes off some area for exploration and discussion. Though I agree with Hollender that the wording has important influence on the patient–analyst inter-actions, I hold that nearly all questions tend to have a stultifying effect on the patient's capacities for free association and symbolic communication. Irrespective of the manifest content or the uncon-scious communications of questions, there is an intrinsic aspect of questioning which tends to be antithetical to open and thera-peutic communication. Questioning shifts the patient's attention from whatever he or she was attending to toward that which the therapist asks about. Because of this, questioning serves as a convenient means by which the therapist can exert some control over the experience, communication, and responses of the patient.

There is another quality of the most common type of questioning used in the analytic situation that often has untoward effects. I refer to an aspect of questioning that is unique to the analytic situation and that rarely occurs elsewhere. Most questioning in the analytic situation is consciously intended for the patient's benefit. The act of questioning directs the attention of the patient toward some topic the analyst believes the patient should think and talk about. This is the type of question that is designed to open up areas for exploration and is supposedly used to prepare the way toward interpretations. Usually analysts communicate directly or indirectly the fact that the question is consciously intended for the patient's benefit.

By way of contrast, in everyday life the questioner seeks something for himself, namely, information. There is no presumption that the one who answers will gain by his answering. The presumption that answering a question is somehow useful to the patient and his analysis puts an additional pressure on the patient. This interpersonal pressure can be variously perceived as an obligation, a duty, an invitation, a promise, or whatever. It is a powerful inducement to a pathological symbiotic mode of relating in which the patient endows the therapist with idealized powers such as knowing how the patient should regulate his thinking and his behavior.

Another disadvantage of this kind of questioning is that often such questions contain contradictory communications disruptive to the patient. The implicit message "I'm doing something good for you in asking about X, since it would be helpful to you to think and talk about X" is contradicted by the unconscious destructive messages (previously described in this chapter) contained in questions which are not good for the patient.

One common subtype in this large category of questions designed to prepare for interpretation is "why" questions. "Why" questions are consciously used to induce the patient to search for reasons and motives of his behavior. Several authors, such as Hollender and Menninger and Holtzman, have recommended caution in the use of "why" questions. Hollender (1965) observed that patients frequently interpret "why" questions as criticisms. According to Menninger and Holtzman (1973), "why" questions can have a stimulating effect, but they can also easily be overworked and often can evoke rationalizations and false reasoning. In my observations of "why" questions, I have not observed a single instance where a "why" type of question had a beneficial effect on the patient or on the analytic process.

Another type of question that is frequently used in psychoanalysis and in psychotherapy is the restating in an interrogative form the last word, phrase, or sentence uttered by the patient. Although this type of question is recommended by a number of analysts, none of them has provided any investigation on the effects of this type of questioning or on the indications or contraindications for its use (Hollender 1965, Olinick 1954).

There are two exceptions to the rule against questioning. In situations where the therapist is uncertain about the meaning of something said by the patient, it may be useful to question the patient in order to clarify or explain the patient's intended meaning. Secondly, a few questions may be needed in intake sessions with a prospective patient. Busch (1986) discussed the advisability of questioning patients during the initial assessment, and he concluded that occasional questions were useful, in contrast to those who advocate adhering to an associative technique from the beginning. However, even in intake interviews, when a therapist is obtaining a history it is advisable to avoid active and repetitive questioning. Repetitive questioning in preliminary sessions tends to establish a Type C field of communication that may be difficult or impossible to later convert into a Type A field. My criticisms of questioning apply mainly to psychoanalytic treatment; some questioning may at times be helpful in supportive psychotherapy and in counseling approaches.

What kinds of techniques and approaches are preferable to questions and can be used instead of questions? Usually, silence is the method most efficacious in situations where clinicians use questioning. A Gestalt therapist, who was aware of the stultifying effects of questioning, suggested to me the simple expedient of transforming questions into statements. I do not believe that his suggestion should apply to all or even most situations where questions are used, because interventions in the declarative form can be as manipulative and antitherapeutic as questions are. Questions can be rephrased as interpretations when the treatment situation is such that the correct conditions and criteria for effective interpretation have been fulfilled. Whenever these conditions do not obtain, silence is nearly always preferable.

The attitudes and beliefs commonly held by many clinicians about questioning are contrary to the conclusions I reached from the findings of this investigation. Next I shall summarize the traditional concepts about questions, and later, in the final section, contrast those ideas with the conclusions of this study.

Traditional psychoanalytic clinicians believe that (1) Questions are useful and necessary investigative tools for the exploration of unconscious transference and resistance reactions; they are a part of the basic model of analytic technique. (2) Questions, like clarifications and confrontations, are technical adjuncts to interpretation, and they effectively prepare the way for interpretation. Here the assumption is that questions, by drawing the patient's attention to something deemed important by the analyst, can prepare and lead the way toward effective interpretation (Dewald 1972). (3) Aside from their function in preparing the way for interpretation, questions have little or no effect on the patient or upon the analytic process.

## CONCLUSIONS

As generally employed in psychoanalytic treatment, questions are seldom useful for opening up unconscious resistances and transferences. Questions rarely prepare the way for interpretation, and they do not assist the analysand toward the attainment of insight.

Frequently, the asking and answering of questions imposes an interactional resistance. Questions tend to shift communication away from derivative communication and toward communication that is matter-of-fact and superficial. Questions often are used in behalf of creating or maintaining pathological symbiotic relations and interactions in which the analyst carries out a directive and controlling position in relation to the patient. Often questions are used as projective identifications, communications unconsciously designed to evoke in the patient the therapist's unwanted affects and ideas.

Far from being a neutral or innocuous technique, questioning can and often does have powerful and far-reaching effects on the patient, on the nature of analyst-analysand transactions and communication, and on the analytic process. Contemporary attitudes and assumptions about questioning overlook the role of unconscious communication in questioning. The clinical vignettes presented in this chapter illustrate some of the unconscious and antitherapeutic messages and projections that may be conveyed by questioning. The findings from this study on questioning in psychoanalytic treatment indicate that questioning seldom has beneficial effects and that it often has detrimental effects.

# Part II

Studies of Psychotherapy and Psychoanalytic Treatment Cases Subjected to Indoctrination Methods

4

# The "Mad Scientist"—
# A Microanalysis of One Analytic Hour

In this chapter, I shall use one analytic hour from an analysis performed by Dr. Martin Silverman (1987) to illustrate one of the most important methods I used for evaluating this and the other cases presented in this book. In the short time since it has been published, Silverman's (1987) case report has evoked much interest and controversy in the psychoanalytic community. (For commentaries and discussions of the Silverman case report, see Dorpat [1991a], Greenberg [1991], and Newsome [1994]). Both the method and the theory of the primary process system which forms the basis for the method has been presented in previous publications (Dorpat 1991a,b, Dorpat and Miller 1992, 1994).

In brief, my theory holds that the primary process system unconsciously analyzes, represents, and communicates the meanings of an individual's interactions with others in primary process derivatives. These derivatives are the end products of a process of unconscious meaning analysis and they include affects, narratives, imagery, metaphors, and nonverbal communications. By listening for and interpreting primary process derivatives, practitioners can achieve some understanding of both what is going on within the patient as well as information about how the patient has unconsciously evaluated his or her transactions with the analyst.

In the final part of this chapter, I shall discuss how clinicians can use the understanding obtained from listening to their patients' primary process communications for purposes of validating their clinical interventions.

The clinical method I use for listening to and understanding primary process communication (i.e., unconscious communication) in the analytic situation is essentially the same as the one I used in examining patients' responses to the interventions made by the ten practitioners in the present study. When, in this book, I describe the short-term psychic effects of the clinicians' covert methods of interpersonal control over their patients, I am doing so mainly on the basis of my examination of their patients' primary process communications (i.e., unconscious communication) in response to their therapists' interventions.

## A MICROANALYSIS OF ONE ANALYTIC HOUR

This case study differs somewhat from others in Part II inasmuch as it provides more clinical details, and it uses a microanalytic approach in which I focus on specific unconscious communications made by both the analyst and the patient together with an account of their unconscious interactions. One reason for presenting this microanalysis of parts of a single psychoanalytic session is to illustrate the method I have used in my studies of the other cases.

The hour I have picked is from a publication by the analyst Dr. Martin Silverman (1987) in which he presents process notes of four analytic sessions. In the publication, edited by Pulver (1987), Silverman's contribution is followed by discussions and by commentaries on the case by thirteen different analyst discussants.

### Case Study

The patient was described by Silverman as a 25-year-old single woman who showed sexual and social inhibition, masochistic tendencies, and chronic depression. Though at first the analysis progressed satisfactorily, it later went into a prolonged stalemate.

## Episode #1

Shortly after this analytic hour began, the patient started talking about her being intimidated by men—a major theme that is repeated often in the four reported analytic hours.

> *Patient:* I get intimidated with men. I always feel that they know they have the knowledge. They have the brains, and I'm dumb. And I always feel like I don't know anything and I can't understand and I get intimidated. It's the same thing here. I feel like asking you, "What does it mean?" I always feel like you know. I feel like asking you now. I know you've told me you don't know anything until I've told it to you, but I don't feel that way. I feel you're always a step ahead of me. You *know*, because you're smarter than I am and all the training and experience you have.
>
> *Analyst:* I don't think that's what it is. I think you feel I know because I'm a man, that as a woman you don't have the brains.
>
> *Patient:* I get intimidated by men [anxiously]. Do you think I signal it to them and that drives them away? So they think, "Who wants her!" I think it started in a way when my father said to me, "Every man is going to want the same thing from you. . . ."

In the above interactional sequence, the patient initially speaks about feeling intimidated by men and about her feeling that she is "dumb" in comparison with men. On this and many other similar occasions, the patient expects to be intimidated by men, and she also, as I plan to demonstrate later, unconsciously behaves in ways that tend to make her expectations and prophecies self-fulfilling. Her prediction is fulfilled inasmuch as the analyst contradicts her view of the situation when he asserts, "I don't think that's what it is." Then he goes on to attribute her sense of intellectual inferiority to her feelings about sexual differences.

The patient responds to the analyst's confrontational intervention by repeating one of her major complaints: "I get intimidated by men." One plausible meaning is that she is telling the analyst in a somewhat indirect way that his intervention was experienced as intimidating. Her next statement, "Do you think I signal it to them and that drives them away?" is a remarkable bit of self-revelation, and it suggests that at some level she knows that she distances herself from men for defensive purposes.

One can also look upon the patient's remarks and questions as an unconscious recognition of the analyst's deprecatory and rejecting intervention. Lichtenberg (one of the discussants) reads her question to mean, "Does my becoming intimidated by and feeling dumb and helpless in your presence drive you away? You seem to me to get irritated when I tell you how dumb I feel at times. Do you only value me if I'm courageous and risk-taking [like my brother]?" (p. 217).

The patient's self-deprecatory remarks unconsciously stem in part, I think, from her unconscious introjection of the demeaning and rejecting attitude conveyed in the analyst's confrontation reported above as well as other previous interventions. Framing her insight in the form of a question rather than a statement is one of several ways in which she devalues her intellectual abilities and idealizes those of the analyst. By expressing herself in the form of a question to the analyst, she defers to his judgment.

Now let us examine the last statement in Episode 1 ("I think it started in a way when my father said to me, 'Every man is going to want the same thing from you . . .'"). It seems highly probable that the patient's last statement contains an unconscious judgment of the analyst's persistent tendency to sexualize her communications. His prior intervention in which he repudiated her reasons for feeling "dumb" sexualized her concerns by placing them on the basis of conflicts over sexual differences ("I think you feel I know because I'm a man, that as a woman you don't have the brains").

There was a fair degree of agreement among the discussants that the treating analyst was at times mistaken in interpreting the patient's communications in terms of oedipal sexual conflicts, at the same time that he tended to overlook or to minimize the importance of conflicts regarding autonomy, aggression and dependency.

My hypothesis is that the memory of her father came to the fore at this time because the analyst's sexualization of her communications is so similar to what her father did with her. Her father's warning that all men want the same thing from her could also apply to the analyst whose persistent and intrusive introduction of sexual themes and contents seems to stem more from his own agenda than from his awareness of the patient's experience.

The analyst's response ("I don't think that's what it is. I think you feel . . .") is the first of several instances of gaslighting in this and the following analytic hours. Here he rejects the patient's judgment and then substitutes his own judgment of what she feels (i.e., "I think you feel I know because I'm a man . . .").

Episode #2

Later in this same analytic hour, the patient tells about feeling intimidated by a male hairdresser and a woman who shampooed her hair.

Patient: I was too intimidated by the hairdresser who cut my hair and I was intimidated about tipping the girl who shampooed my hair. Why [slight pause] I can't figure it out. There's no rhyme or reason. I don't understand it.

Analyst: So long as you take that attitude, so long as you don't think it out and find out the rhyme and reason. . . .

Patient: Well, *he* cut my hair. He *cut* me. But she just put her fingers into my hair. I don't understand.

Analyst: He stuck scissors into your hair and she stuck her fingers into your hair. You were talking before that about avoiding sexual excitement. Scissors and fingers into your hair *sounds* sexual. You turn away and avoid the excite-

> ment, pain and hurt with men, and when you turn away
> from men altogether and turn toward a woman you get
> scared all over again.

In Episode 2, the patient says she cannot understand why she felt intimidated by the hairdresser who cut her hair and by her tipping the girl who shampooed her hair. Silverman responds by shaming and scolding her ("So long as you take that attitude . . ."). Apparently he has forgotten that her difficulty in understanding is something to be understood and analyzed, rather than dealt with by criticism and exhortation.

### The Sadomasochistic Interaction

The process notes of this session, as well as the other three sessions, reveal a repeated and consistent pattern of analyst–analysand relations like those in Episodes 1 and 2 and best described by one of the discussants, Gill, as a sadomasochistic interaction.

Often, when an individual's expectations and prophecies are enacted in interpersonal situations, there occurs a vicious circle in which the subject evokes responses from the object that confirm the subject's expectations and prophecies (Dorpat 1992). This is precisely what is going on between the patient and the analyst. Her masochistic behaviors tend to elicit sadistic responses from the analyst (e.g., controlling, patronizing, coercive, and the like) and these sadistic behaviors, in turn, provoke a renewed expression of masochistic behaviors by the patient. The masochistic partner in these sadomasochistic interactions stimulates the partner to behave sadistically and vice versa.

There is something about the patient's characteristic anxious expectation that men will be sadistic with her that evokes in them the very emotions and behaviors that she fears. From Dr. Silverman's case study, we learn that this interactional pattern apparently began in the patient's childhood relations with her father who was often impatient and harsh with her. The father is pictured as an emotionally restrained man with a quick temper. Of the father, Silverman writes:

> He had a way of explaining things unclearly but was impatient with her and intolerant when she failed to understand him. She had developed a kind of pseudo-stupidity with him so that she found herself incapable of answering even his simplest questions and ended up in tears. She had looked up to and loved her father, with whom she had subjected herself to repeated disappointments and pain [pp. 147–148].

### The Patient's Symptom of Not Understanding

In response to the analyst's scolding remarks ("So long as you take that attitude; so long . . ."), the patient focuses her attention on the details of what happened to her ("Well, *he* cut my hair. He *cut* me. . . . I don't understand") Her literal and concrete response is not responsive to the verbal content of the analyst's communication, and it appears that she may have not actually "heard" what he had just said to her.

The hypothesis that her concrete response stems from her temporary inability to understand the meaning of the analyst's confrontation is somewhat supported by the last sentence in her response to the analyst's scolding, where she said, "I don't understand." Most probably what is occurring here is an example of what the patient repeatedly complains about—when she becomes intimidated by men she becomes anxious and unable to understand them. The patient defends herself by avoiding symbolic discourse, by not acknowledging or representing consciously the meaning of the analyst's previous communication and by retreating to a literal and concrete account of what happened to her (e.g., "Well, he *cut* my hair").

Most probably the anxiety and fear engendered by the analyst's deprecating remarks triggered a shift in her mode of communication from what Langs (1978a) calls Type A and Type B modes to a Type C mode in which there is a relative absence of affective expression and other primary process derivations.

In previous publications, I presented evidence for the hypothesis that the absence of primary process derivatives in the Type C mode of communication derives from a defensively motivated suspension of both expressive and receptive functions of the primary process system (Dorpat 1993d). This defensive suspension of specific primary process functions explains her affectless expression, as well as her temporary inability to understand what is being said to her by others.

The patient's constricted and defensive mode of communication is probably linked developmentally with what Silverman describes as the patient's inability to understand her father when he became abusive and impatient with her. By being concrete, she defensively avoids the anxiety and other disturbing affects engendered by ideas concerning what is transpiring between herself and men like her father who intimidate her.

Earlier in this hour, as well as in the hours immediately prior to this one, the patient had expressed concern about feeling intimidated by men and then not being able to understand what they said. Silverman told of a previous hour in which the patient told of an "intimidating" tennis lesson with a tall tennis pro. Silverman states, "She found that she could not understand him no matter how he phrased and rephrased his instructions" (p. 150). She compared her difficulty in understanding the tennis pro with similar problems she had in understanding her father when he was angry with her.

Silverman mistakenly, I think, describes her symptom as pseudo-stupidity, implying that there is something not real, pretended, or ungenuine about her complaints of not understanding. In my opinion, her complaints should be taken seriously, because, in addition to her repeated subjective complaints of not understanding, there is objective evidence (such as her concreteness) that her higher level psychic functions have been temporarily suspended or impaired in situations where she feels intimidated by men.

## Interactional Elements in Symptom Formation

Her repeated difficulties in understanding the communications of certain men such as her father, the tennis teacher, and the analyst are a symptom that has significant unconscious interactional elements. The traditional psychoanalytic theory of symptom formation emphasizes endogenous causes such as unconscious psychic conflicts and tends to minimize and discount interactional elements. The tendency of analysts to ignore interactional elements in symptom formation is illustrated by the fact that not one of the thirteen prominent analysts who studied and discussed this case mentioned the possibility that some of the patient's difficulty in understanding and her so-called "pseudo-stupidity" during the analytic hours stemmed in part from her transactions with the analyst (Pulver 1987).

Langs (1982a) holds that disturbing unconscious percepts and introjects generated in the patient by the therapist's interventions may be important sources and causes of the patient's symptoms. Symptoms may be founded and sustained by the introjection of the implications of the therapist's interventions, and Langs defines *interactional symptoms* as "emotional disturbance[s] in either participant to the therapeutic dyad with significant sources from both participants" (1982, p. 529).

Though the causal significance of interpersonal and social transactions in symptom formation has been studied by family therapists and others, few psychoanalytic investigators have recognized the crucial importance of *unconscious* interactional factors in both the formation and maintenance of psychiatric symptoms. In a previous publication, I proposed a dyscontrol hypothesis of psychiatric symptom formation that attempted to integrate interactional elements with dispositional elements (Dorpat 1983, 1985). (For another example of the interactional aspects of symptom formation, see the case of Mrs. E. in Chapter 5 of the present work.)

The patient's symptom of not understanding what the analyst said to her may be viewed as the pathologic end-product of the patient's unconscious sadomasochistic interactions with the analyst and of the affective and cognitive dyscontrol evoked in the patient by those interactions. Embedded in the symptom are traces of the patient's unconscious introjection of her relations with the analyst. She first introjects and then enacts in the symptom of not understanding the image of being stupid contained in the analyst's use of gaslighting interventions and other methods of interpersonal control.

### Episode #3—Who is the mad scientist?

Episode 3 follows immediately after Episode 2. In the next quotation from the process notes, the patient responds to Silverman's sexual interpretation about the scissors and fingers in her hair by telling him in a halting way about what she describes as a "masturbation fantasy."

> *Patient:* Yes. But there's something that doesn't fit. I had no problem about tipping the woman who gave me a manicure. And she massages my fingers. And that didn't get me anxious. I like it. It's relaxing. I thought of something. I told you about it a long time ago and then I dropped it and avoided it. It's a masturbation fantasy.

The analyst comments in the text. "Now her voice changes, becomes more hollow, tending toward a chilled monotone, drained of all emotion." The patient begins pausing between words and in the quotations that follow, Silverman indicates short pauses by the use of dashes and longer pauses by the word 'pause' in brackets.

> *Patient:* There's—a doctor—a mad scientist—and his nurse and—he ties me down to—do things to me. I don't know what this has to do with being intimidated by the hairdresser and feeling inhibited tipping the girl who washes my hair but not the manicurist. It makes no sense [pause].
> *Analyst:* You've blocked yourself from hearing the answer you gave: the hairdresser sticking scissors in your hair and cutting you; the young woman preparing you for the haircut; they're the mad scientist doctor and his nurse.

*Patient:* The fantasy had to do with—something—it had to do with getting bigger breasts. It's foolish—I feel sheepish [pause]. It's so silly [pause].

*Analyst:* There's nothing silly about it; you mobilize those feelings to push away and avoid looking into the fantasy and the feelings.

The patient's presentation of the "masturbation fantasy" was, I think, a gift to the analyst and a compliance with his repeated pressures to express sexual material.[1] Just prior to her relating the mad scientist story, he had made a sexual interpretation of her accounts about scissors and fingers in her hair. As one of the discussants, Goldberg, suggests, the patient was probably incredulous at Silverman's attributing a sexual connotation to scissors and fingers and so she unconsciously equates the analyst with the mad scientist in her "masturbation fantasy."

What is most surprising is that Silverman does not consider the possibility that the communication about the mad scientist might be an allusion to himself. Analysts are taught that references to doctors and scientists may well be indirect references of the patient's transferences to the analyst. For the analyst to recognize that the patient experiences him as the mad scientist, he must consider this a plausible experience on the patient's part. In his discussion of the case material, Gill provides a convincing argument for the proposition that the analyst's previous interpretation of shampooing and haircutting as sexual could be plausibly interpreted as the "ravings of a mad scientist" (p. 251.) For similar interpretations, see Dorpat and Miller (1992) and Greenberg (1991).

The patient's fantasy of being bound and manipulated in the mad scientist story may be considered to be a concrete metaphor describing in visual imagery disturbing aspects of her interactions with the analyst. Though Silverman views the mad scientist fantasy as oedipally sexual, in my view and some of the discussants

---

1. I am grateful to Dr. M. Miller for suggesting that the patient's presentation of the "mad scientist" fantasy was a kind of gift to the analyst and a compliance with his repeated pressures to bring forth sexual contents.

such as Modell, this fantasy is a sexualized expression of object relations conflicts and developmental defects having to do with autonomy and dependency. In the fantasy, the fear of being sadistically controlled is sexualized and expressed in erotic images of bondage. Here I am using the term sexualization to denote a defense in which some disturbing and disavowed psychic content is disguised by sexual feelings, ideas, and overt actions that serve a screen function.

Why did she remember the image of the mad scientist at this particular time? The controlling and demeaning communications of the analyst toward her preceding her remembrance of the mad scientist image were, in my opinion, the proximal causes for recalling this memory. In other words, she remembers the sadistically manipulative behaviors of the mad scientist because they are similar to the current behaviors of the analyst toward her.

The patient's recall of her masochistic masturbation fantasy and her telling it are *responsive to* and *representative of* the sadistic and controlling elements in the analyst's previous interventions and the patient's affective reactions to those interventions. The patient's telling the story about the mad scientist contains an incisive unconscious commentary and a basically veridical appraisal of the sadomasochistic interaction between herself and the analyst. Her account of what the mad scientist does to her is the product of a primary process meaning analysis in which the patient has correctly, though unconsciously, evaluated the meaning of what is going on in her relationship with the analyst.

### Another Gaslighting Intervention

In the last interchange of Episode 3, the patient said she felt sheepish because the mad scientist fantasy had something to do with her getting bigger breasts. Then the analyst contradicted her by saying to her, "There's nothing silly about it." This intervention, like others in the four reported analytic sessions, had some gaslighting properties, inasmuch as Silverman repudiated the patient's experience and judgment at the same time that he insisted that his experience of what was going on with her was more valid.

Silverman's gaslighting interventions violate a cardinal psychoanalytic rule of initially accepting a patient's experience to understand it further, rather than rejecting it and substituting one's own opinions. Because Silverman is an experienced analyst, it seems improbable to me that this technical blunder arises from inexperience. Rather, a systematic scrutiny of the process notes reveals that the patient has skillfully and unconsciously maneuvered the analyst into a sadomasochistic exchange, and that he has allowed himself to fall prey to the pressures of her repeated masochistic provocations.

### How the Patient Provokes Men to Treat Her Sadistically

As Lichtenberg and other discussants indicate, the patient has a highly evocative array of interpersonal techniques, such as inappropriate compliance, withholding, stalling, and obfuscation. By these and other methods of interpersonal manipulation and pressure, she repeatedly evokes in her analyst and others, responses of anger, impatience, and condescension as well as various patronizing and demeaning attitudes. Her modes of provoking others (predominantly men) to behave sadistically serve the ends of actualizing and confirming her expectations as well as insuring that her prophecies about her interpersonal relations are self-fulfilling.

### Episode #4

Episode 4 continues without interruption from Episode 3. Recall that the last interchange in Episode 3 was the analyst's statement that there's nothing silly about the patient's mad scientist fantasy and that she was using the feeling of being silly to avoid looking at the fantasy.

> *Patient:* I'd try not to think the fantasy. I didn't want to dig into it. You're right. I feel sheepish to push it away.

*Analyst:* And what happens to sheep?
*Patient:* They get sheared; their hair cut off.
*Analyst:* And so do "fallen women."
*Patient:* In old times, they did. I know about that. The hairdresser was cutting *my* hair off. Maybe it was my "crown-
   ing glory." And sheep certainly get their hair cut off.
   When I was in New Zealand, I saw the sheep getting
   sheared. There was one brown one I remember. They
   held it and sheared it, and piled the wool, and all that.

The analyst comments in the text: "The emotions's gone from her voice; she's shearing the sheep to pull the wool over our eyes."

Silverman diverts the patient by his own associations to sheep and to fallen women. He avoids dealing with the patient's experience. Often when the patient begins to feel something and to explore what she is feeling, an intrusive interpretation by the analyst of the manifest content of what she is communicating turns her off.

To the analyst's query "What happens to sheep?" the patient responds with, "They get sheared, their hair cut off." Again, Silverman leads and directs the interchange with his terse comment laden with sexualization "and so do fallen women." In response to Silverman's intrusive interventions about the shearing of sheep and the "fallen women" who get their hair cut, the patient again (as she did in Episode 2) defensively retreats to a literal and affectless report (i.e., Type C mode) about observing the shearing of a brown sheep in New Zealand.

## The Type C Mode and the Defense of Affective Non-Relatedness

In my earlier discussion about Episode 2, I hypothesized that the patient's literal response (i.e., "Well, *he* cut my hair") to the analyst's prior scolding intervention served a defensive function. My hypothesis is supported by what occurred in Episode 4, where a similar interactional pattern takes place in which the analyst's repeated controlling interventions again lead to the patient's shift to a Type C mode of communication.

The patient stonewalls the analyst by responding to his intrusive communications in a literal and affectively lifeless way. Silverman notes that emotion has left the patient's tone of voice when she tells of watching sheep being sheared in New Zealand, and he describes the defensive nature of her communication with this written comment, "She's shearing the sheep to pull the wool over our eyes." His use of metaphor and symbolic discourse in this comment on the patient highlights, by contrast, the stark, literal quality of the patient's report about sheep shearing.

Her Type C mode of communication and her concreteness defend against both the arousal and awareness of disturbing emotions such as shame and anger evoked by the analyst's controlling and demeaning interventions. What she repeatedly says about herself in these four analytic hours is, as I discussed earlier, probably true—when she feels intimidated by men she is unable to understand them. Modell (1984) calls her defensive response the defense of affective nonrelatedness. The patient, in effect, breaks off meaningful, affective communication with the analyst by suspending both the expressive and the receptive functions of her primary process system. What first Langs (1979a) and later Dorpat (1993d) call the Type C mode of communication is essentially the same as what Modell (1984) calls the defense against affective relatedness. According to Modell (1984), the defense against affective relatedness is not an intrapsychic defense such as repression, but a defense in the context of a two-person psychology. (For a comprehensive discussion of an interactional perspective on defensive activity, see Dorpat 1985.)

## Episode #5

Episode 5 follows immediately after Episode 4. After the patient had retreated to a literal report of watching sheep being sheared, the analyst made the first of five interpretations about the patient's defensiveness, all of which had essentially the same content. The five interventions follow.

1. You're getting away to avoid uncomfortable feelings.
2. Notice you're interrupting yourself, stopping yourself?
3. Notice you switched from uncomfortable thinking about the wish for the mad scientist to give you bigger breasts to the slave and master theme?
4. I notice you keep interrupting yourself and stopping yourself.

[At this place in the text, the analyst adds a parenthetical comment about his own feelings. He writes, "There's a tightness in my belly, and I'm getting irritated at her excruciating stopping and starting and hesitating."]

5. You're having all that trouble talking about, thinking all those thoughts about pain and hurt, S & M, bondage, because of a wish to enact the fantasy with me rather than think and feel it out and understand it. You want *me* to be the mad scientist doctor forcing and hurting you and making changes in you.

In these five defense interpretations, the analyst follows the classical psychoanalytic view of defenses as intrapsychic functions determined by internal conflicts. This traditional notion of defense overlooks consideration of interactional elements that, together with pre-existing conflicts and other dispositions, determines the final form of an individual's defensive activity.

The patient's defensive retreat to a Type C mode of communication has been triggered by the analyst's controlling and intrusive interventions.

### "Master-Slave" Relations

For much of this hour, as Lichtenberg, Gill and other discussants point out, the patient and the analyst have been engaged in a power struggle as to what issues they are to talk about. The patient repeatedly, in this hour and to some extent in other hours, returns to the related concerns about feeling intimidated and not understanding. She wants to pursue the question—why did she feel inhibited tipping the girl who washed her hair but not the manicurist? Silverman continues to push sexual themes and in this fifth episode he makes five interpretations in a row that interpret her defensiveness.

In response to the second of the five defense interpretations made by Silverman in Episode 5, the patient complains:

> I don't want to talk about it, think about it; I'm afraid you'll think I'm foolish. I had to submit to the mad scientist, like I was his slave and he was my master. When I'm intimidated by men, it's like I have to put up with anything, like I'm a slave and he's a master and it makes me angry [pause] . . .

Here again the analyst fails to understand or to interpret the references to master–slave issues as allusions to his current relations with the patient. In his interpretations, Silverman continues to ignore what is taking place in his interactions with the patient, and he persists in making the same kind of intrapsychic defense interpretation.

Discussant Gill criticizes Silverman's rejection of the patient's experience and his insistence that his judgments about the patient are more valid than the patient's. After noting that Silverman made essentially the same defense interpretation five consecutive times, Gill concludes, "Can one doubt that she experiences him as misunderstanding her, failing to appreciate her, and forcing his views on her?" (p. 251).

## Fantasy or Actuality?

Though in the fifth defense interpretation of Episode 5, Silverman interprets the patient's difficulty in talking as arising from her wish to enact with him the mad scientist *fantasy*, he does not acknowledge the *actuality* of his sadomasochistic enactment with the patient.

In his interpretations and in his discussions of this case, Silverman repeatedly refers to the patient's cognitions about the mad scientist as a wish-fulfilling fantasy. Unfortunately, Silverman focuses on the manifest content of the mad scientist fantasy, and he appears to be unaware that the important unconscious meaning of a patient's verbal communication resides in the latent content and not the manifest content. My study of the patient's derivatives and the context in which they are communicated reveals the unconscious meaning (i.e., the latent content) of what she is saying.

Studies by Dorpat (1991a), Dorpat and Miller (1992), and Mitchell (1993) of the interactions between the analyst and the analysand indicate that the central unconscious meaning of her discourse about the mad scientist at this particular time is an essentially veridical though unconscious commentary about the patient's *actual* (not fantasy) relations with the analyst. In her account about the mad scientist, the patient uses sophisticated primary process imagery and narratives to represent the sadomasochistic nature of her current relations with the analyst. The immediate and foremost dynamic significance of the cognitions that both the analyst and patient refer to as a "fantasy" is their implicit reference to the *actuality* of what is occurring in the patient-analyst transactions.

One may consider the patient's image of being bound and manipulated in the mad scientist story to be a concrete metaphor about the disturbing aspects of her interactions with the analyst. Her fear of being sadistically controlled is sexualized and expressed in erotic images of bondage.

In sum, a systematic microanalysis of the few analytic hours reveals (1) the analyst's use of a variety of covert methods of interpersonal control (including gaslighting, confrontations, and shaming interventions) carried out to discredit the patient's judgments and to induce her to accept his ideas, (2) the harmful effects of these interventions on the patient and the analytic process, (3) the sadomasochistic interactions between the patient and the analyst, and (4) what seems most remarkable is the fact that, though all of the above three issues are seldom if ever openly discussed, explicitly addressed, or analyzed by either the patient or the analyst, the patient nevertheless through her communication of primary process derivatives demonstrates that she has been unconsciously analyzing and representing her unconscious judgments about these pathological interactions.

## Some Notes on the Shared Denial of the Discussants

I strongly suspect that all of the thirteen analyst discussants in the Pulver (1987) publication except Merton Gill share a kind of collective denial about Silverman's repeated use of controlling and directive methods. Though the sadomasochistic nature of the interaction between the analyst and patient is readily apparent to any reasonably well-educated person, only Gill was able to evaluate and discuss it. Together with Gill, I view the sadomasochistic nature of their interactions as the central issue, and one that provides a unifying frame of reference for understanding what is occurring in the analysis as well as explaining the prolonged analytic stalemate.

One discussant, Brenner, avowedly shares the same theoretical perspective as Silverman, and he finds nothing in Silverman's conduct of the analysis to criticize! Could it be that what discussant Schwaber faults in the entire group of discussants (except Gill) about their imposing their theoretical point of view without adequately attending to the clinical material is related to what I hypothesize to be their collective denial of Silverman's verbally abusive treatment of the patient? How else can one explain the disturbing fact that only one analyst, Gill, out of a group of thirteen eminent clinicians, wrote much about what was actually taking place in the analysis?

According to Schwaber all of the discussants save Gill allow their theoretical model to determine how the material is understood and what is to be interpreted. In Schwaber's view, all of the discussants (but Gill) assigned to their theoretical preconceptions "a primacy that goes beyond serving its purported function of organizing the data and broadening our perceptual scope" (p. 262).

Except for Gill, the other discussants provide inferences and speculations about the unconscious dynamics and conflicts *in the patient*. Few of them discuss what is going on in the interactions between the patient and the analyst.

The startling unawareness of the discussants about what was going on between Silverman and his patient stands in marked contrast to the responses of nonanalyst mental health professionals who have studied the process notes of this case. In our efforts to teach mental health professionals about our interactional theory and especially the theory of primary process meaning analysis, my colleague, Dr. Michael Miller, and I have presented the process notes of the Silverman case to ten groups ranging from nine to fifty participants. Even the least experienced trainees (e.g., first-year psychiatric residents) could, with less than thirty minutes of instruction on how to detect and decode primary process derivatives, readily understand not only the important elements of the sadomasochistic interaction but also how the patient was unconsciously analyzing and then representing these interactions in her unconscious (i.e., primary process) communication.

One of the aims of this book is to induce analysts and other mental health professionals to examine their clinical work in order to ascertain to what extent, if any, are they denying their use of covert methods of interpersonal control.

# 5

## The Effects of Indoctrination Methods—Six Case Studies

My aim in this chapter is to use six case studies for describing and discussing the effects of covert methods of interpersonal control and stereotyped approaches in psychoanalytic treatment. Though all of these cases were ostensibly in either psychoanalysis or psychoanalytic psychotherapy, the actual process was often one of indoctrination. Four of the six case studies are based on my examination of published articles and books. Five cases were analytic cases, and one case (Mrs. E.) was in intensive psychoanalytic psychotherapy for over ten years.

The major focus of my study is on covert methods of interpersonal control and other methods of indoctrination and both their short-term and long-term effects on patients. Though I emphasize the effects of the psychotherapist's interventions, I have tried to use an interactional perspective throughout my investigations, a perspective that includes the contributions of both members of the therapeutic dyad to their interactions. An interactional or relational point of view acknowledges the powerful, largely unconscious ways in which analysand and analyst influence each other and help shape the communications of each other.

A secondary and subsidiary aim is to discuss and illustrate stereotyped approaches and their role in bringing about a process of indoctrination. I suspect there may be a link between the use of stereotyped approaches and the use of covert methods of interpersonal control, because all of the analysts and psychotherapists I have known who extensively employ stereotyped approaches also use covert methods of interpersonal control. Though Peterfreund (1983) in his writings on stereotyped approaches did not write about covert methods of interpersonal control, he did indicate that stereotyped approaches led to a process of "indoctrination."

This chapter is divided into two parts, with Part I devoted to an intensive study of two psychoanalytic treatment cases. Some of the descriptions of persons written about in Part I have been disguised in order to protect the privacy and identity of both the patients and clinicians. Part II summarizes my investigations of four analytic cases reported in the psychoanalytic literature.

## PART I

### The Case of Mrs. E.—A Study of an Iatrogenic Syndrome

Mrs. E. is a middle-aged married mother of two children. She became increasingly more emotionally disturbed during more than ten years of psychoanalytic psychotherapy conducted on a two or three times a week basis by a psychoanalytically oriented therapist I shall call Dr. X. Mrs. E. had anxiety and depressive symptoms when she began therapy with Dr. X. The patient is the second of three children, all of whom have serious psychiatric impairments caused in a major way by prolonged verbal and physical abuse from their father.

About a year after her therapy with Dr. X. was terminated, she resumed intensive psychotherapy with another therapist, Dr. Y. The story which I am about to summarize of her treatment with Dr. X. emerged gradually in her therapy with Dr. Y. A major method for discovering the nature of her interactions with Dr. X. was by the working through of her transferences to Dr. Y. With

Dr. Y., she quickly attempted to establish the same kind of submissive and masochistic bond as she previously had with her tyrannical father and later with Dr. X.

Mrs. E. repeatedly asked questions which invited Dr. Y. to assume direction and control over the conduct of her life. She often would ask her new therapist what she should do, think, or feel about such-and-such. In one session she told about her husband wanting her to go on a vacation, and she asked Dr. Y. whether the vacation would be good for her. Then she asked Dr. Y. whether he would give his permission for her to leave. When Dr. Y. attempted to understand and interpret the patient's need for "permission" he discovered that Dr. X. had "forbidden" the patient to go on vacations. Moreover, Dr. X. had criticized her desire to leave on vacation as showing inadequate loyalty to him and to her treatment.

On another occasion after she began reading some articles and books on mental health topics, she told her new therapist, Dr. Y., how pleased she was that he "had *let* her read psychiatric and psychoanalytic books." Dr. Y. made the following interpretation to Mrs. E. "Your statement about my 'letting' you read the psychoanalytic book suggests you believe I have some power to regulate your reading." In reply, Mrs. E. told him about Dr. X.'s prohibition against her reading psychiatric and psychoanalytic publications.

Over time, Dr. Y. was able to help the patient understand how she had contributed to her pathologic symbiotic relation with Dr. X. She gradually developed more insight into ways she had invited or evoked directive and sadistic responses from Dr. X. as well as other men in her life. For several years, Mrs. E. continued to test Dr. Y. in various ways to determine whether or not he would assume the same type of oppressive control over the conduct of her life as had her father and her previous therapist, Dr. X.

Her therapy with Dr. Y. was similar in some ways to the reparative therapies used by some professionals for the rehabilitation and psychotherapy of individuals who have been subjected to brainwashing and other forms of indoctrination in religious cults such as the Moonies. (See Chapter 9 for a comparison between cults and the eleven cases of indoctrination presented in this book.)

During the therapy, Dr. X. persistently attempted to direct and control the patient's thinking and behavior, especially through the use of covert methods of interpersonal control. In addition to the prohibitions mentioned above, Dr. X. issued a number of other prohibitions and injunctions. What he called interpretations were actually gaslighting interventions in which he systematically and repeatedly attacked her judgments, beliefs, and perceptions about herself and those who were close to her. He undermined her confidence in her psychic abilities by labeling her judgments and perceptions as illusions, distortions, transferences, wish-fulfilling fantasies, and the like.

For example, she told him she believed she was a sociable person. He negated this belief in herself and described her as "reclusive." Her desire to practice her profession was attacked as stemming from her rejection of femininity and her desire to be a man. Her dedication to the Catholic religion was described as "hysteric," "fanciful," and "irrational." His practice of attacking and demeaning her judgments and beliefs extended across a wide range of her attitudes, relations, and belief systems. She gradually became more subservient to him much in the same way as she and other members of her family had been to her abusive father.

Even in the last years of her long treatment, she continued to think that Dr. X.'s task was to point out to her what was wrong with her thinking. She believed she had to accept what he said because he was the expert. In her view, she could only overcome her illness by learning from him what was wrong with her and then correcting it.

A major personality change in her therapy with Dr. X. was a growing and ominous constriction of her life and affectivity to the point where her capacities for critical and reflective thinking were inoperative or suspended. She did not consciously realize how much she had blindly followed Dr. X. until several years after she had stopped treatment with him. In her pathological and destructive symbiotic relation with Dr. X., she increasingly turned over various ego and superego functions, such as judgment, decision making, establishing values, and the like to him. In so doing she was unconsciously trying to support and gratify her therapist by her "compassionate sacrifice" as she and her submissive mother had done for her tyrannical father.

The concept of "the compassionate sacrifice" as presented by Feiner and Levenson (1968–1969) and Searles (1975) refers to the profound sacrifices some individuals make to provide narcissistic supplies to members of their families and sometimes later to their therapists. Whether expressed through the symptomatology of school phobia in latency, the school dropout in adolescence, or the regressed behavior of the schizophrenic or in other ways, the patient who is making a "compassionate sacrifice" gives up much of his or her autonomous strivings in order to gratify the narcissistic needs of some other family member.

Here is an example of the many gaslighting interpretations made by Dr. X. She told Dr. X. about how anxious she felt in the company of her father, and she attempted to explain her anxiety as arising from memories of herself and her siblings being spanked by him for trivial offenses. Dr. X. summarily rejected this explanation of her anxiety and attributed her anxiety to fears of losing control over her incestuous sexual drives.

Several new iatrogenic interactional psychiatric[1] symptoms developed from Dr. X.'s abusive treatment of Mrs. E. For example, after he mistakenly interpreted her anxieties in social situations as arising from repressed homosexual impulses, she developed obsessive thoughts and fears of being homosexual. As Dr. X. continued his assault on her personal value-system and her psychic functions, she became more and more mistrustful of herself and confused about her beliefs. She developed new symptoms of derealization and claustrophobia that were in part caused by her pathological interactions with Dr. X.

---

1. The term *iatrogenic interactional symptoms* is used here to describe psychiatric symptoms arising from pathological patient-therapist interactions.

Her unconscious conflict between accepting her beliefs and perceptions or those of Dr. X. was expressed in a new symptom of derealization. At times the world seemed "fuzzy," "unreal," and "out of focus." When Dr. X. spoke to her the derealization symptom became exacerbated and she then seemed detached and removed from him and from what he was saying to her. The "unreal" and "fuzzy" symptom was a representation of her experiences with the analyst inasmuch as they repeated interactions with her in which he repudiated her perceptions and judgments.

Another iatrogenic psychiatric symptom, claustrophobia, developed out of her interactions with Dr. X. This symptom was a product of her unconscious meaning analysis of her interactions with Dr. X. Her feelings of being smothered, restricted, and constrained by him were symbolically expressed in the claustrophobia symptom. The claustrophobia symptom began in the fifth year of her treatment with Dr. X. and was not resolved until after a year of treatment with Dr. Y. With Dr. Y. she presented sufficient data to make it possible for him to interpret to Mrs. E. how the symptom arose out of her interactions with Dr. X. and how it unconsciously symbolized her experience of being oppressed by him. The symptom disappeared after the patient was able to avow how much she felt oppressed and restricted by Dr. X. From then on, she could express in words the same basic idea of being constrained which she previously unconsciously had expressed in the symptom of claustrophobia.

## Conclusions

Both the patient and Dr. X. contributed to what occurred in the psychoanalysis including the psychiatric symptoms discussed above. By her compliant and submissive attitudes and communications the patient brought repeated pressures on first Dr. X. and later Dr. Y. to be directive, controlling, and sadistic. Her masochistic modes of relating were powerful inducements and evocations of sadistic responses in her therapist as well as other men in her life. What happens in psychoanalytic treatment is a function of what both parties contribute to the intersubjective field. Her sado-masochistic modes of relating to her therapists were, of course, enactments and repetitions of similar pathological and destructive childhood relationships.

### The Consolidation of False Self Pathology through the Use of Indoctrination Methods—The Case of Mrs. G.

The patient (Mrs. G.) was a young married woman who sought psychoanalytic treatment for anxiety symptoms and several inhibitions. A major purpose of this case study is to highlight the role of covert methods of interpersonal control and other indoctrination methods in facilitating and consolidating the formation of inauthentic communication and a "false self" in Mrs. G. For further discussion about the relationship between inauthentic communication and false self psychopathology, see Dorpat (1994a).

In addition to the accepted methods of psychoanalytic treatment, the authoritarian Dr. A. often used nonanalytic and antianalytic methods including advice, limit setting, extensive use of educational methods, and directives on such matters as what she should and should not read, how she should behave during sexual relations, and the like. She was forbidden to masturbate or have sexual relations during the daytime hours prior to her analytic hour because, as he explained to her, such "frustrations" were helpful to her analysis. Furthermore, he warned her, the genital satisfactions of the forbidden activities would interfere with the development and working through of her transferences to him.

His method of interpreting unconscious contents constituted a highly effective method of gaslighting. He prided himself on being a classical analyst who could quickly detect distortions of reality and unconscious fantasy in his patients. He frequently interpreted Mrs. G.'s judgments, feelings, and ideas as distortions of reality stemming from repressed childhood fantasies. He then would explicitly or by implication present his own view of what he considered was the true and objective reality of the patient's situation. By his interpretations about her defensive and trans-ferential distortions of reality, as well as other so-called derivatives of unconscious fantasy, he succeeded in undermining her confi-dence in her own cognitive and perceptual capacities.

Through his interpretations about what he considered to be the objective and undistorted truth about her, he substituted his own beliefs and perceptions for hers. Under these pressures, the patient gradually gave up self-reflection and introspection about anything emotionally charged and then, as a defensive substitute for her own discredited views, she began to compliantly adopt his views. Once, when she offered an interpretation of her own be-havior, he ignored what she had said except to criticize her for being competitive with him. In the above and other ways, he often unconsciously undermined both her self-esteem and her confi-dence in her own capacities for reality-testing and for understand-ing herself.

As a result of childhood traumas, the patient had developed a highly effective ensemble of skills for pleasing others and adapt-ing to their needs and desires for her. Unfortunately this pleasing and seemingly attractive demeanor was frequently inauthentic[2] and defensive—it did not arise spontaneously from her own desires. Rather, her preconscious sense of what others wanted of her acti-vated and regulated her participation in most interpersonal and social interactions. Early in life she became acutely attuned to de-tecting and meeting the needs of others while at the same time disavowing what she desired for herself. What I have briefly de-scribed above is, of course, essentially the same as what Winnicott (1960) called a false-self organization developed in childhood on the basis of compliance with others.

---

2. In a previous publication, I described inauthentic communication as a defining property of the false self organization, and I labelled it as Type D com-munication (Dorpat, 1994a). The Type D category is an addition to and modifi-cation of Langs's (1976a) classification of three communicative modes, Types A, B, and C. Type A mode is normal symbolic communication. Projective iden-tification is the defining characteristic of the Type B mode. Communication lacking in affect and other primary process derivatives is called the Type C mode.

The analyst's use of gaslighting and other methods of covert interpersonal control supported the maintenance of her false self at the same time that his oppressive and dominating mode of relating to her reinforced her unconscious anxieties about revealing and expressing her true self. A second analysis performed many years after the first analysis induced her to understand and reconstruct what had taken place in her first analysis with Dr. A. and especially to understand how the first analysis had supported her false self at the same time causing her true self to become more deeply buried.

## On Normopaths and Functioning as a Mirror for Others

People who did not know Mrs. G. well erroneously thought of her as being exceptionally "normal." This erroneous judgment was based partly on her surface agreeability and appearance of being "normal." Her sense of security was founded on her ability to understand and meet the expectations of others, and this is what she initially believed meant being normal. She was a "normopath" —one of many in our culture who want to appear normal and who confuse the appearance with the substance of normality. Though she was extraordinarily sensitive and vigilant to the desires of others, she was most often vague or unaware of her own desires and needs. She gave to others what she unconsciously wanted for herself, and frequently in her interactions with others, she provided selfobject mirroring functions for them.

In her interpersonal relations she behaved like a mirror reflecting back to others what they wanted and at the same time (again, like a mirror) concealing from the view of others whatever was going on inside of her and behind, as it were, the exterior reflecting surface of the mirror.

## A Vertical Split—The True and the False Self

A vertical split of the kind Kohut (1971) described was constructed early in her life from her traumatizing interactions with her disturbed and disturbing parents. The false self organization of feelings, ideas, representations, and responses on one side of the vertical split was split off by the defense of disavowal from the complex of psychic contents, perceptions, attitudes, and the like on the other side of the split.

By his use of covert methods of control and other methods of indoctrination, Dr. A. supported the maintenance of the vertical split. Her defensive need to comply with the analyst and to ingratiate herself with him was regulated by her false self organization.

She manifested a surface level of compliance and affability split off from a deeper level of disavowed rebellion, autonomy, and independence. The vertical split also determined and regulated her affective responses and expressions. One aspect of her false self organization included a highly developed and refined set of emotional expressions which, though often entertaining and engaging, were not authentic. Rather they were contrived performances regulated by her needs for attracting attention, for manipulating others, or for complying with what she believed others wanted of her. The genuine emotional expressions of her true self were for the most part rigorously controlled, often concealed, and usually subjected to repression and/or denial. Few persons even suspected how successfully and expertly her affective expressions and surface charm stemming from the false self concealed a profound defect in personal integrity.

Early on in her analysis, Dr. A. assumed that the patient's problems in living and symptoms were reflections of unconscious penis envy and unresolved oedipal conflict, and he saw his analytic role to be one of getting the patient to understand the analyst's initial formulation. Her disagreements, avoidances, and defenses to her acceptance of his initial formulations he viewed as resistances. In Chapter 10, I discuss the stereotyped approach of viewing the patient's disagreements with the analyst as resistances. Dr. A.'s avowed aim was to overcome her resistances. Usually he was unaware of the coercive and sometimes even abusive quality of these covert methods of interpersonal control. He rationalized and justified his use of these controlling methods. For example, he maintained that his directives (such as forbidding masturbation) were necessary for her learning. What I call gaslighting interventions he rationalized as interpretations of reality and corrections of the patient's distortions.

Considerable analytic effort was directed toward interpreting and working through what Dr. A. believed were the patient's deepseated repressed conflicts concerning penis envy. As in so many other instances with Dr. A., the notion of "penis envy" was in his usage a cliché. As evidence for what he mistakenly believed were derivatives of penis envy he cited the patient's feeling of anger toward men and envy for the power and advantages they maintained in the social order.

Dr. A. negated the patient's opinions about her envy of male power and her resentment over the abuses she had suffered at the hands of men (especially her father), and he repeatedly attempted to get her to accept his erroneous view that all her protestations about men could be reduced to and explained by her unconscious penis envy. The patient was in a no-win situation with Dr. A. The fact that she was not aware of having envious attitudes about the male organ Dr. A. used as evidence of its repressed existence and its perniciously widespread influence on her mental functioning and relationships. In sum, Dr. A. used gaslighting techniques and other covert methods of interpersonal control in order to induce the patient to overcome her resistances and to accept his formulations regarding her supposed penis envy.

He made the mistaken inference that the underlying cause for her negative feelings toward men was her envy of their external genitalia. She was initially puzzled and shocked by his interpretations of her penis envy. Later her feelings of humiliation and shame engendered by Dr. A.'s interpretations led her to suppress her concerns about her sexuality and about her marriage.

She gradually came to believe that her alleged penis envy, as well as what she increasingly viewed as her unjustified anger to men, were the major sources of her marital problems. Then, in identification with previous generations of women in her family, she chose to quietly suffer and sacrifice herself for the sake of preserving her marriage.

Dr. A. characteristically made the error of seeing the gradual lessening of complaints about her marriage as evidence for his hypothesis that his interpretations and firm confrontations about her penis envy had assisted her in resolving her unconscious conflicts about penis envy. What actually occurred in their interactions was much different. Through his repeated use of covert methods of interpersonal control, he succeeded in getting the patient to feel guilty about her anger to men and ashamed about herself for her so-called "penis envy." To please Dr. A. and to avoid further shame and helplessness in her analytic hours, she suppressed her concerns about her marriage and stopped talking about them.

Dr. A. usually employed the stereotyped approaches described by Peterfreund (1983) and he seldom used heuristic approaches toward understanding and interpretation. He was unaware of his failure to establish and maintain a therapeutic alliance with the patient. The patient was not supported in her efforts toward self-analysis or in forming a relationship with him based on collaboration and cooperation rather than surface agreeability and compliance to the analyst's directives.

Circular self-confirming processes are at the heart of stereotyped approaches and indoctrination methods. For example, Dr. A. used a number of indoctrination methods to suppress her sexual and marriage concerns. He then mistakenly construed the gradual decrease in her communications about these issues plus her statements which indicate compliance or agreement with his interpretations to mean that his initial formulation about her was correct. Furthermore, he concluded that his interventions had helped her to resolve and work through her unconscious conflicts.

## Discussion

Stereotyped approaches are self-confirming in two ways. First, they are self-confirming because the therapist who uses stereotyped approaches tends to see only what his theory permits and communications from the patient that are new, unexpected, or different from the theoretical presuppositions of the therapist are discounted or ignored. Second, the continued use of covert methods of interpersonal control tends to regulate and shape the patient's communications so that they conform to the analyst's theoretical expectations.

My opposition to the use of covert methods of interpersonal control in psychoanalytic treatment should not be construed to mean that I proscribe the use of suggestion. Contrary to what Freud and other analysts have thought, it is not possible in psychoanalytic treatment or elsewhere for one person to verbally communicate with another person without suggesting. Defined in a broad sense, suggestion is an aspect of all affective (primary process) communication (Dorpat and Miller 1992). And since affective communication is an inseparable part of all verbal communication, it is not possible to speak to others without suggestion.[3] The indirect kind of suggestion that is an aspect of all nonverbal (affective) communication is not necessarily coercive or controlling. It may simply convey meanings such as, "Please listen; this is important." (For similar views on suggestion in psychoanalysis, see Oremland 1991, Stolorow et al. 1994.)

Therefore, it is not my purpose to have practitioners eliminate any kind of conscious or unconscious suggestion or influence, because it would not be either possible or desirable to do so. But the interpersonal influence of covert methods of interpersonal control and other methods of indoctrination includes, but goes beyond, suggestion. Much of the interpersonal power of these methods resides in the evocation of painful affects including, among others, anxiety, fear, guilt, and shame. The effect of these covert methods of interpersonal control and other indoctrination methods is most often antitherapeutic, antianalytic, and harmful to patients.

---

3. The indirect kind of suggestion I have just described should not be confused or conflated with the direct and explicit kinds of verbal suggestions used in some kinds of supportive psychotherapy or hypnosis therapy in which the therapist may, for example, explicitly suggest to the patient certain attitudes or types of overt actions.

Of the six cases in this chapter and five cases described in other chapters, the three patients treated by Drs. A., T.,[4] and X. were, in my opinion, the most seriously and to some degree permanently damaged by the treatment they sustained. The traumatic effects of their treatments by Drs. A., T., and X. were partly relieved and overcome by the therapeutic benefits they received years later from psychotherapy or psychoanalysis following their care by Drs. A., T., and X.

The various iatrogenic anxiety, depressive, and psychoneurotic symptoms engendered in these patients by Drs. A., T., and X. were only the tip of the iceberg of the psychopathology formed out of their interactions with these clinicians.

During the time the patients were in treatment with these authoritarian clinicians and for a prolonged time afterwards, they showed marked pathological changes in personality functioning. Their psychic development was stalemated and fixated to their traumatogenic therapy. To some extent their lives became simpler, inasmuch as they escaped personal responsibility, uncertainty, and ambiguity by their masochistic and submissive merge with their therapists. Under the direction of their therapists, they constructed a rigid organization of experience in which they would think in stereotypes and cliches. Individuality, flexibility, and critical thinking were suspended, and they lost some of their capacities for initiative and autonomous thought and action. All three showed a progressive constriction of their personalities and a loss of positive freedom. (For a discussion of the psychological significance of positive freedom and how successful psychoanalytic treatment enhances the patient's positive freedom, see Dorpat 1987a.)

The constricting and inhibiting effects of the use of indoctrination methods was shown by the impairment of their abilities for creativity, leadership, and artistic sublimatory pursuits. John (Dr. T.'s patient) had a history of being a successful and effective

---

4. Dr. T.'s treatment of Bill was discussed in Chapter 2. Bill became severely depressed and suicidal while being treated by Dr. T., who also was the charismatic leader of a psychotherapy cult which included Bill and Bill's wife.

leader in several areas of his life, a capacity which was lost both during his treatment with Dr. T. and for at least five years afterward. Mrs. E. and Mrs. G. had artistic interests and talents which were set aside during their treatment and these sublimatory activities and talents were not recovered for many years after their traumatic interactions with Drs. A. and X.

As I indicate in Chapter 9, the long-term psychopathologic effects of indoctrination on these three patients were similar to the long-term effects on followers of membership in cults.

## PART II

In Part II, I shall present four analytic cases reported in the psychoanalytic literature in which covert methods of control and other indoctrination methods were used. These brief reports will include some vignettes and case summaries, as well as some relevant comments about the cases written by other analysts.

### An Analysis Conducted by Dr. Dewald

In a previous study of an analysis conducted and reported by Dewald (1972), I described and discussed some of the effects his use of gaslighting and directive questioning had on the analytic process and on the patient (Dorpat 1985).

Questioning was the most frequent type of intervention made by Dewald (1972) in the case he reported, and over 70 percent of all of his interventions were questions. His avowed purposes in questioning the patient were to not allow prolonged silences, to point to promising avenues of exploration, to direct the patient's attention, and the like. In his extensive commentaries on the analytic case and in his discussion of the analytic process, he was evidently unaware of the antitherapeutic effects on the patient of his repetitive and directive type of questioning.

In the following vignette, my aim is to illustrate and discuss some effects on the patient of Dewald's use of various covert methods of interpersonal control. This vignette is taken from Session 4 as described by Dewald (1972).

> *Analyst:* What comes to your mind about wanting to hide here?
>
> *Patient:* I could make Mr Harris like me, but I can't do that with you. So I'm not even going to try. I know that I can't. I feel very hostile to you, and I don't understand what I'm supposed to do.
>
> *Analyst:* I think that really you do understand what you're supposed to do here in analysis, but you can't believe it.
>
> *Patient:* I don't really understand this. Somehow we don't seem to be discussing things and it seems as I'm doing all of the talking. . . .I've felt anxious all day [Elaborates symptom.] I don't know why.
>
> *Analyst:* Let's see what your associations are without jumping to conclusions about it.
>
> *Patient:* I feel as if someone is trying to overpower me. As if they are trying to. . . .
>
> *Analyst:* What is it that you're afraid to say?
>
> *Patient:* As if you are trying to sit on me and squash me.
>
> *Analyst:* I think this is one of your fears about starting analysis. It's as if you fantasize that you're going to end up in my power and that you're going to be helpless.

Immediately after the patient said "I don't understand what I'm supposed to do," the analyst countered with a gaslighting[5] confrontation in which he rejected her judgments about her own and aggressively tried to get her to accept his judgment. "I think that really you do understand what you're supposed to do here in analysis, but you can't believe it." Actually, Dewald was the one

---

5. For other examples of Dewald's use of gaslighting interventions with this patient, see Chapter 2.

who would not believe what she said. Most probably he denied his disbelief and projected it onto the patient by saying she was the one who "can't believe it." She replied, "I don't really understand this," and she described her anxiety and other symptoms experienced before the session. What is most striking here about her reply (i.e., "I don't really understand this") is to what extent it follows both in its form and its content the analyst's previous utterance. The patient contraindicated Dewald, just as he had just done to her, and she used the word really just as he had done. My point is that patients tend unconsciously to adapt more or less temporarily the same communicative mode (Types A, B, or C) as used by their analyst. (For more on this, see Langs 1978a.) A careful study of Dewald's book reveals that frequently the patient temporarily switched from a predominantly Type A mode to a Type B mode under the influence of the analyst's all-too-frequent use of *controlling* interventions (such as directive questions, confrontations, and gaslighting interventions) that had marked Type B qualities. (For a brief description of these communicative modes, see footnote number 2 in this chapter.)

In another effort to assert his control over the patient and the analytic situation, Dewald criticized her with, "Let's see what your associations are without jumping to conclusions about it." As in so many other of his interventions, Dewald did not acknowledge to the patient that what she had protested about may have had some measure of validity. He directed her to continue talking, while at the same time implicitly negating the significance of what she had said. She anxiously responded with, "I feel as if someone is trying to overpower me. As if they were trying to. . . ." The patient hesitated and the analyst asked, "What is it you're afraid to say?" She replied, "As if you are trying to sit on me and squash me."

The patient's visual image of being physically squashed was a concrete metaphor that depicted actual aspects of her interactions with Dewald. Her image of being "squashed" was a derivative of a process of unconscious meaning analysis in which she accurately though mainly unconsciously evaluated the meanings of her ongoing disturbing interactions with the analyst in which he repeatedly used various covert methods of interpersonal control.

In response to her protests the analyst made the following transference interpretation, "I think this is one of your fears about starting analysis. It's as if you fantasize that you're going to end up in my power and that you're going to be helpless." In his interpretation of her protest about being overpowered as a transference fantasy, he implicitly denied that her protest and visual image of being squashed by him had actually something to do with their actual (and *not* fantasy) relations with her. Dewald's transference interpretation employed a gaslighting manipulation inasmuch as it first repudiated the patient's judgment about what was occurring in their relationship and secondly he substituted his own judgment of those events. His controlling tactic of negating her judgments and attempting to manipulate her into accepting his judgments instead of her own is one of the methods Searles (1959) mentioned for driving another person crazy. The analyst's transference interpretations disavowed the actuality of his use of covert methods of interpersonal control as well as the antitherapeutic and oppressive affects on the patient. Both his interventions and his discussions of this hour immediately following the process notes of this session ascribed her mounting anxieties over being controlled to the emergence of transference fears and fantasies. Dewald used the term transference to denote irrational ideas caused by the distorting effects of unconscious fantasies.

Now I propose to switch from the microanalytic perspective used in the foregoing vignette to a more macroanalytic perspective on the important effects Dewald's use of indoctrination methods had on the entire analysis.

Initially, the patient responded to these directive and controlling interventions by both conscious and unconscious protests and commentaries on the ways he was relating to her, as well as her responses of anger and helplessness. In response to the patient's conscious as well as unconscious communications regarding his controlling interventions, the analyst denied both that he had been controlling. Also he failed to recognize that her negative responses were to some degree understandable and appropriate reactions to his directiveness. By gaslighting, he attempted to induce her to relinquish her own judgments about their interactions and to accept his judgment about what was occurring both within herself and in her relationships with him. His efforts apparently succeeded, and after the fourth session, the patient seldom complained about his directiveness.

During the remainder of the analysis, an interaction pattern was gradually established in which both the analyst and patient unconsciously colluded in denying some important meanings and realities of their interactions (such as Dewald's use of covert methods of interpersonal control).

Dewald's theoretical stance was a traditional one in which he viewed the sources of his patient's disturbed thoughts and actions as intrapsychic and isolated from environmental influences. Through his covert methods of interpersonal control (especially gaslighting and repetitive questioning) he induced her to drop her complaints about his directiveness. She complied with him as he gradually shaped her responses to conform to his theoretical stance. This included her abandoning her interactional point of view in which she attempted to assess the meaning of her interactions with the analyst. She complied with his position of viewing fantasies, feelings, and ideas as wholly endogenous and disconnected from her interactions with the analyst. Through his use of covert methods of interpersonal control, a mode of relating and communicating was unconsciously established and maintained throughout the analysis wherein the patient complied with the analyst's directives and controls.

The repeated use of these various covert methods of interpersonal control made for a kind of treatment best described as a subtle type of indoctrination. There was little resumption of psychic development, enhancement of positive freedom, or the creation of insight. She attained some symptom relief and what could be called a transference came through an unresolved idealizing transference. For similar interpretations of the Dewald (1972) case, see Levenson (1991) and Hirsch (1993, 1994), both of whom point out the unanalyzed romantic idealization of Dewald by the patient and the analyst's unacknowledged contribution to the patient's transference.[6]

Dewald presented himself as a strong, idealized man to a woman whose history indicates she was devoted to compliantly pleasing men. She complied with Dewald's directives by presenting the sort of analytic material he could use to validate his preferred traditional drive-conflict analytic model. The latter is an example of the stereotyped approach involving circular self-confirming processes. Furthermore, as Hirsch (1994) indicates, "This counter-transference enactment never came close to being analyzed since the analyst, based on his theoretical schema, could not have possibly seen this sadomasochistic, sexually charged interaction from a two-person psychology point of view" (p. 175).

## Melanie Klein's Narrative of a Child's Indoctrination

Melanie Klein's (1961) book, *Narrative of a Child Analysis*, is a daily account of the analysis of a child of 10 which lasted four months during World War II. Klein had an intensive and unrelenting need to control the analytic hours as shown by her shocking, persistent id interpretations and her repeated use of covert methods of inter-

---

6. Though others including Hirsch (1994) and Levenson (1991) have presented negative opinions about the methods Dewald used in treating this patient, in fairness to Dewald I should note that two analysts (Drs. Fleming and Anthony), after their study of the case and follow-up interviews with the patient, gave a positive judgment about the outcome of this case and their views are presented in Dewald's (1972) book. Also significant is the fact that both the patient and Dewald gave a favorable assessment of the outcome both when the analysis was terminated and later after the conclusion of a follow-up study. In addition to attaining some symptom relief, the patient apparently was able to use the analysis to work through some early traumas. Dewald was less controlling and more benevolent to the patient than the significant persons in the patient's childhood were, especially her tyrannical father.

personal control. Bion (1985), Kernberg (1980), Gedo (1988), and others have commented on the dogmatic and dominating quality in Klein's attitude and analytic methodology. Bion's (1985) critical account of his analysis with Klein supports the conclusions others, including I, have made about her use of indoctrination methods. Bion (1985) claimed that he learned from Klein what he did *not* want to do as an analyst with his patients, such as speaking as if he always knew the correct interpretation.

The patient's conscious and unconscious commentaries about her controlling methods apparently were ignored by Klein. For the most part, Klein bypassed interactional dynamics in her search for unconscious phantasies and intrapsychic dynamics. The patient's cognitive and affective responses to her interventions were reduced to the distorting effects of his unconscious phantasies about Mrs. Klein. If the patient turned his attention to someone else, Klein would immediately interpret this as a displacement of feelings that really belonged to the consulting room. Using various methods of covert interpersonal control the analyst steadfastly and repeatedly directed and shaped both the mentation and communications of the patient, who at first meekly demurred and later followed and complied with the analyst.

Gedo (1988) wrote:

> Klein responded to the patient's failure to accept interpretations in the fifth session with a barrage of arguments in which she arbitrarily asserted that all the patient's subsequent associations confirmed her prior statements. When, in the next session, the boy reported that he had been afraid to return, Klein interpreted . . . that he wanted to have intercourse with her (pp. 35–36). Under the circumstances, most analysts would have considered the possibility that the child might simply have been frightened by her insistence on interpretations that made no sense to him. Some weeks after this incident, when the patient expressed doubt that Klein knew everything about him and made *only* valid interpretations, she understood these statements as signs of his paranoid mistrust [pp. 111–112].

Kernberg (1972) asserts that the following approaches used by Klein tend to bring about a process of indoctrination: "The consistently active behavior of the analyst . . ." (p. 78); "The atmosphere of certainty within which interpretations are given . . ." (p. 78); "The premature deep interpretations of unconscious fantasies and transferences which bypass defenses" (p. 77).

Melanie Klein's *The Narrative of a Child Analysis* is the disturbing record of the indoctrination of a young boy by an analyst who apparently had an unshakable need to control the patient.

### Who Was Detribalized?

The following analytic case was reported in a book titled *Panic— The Course of a Psychoanalysis* written by a Danish psychoanalyst, Thorkil Vanggaard (1989). The patient was a 44-year-old physician who suffered all of his life from panic attacks and who was seen three times weekly for five and a half months and then with sporadic sessions for another six months. The book provides process notes made immediately after each session. A close reading of these process notes reveals some repeated pathologic interactional patterns, patterns that were not addressed or interpreted in Vanggaard's book.

Vanggaard repeatedly deflects the patient from dealing with sensitive emotional topics such as conflicts over submission and dominance by engaging in a kind of instruction, education, and coaching. After about a month of this pedagogy, the patient reveals his unconscious judgment about the analyst's indoctrination methods with the following comment. He tells the analyst that there is a misconception prevailing among white men, "that if you take a native and pull him in at one end of a white educational system he will come out at the other as an excellent character. Very often what happens is exactly the reverse, because he is detribalized and, as a result, loses something of value which we do not possess" (p. 39).

The patient's story about the native who is subjected to the white man's education system is, in my opinion, a derivative of the patient's primary process meaning analysis of his interactions with the analyst. I believe it is highly probable that the term "white educational system" refers to the analysis. The statement "if you take a native and pull him in at one end of a white educational system," refers to the patient's unconscious meaning analysis of his own experience with the analyst. Similarly, his references to the native being "detribalized" and "losing something of value" refer to the loss of autonomy and freedom the patient experienced under the repeated impact of Vanggaard's indoctrination methods.

My interpretation of the foregoing passage and of Vanggaard's use of indoctrination methods is supported by David Sachs (1991), who made similar criticisms of Vanggaard's conduct of the analysis. As Sachs asserts, Vanggaard repeatedly demonstrates the stereotyped approach of suggesting the conclusions he wants the patient to reach. Vanggaard transforms the voyage of discovery that an analysis should be into a technology in which the patient proves what the analyst already believes. Sachs (1991) concludes, "Vanggaard's approach exemplifies how analysts can convert their own science into a religion of beliefs while claiming that they do not" (p. 749).

Throughout the analysis Vanggaard uses nonanalytic methods of education, exhortation, lecturing, and various other pressures to get the patient to endorse and confirm his (Vanggaard's) beliefs. Vanggaard succumbs to the temptation to use authority as a substitute for interpretation. The so-called cure of the patient was most probably a "transference cure" obtained through the repeated use of stereotyped approaches and methods of indoctrination.

### From Richard to Renee

The information for this tragic story about Richard's analysis comes from an article by a psychoanalyst, Bloom (1991), and an autobiography, *Second Serve*, written by Dr. Renee Richards (1983). Renee was born Richard H. Raskind and raised by two parents who were both physicians. As a young man, Raskind was plagued by the desire to cross-dress and by fantasies of being a woman. During this time, he underwent years of psychoanalysis with several eminent analysts, including Dr. Robert Bak, one-time president of the American Psychoanalytic Association. Raskind eventually fled treatment, underwent a transsexual operation, assumed a female identity, and became Renee Richards.

Richards book provides an in-depth and comprehensive report of his early development and the events leading up to his transsexual surgery. His account clearly describes how his mother and sister traumatized him in his childhood development by dressing him as a little girl and used any means, including force, to get him to comply with their demands. His mother dressed in a masculine manner and literally wore the pants in the family. Richard's father was passive and submissive to his controlling and sadistic wife.

Richard felt loved and accepted by his mother and sister only when he was dressed as a little girl. As an adult, he felt tense and unhappy as a male but enjoyed more positive feelings only when he dressed as a woman. He worked hard as an analytic patient to utilize the concept of castration anxiety, which at the time was believed to be of central importance in the psychogenesis of the perversions.

The latter part of his analysis deteriorated when Bak made repeated use of directives and threats of psychosis if the patient "acted-out" by trying to solve his problem by surgery.

Bloom (1991) concludes his case study with these remarks.

> There was little indication of any empathic understanding on the part of his world-famous psychoanalyst; rather, Richard was implored to grow a beard, date women, get married, have a son, work as a doctor—in other words, conform to social expectations. These directives and threats evidently did not work, despite the fact that the patient gamely went along with social pressures for years. Like his mother, Richards's analyst was dominating, controlling, and relentless. The transference-countertransference impasse that resulted precluded the nec-

essary empathy, and Richards had to flee treatment and seek transsexual surgery. The empathic approach would have been to maintain the analytic nondirective and nonjudgmental position, while empathizing with the little boy's need to be loved and not controlled. [p. 11]

In this case, the treatment floundered partly because the analyst turned away from using empathic understanding and interpretive methods and instead used various methods of covert interpersonal control, including gaslighting, confrontation, directives, and threats. The analyst's use of these coercive methods repeated the patient's childhood pathological relationships rather than helped him to understand them and develop beyond them.

## CONCLUDING COMMENTS

My careful review of the information about the analyses of all six patients discussed in this chapter convinces me that all of them were harmed by their clinician's indoctrination methods and stereotyped approaches. However, as I shall indicate in Chapter 8, I doubt that the pathological effects on the four patients discussed in Part II were as severe as the two cases discussed in Part I and the case of Bill treated by Dr. T. (see footnote number 4 in this chapter) and discussed in Chapter 2.

Unlike the patients discussed in Part I of this chapter, there are no published follow-up studies of the analyses conducted by Drs. Bak, Klein, Silverman, or Vanggaard. Whether the supposed positive therapeutic results reported by Drs. Fleming and Anthony in their follow-up studies on Dewald's patient outweighed the antitherapeutic effects of Dewald's indoctrination methods is problematic.

# The Wolf Man's Analysis—
# An Interactional Perspective

This review of Freud's analysis of the Wolf Man focuses on the nature of the conscious and unconscious interactions between Freud and the Wolf Man, on Freud's use of deviations, and on pressures he brought to bear on the patient to accept his (Freud's) formulations. Particular attention is given to Freud's interpretations regarding the Wolf Man's childhood nightmare about wolves as arising from early primal scene experiences. The interactional perspective used here and the revised psychoanaltyic theory supporting this approach are provided in previous publications (Dorpat and Miller 1992, 1994).

As the most famous as well as the most controversial of Freud's (1918) patients, the Wolf Man, whose real name was Dr. Serge Pankejiff, is the subject of the best and the largest of Freud's five major case histories. In reviewing the case, we have available not only Freud's (1918) monumental case study, "From the History of an Infantile Neurosis," but also additional accounts of the patient's life and treatment by Pankejiff and by others who knew him and treated him for many years after his analysis with Freud. The Wolf Man's memoirs, Ruth Mack Brunswick's (1928) account of her re-analysis of the Wolf Man, Muriel Gardner's memoirs of her long association with him, and other information about Panke-jiff have been gathered together into a single volume: *The Wolf-Man by the Wolf-Man* (Gardner 1971). Also, we have at our disposal the record of the extensive interviews conducted by the German journalist Karen Obholzer (1982), which she published after Pankejiff's death as *The Wolf-Man Sixty Years Later*. Mahoney's (1984) monograph, *Cries of the Wolf-Man*, provides a brilliant review of Freud's handling of the case.

The Wolf Man had originally been in treatment with Freud from February 1910 until June 1914, and he returned for several additional months of analysis in 1919. When he again decompensated and returned to see Freud in 1926, Freud referred him to Ruth Mack Brunswick, who conducted another analysis lasting five months. For most of his adult life, Pankejiff received some kind of care from psychiatrists or psychoanalysts, and the last two years of his unhappy and troubled life were spent in a psychiatric hospital in Vienna.

## THE NATURE OF THE WOLF MAN'S INTERACTIONS WITH FREUD

In recent years, there has been a deluge of publications criticizing Freud for deviations from acceptable analytic technique and other mistakes in the conduct of the analysis of the Wolf Man. Freud brought relentless pressures on the Wolf Man to accept and to confirm Freud's reconstructions and formulations, such as the primal scene interpretation of the Wolf Man's nightmare about wolves.

Frustrated by the patient's seemingly intractable resistances and the slow progress of the analysis, Freud arbitrarily imposed a fixed time limit on the analysis. In the closing stage of his first analysis and under unremitting pressures from Freud to produce material confirmatory of Freud's theories, the Wolf Man came forth with associations which appeared to support Freud's theories about infantile sexuality and about the primal scene reconstruction of the nightmare about the wolves (Magid 1992, Mahoney 1984). The patient's false and compliant self gave Freud what he was looking for with the result that the patient's true self remained untouched, a false-self maneuver which, as Meissner (1977) noted, "settled several critical dilemmas, and satisfied narcissism at both ends of the couch" (p. 68).

Freud (1918) stated:

> Under the inexorable pressures of this fixed limit his resistance and his fixation to the illness gave way, and now in a disproportionately short time the analysis produced all the material which made it possible to clear up his inhibitions and remove his symptoms. All the information, too, which enabled me to understand his infantile memories is derived from this last period of the work, during which resistance temporarily disappeared and the patient gave an impression of lucidity which is usually attainable only in hypnosis. [p. 11]

Freud used the forced termination as a last-ditch effort to force the facts of this difficult case to conform to his expectations about the centrality of infantile sexuality in neurosogenesis. Magid (1992) concludes: "Only under the pressure of this deadline will his patient accede to the reconstruction of the primal scene as the key to his illness and of the famous dream" (pp. 181–182). Freud (1937b) was frank about the pressures the forced termination placed on the Wolf Man when he called it "blackmailing." He said, "There can be only one verdict about the value of the blackmailing device: it is effective provided that one hits the right time for it" (p. 218).

Freud (1918) said, "The patient related the dream at a very early stage of the analysis and very soon came to share my conviction that the causes of his infantile neurosis lay concealed behind it" (p. 117). He continues, "In the course of the treatment the first dream returned in innumerable variations and new editions," but "it was only during the last months of the analysis that it became possible to understand it completely, and only then thanks to the spontaneous work on the patient's part" (p. 181).

Freud's description of the process of interpretation in the Wolf Man case is disingenuous and at odds with what he wrote elsewhere (Fish 1989, Magid 1992). Freud indicates that his patient "required a long education to induce him to take an independent share in the work" (p. 157). In light of knowledge we have about the Wolf Man's deep fixations to passive attitudes and ways of relating, it is highly improbable that Freud, or anyone else for that matter, could by a "long education" induce the Wolf Man to take an "independent share" in the work.

Note the contradiction in Freud's account about how "spontaneous work" on the patient's part came about as a result of the "inexorable pressure" of the forced termination. All analysts who have written about this issue agree that most probably the Wolf Man did *not* take an independent share of the work. Rather, as was his characteristic tendency in other relationships, he defensively complied with Freud's pressures to bring forth associations Freud could use to confirm his theory of infantile sexuality and his primal scene reconstruction.

Fish (1989) describes how Freud disclaims his repeated actions of controlling the patient. His disclaimers tend themselves to extend his controlling influence on the patient. His efforts to induce the Wolf Man's independence actually undermined what little capacity he had for independent action. All of the time Freud is proclaiming the autonomy of the patient and of his readers, he is at the same time covertly attempting to control them. Fish declared that Freud is engaged in establishing his power by means that could not be more rhetorical (p. 190).

Freud presents himself as a disinterested researcher and at the same time works energetically to extend his control until it finally includes everything: the behavior of the patient, the details of the analysis, and the performance of the reader (Fish 1989).

Fish (1989) concludes:

> . . . the true story of domination and submission is the story of Freud's performance here and now, the story of a master rhetorician who hides from others and from himself the true

nature of his activities. Once more Freud contrives to keep that secret by publishing it, by discovering at the heart of the *patient's* fantasy the very conflicts that he himself has been acting out in his relationships with the patient, the analysis, the reader, and his critics. In all of these relationships he is driven by the obsessions he uncovers, by the continued need to control, to convince, and to seduce in endless vacillation with the equally powerful need to disclaim any traces of influence and to present himself as the passive conduit of forces that exist independently of him. [p. 197]

Fish's (1989) unique contributions are the insights he gives into not only how Freud covertly controls the Wolf Man, but also his detailed and well-documented explanations about Freud's rhetorical gifts for seducing and controlling his readers.

The following examples from Freud's (1918) study of the Wolf Man give further examples of the kind of pressures he made on the Wolf Man. "But the patient would not hear of this *correction*; I could not succeed, as in so many other differences of opinion between us, in *convincing* him" (p. 62, the italics are mine). "Out of critical interest I made one more attempt to *force* upon the patient another view of his story" (p. 9, the italics are mine). In his discussions with Obholzer (1982), the Wolf Man complained that Freud told him, "Don't seek after contradictions but accept what I tell you and improvement will set in by itself" (p. 46).

Between the two members of the analytic dyad there was a complementary interplay between the aggressive Freud with his insistent manner and the Wolf Man's yielding, compliant, and obliging nature. Severe trauma in childhood brought about a vertical split in Pankejiff in which, as Mahoney (1984) states that "part of the Wolf Man's self could falsely cooperate with Freud and hunt down corroborating evidence in bookshops; another part was skeptical and ultimately impenetrable" (p. 106).

Freud had professional as well as personal reasons for seeking evidence to support his theory of infantile sexuality and to defeat his rivals. He was strongly invested in refuting the arguments of his former followers Jung and Adler, who would not accept Freud's concept of infantile sexuality and its central role in neurosogenesis.

The picture that emerges is one of Freud weaving a complex reconstruction about the primal scene interpretation of the nightmare that the Wolf Man "must be educated in, and then progressively comply with, in all its implications, no matter how farfetched they seem, as the price for maintaining his desperately needed selfobject ties to Freud" (Magid 1992, p. 184).

Magid (1992) presents a self psychology perspective on the nature of the relations between Freud and the Wolf Man. He states, "The Wolf Man was able to maintain selfobject ties almost solely via a masochistic surrender to the other. This pattern, unfortunately, seems to have characterized his relationship with Freud, when his own reality was continually sacrificed to the necessity of making his experience conform to Freud's preordained theories of sexuality" (p. 191).

Among the many investigators who have written about Freud's analysis of the Wolf Man, there is some consensus about the central unconscious interactional dynamics concerning the Wolf Man's analysis with Freud. In order to win Freud's approval and to maintain his relationship with Freud, the Wolf Man unconsciously complied with Freud's pressures to accept Freud's interpretations, as well as to even bring forth memories and the other information supporting Freud's reconstructions and theories (Fish 1989, Flarsheim 1972, Langs 1980b, Magid 1992, Mahoney 1984, Meissner 1977).

Given Freud's forceful personality, the pressures he placed on the Wolf Man, and his intense personal and professional investment in the case, it comes as no surprise to learn that the Wolf Man years later bitterly complained about the treatment and Freud's charismatic influence on him (Obholzer 1982).

In Flarsheim's (1972) view, the Wolf Man's residual paranoidal transference reactions to Freud stemmed from the latter's controlling interventions on the Wolf Man and especially what Freud (1937b) called the "forcible technical device" of setting a fixed time limit before termination.

## INTERACTIONAL DYNAMICS

The Wolf Man's psychoanalytic experience with Freud resulted in the maintenance and reinforcement of a false self organization which represented a compliance with Freud's expectations and served to defensively conceal an undeveloped and vulnerable true self. Meissner (1977) emphasizes how the Wolf Man's false self organization entails internal fragmentation, a lack of integration (or "splitting"), and represents a failure in the capacity for integration both of a cohesive sense of self and of the internalization of stable psychic structures.

Freud's active and aggressive efforts to "educate," "correct," "pressure," and "blackmail" the patient were antitherapeutic and counterproductive to the goals of psychoanalytic therapy. As Fish (1989), Mahoney (1984), and others convincingly demonstrate, Freud denied how much he had used controlling and suggestive methods by rationalizing these "forceful" techniques as necessary to "educate" the patient, to induce the patient to take independent action, and to overcome the patient's resistance. Freud tended to view the patient's occasional ambivalences and failures to agree with Freud's ideas as resistances to be aggressively surmounted with the use of indoctrination methods.

In what follows, I shall provide a brief outline of the predominant pathological unconscious interactions between Freud and the Wolf Man, interactions that not only prevented the formation of a therapeutic alliance but also contributed to the failure of the treatment. Their interactions could be described in terms of a vicious circle, an unconscious and closed system of self-repeating interactions in which the action of each person unconsciously elicits a complementary response in the other person. Under the repetitive impact of the patient's unconscious masochistic communications, narcissistic demands, and provocations, Freud put aside the use of nondirective interpretive methods and began to employ covert methods of interpersonal control in order to induce the patient into changing his beliefs and his behavior.

Motivated by the anxiety, shame, and guilt engendered by Freud's use of covert methods of interpersonal control and fearful of losing his relationship to Freud, the Wolf Man complied with the pressures placed upon him and formed a misalliance with Freud.

In other words, Freud's directive and controlling communications evoked the Wolf Man's passive submissive responses and these in turn triggered directive and controlling responses from Freud. The latter's response initiated another cycle of these repetitive and for the most part unconscious pathological symbiotic relations between the Wolf Man and Freud. Often Freud and the Wolf Man were engaged in what Langs (1978a) calls a Type B field, a type of interpersonal interaction marked by the repeated use of projective identifications by both parties of the dyad.

### Freud's Primal Scene Interpretation of Pankejiff's Nightmare

My aim here is to critically review Freud's (1918) primal scene interpretation of a nightmare Pankejiff had when he was 4 years old and which he first told to Freud early in his analysis. He dreamed it was night and he was lying in a bed which had its foot toward a window. Suddenly, the window opened and Pankejiff was terrified to see some six or seven white wolves sitting on a big walnut tree in front of the window. They had big tails like foxes, and their ears were pricked like dogs when they pay attention to something. In terror of being eaten up by the wolves, he screamed and woke up.

Freud interpreted the dream as having been unconsciously derived from an earlier primal scene experienced when Pankejiff was 18 months old. According to Freud's (1918) famous reconstruction, the patient, when he was 18 months old, woke up one afternoon at the peak of his malaria fever and watched his parents having *coitus a tergo*. While observing his parents' genitalia, his father's heavy breathing, and his mother's facial expression, the guardedly passive baby resorted to having a bowel movement, which gave him an excuse for the screaming which interrupted his parent's sexual intercourse.

There exists a consensus among those who have reviewed Freud's writings, as well as Pankejiff's later remarks about the dream and Freud's interpretation of it, that Freud's primal scene interpretation about the nightmare is most implausible. Blum (1974) expresses deep skepticism over Freud's primal scene reconstruction. He reviewed Freud's reconstruction of the Wolf Man's primal scene at eighteen months with particular attention to the possible role of the infant's malaria. There is good reason to doubt that an 18-month-old child could perceive or remember the details of his parents' sexual activity while suffering from malaria and a high fever.

In his reconstruction of the Wolf Man's primal scene, Freud (1918) insisted that the primal scene was one of *coitus a tergo* because, in Freud's opinion, it "alone offers the spectator a possibility of inspecting the genitals" (p. 59). Freud was incorrect in his claim that the *a tergo* position allows a spectator an opportunity for viewing the genitals. Videman (1977) wrote, "The position *a tergo* is the least favorable to observe the female genitals, unless the child enjoyed the optimal position neither behind nor before the couple but at their very juncture" (p. 306). Mahoney (1984) concludes, "The amount of perceptual acrobatics in Freud's reconstruction is staggering, for the observability assigned to the Wolf-baby's angle of vision would exceed the ingenious staging of any pornographic film producer" (p. 52).

Mahoney (1984) and others describe the "climate of suggestion and mutual deception" (p. 117) in which both the analyst and the patient accepted a bizarre conception of a physically impossible primal scene. (For a similar interpretation, see Videman 1977).

Mahoney suggests that Freud's case history about the Wolf Man's nightmares and his primal scene reconstruction is mainly and unconsciously Freud's own dream and his concerns about the primal scene. As a young child, Freud *did* sleep in his parents' bedroom, whereas the Wolf Man, according to the Wolf Man, did *not*. Using various sources, including of course Freud's writings plus later writings on this famous case, Mahoney (1984) concluded that Freud was "the originator of his own primal scene; he begets the scene, witnesses it, and repeatedly engenders it in his patient, tries to 'convince' him of this construction or creation" (p. 113). Like Mahoney, Kanzer and Glenn (1980) argue that Freud's special interest in the Wolf Man and the Wolf Man's dream was prompted by Freud's own need to work out primal scene residues and particularly to repress aggression against his own father.

In one of his interviews with Obholzer (1982), the elderly Wolf Man described Freud's primal scene interpretation of his nightmares about wolves as "terribly farfetched." Freud's reconstructions and especially the primal scene notion had little plausibility for the Wolf Man, even though at the time of his first analysis his need to idealize and please Freud overrode all other considerations. In sum, he complied with Freud, brought forth confirming material at the same time that he more or less consciously knew that Freud's formulation was "farfetched." Pankejiff told Obholzer, "The whole matter is improbable, because children in Russia slept with the nurse in her room and not with the parents in their room." (This quotation appears in Magid 1992, p. 185).

The Wolf Man told Obholzer, "In my story, what was explained by dreams? Nothing, as far as I can see. Freud traces everything back to the primal scene which he derives from the dream. But that scene doesn't occur in the dream" (quoted in Magid 1992, p. 188). After a careful review of the clinical evidence, I, too, must conclude with the emerging majority of opinions that Freud's primal scene interpretation of the nightmare was beyond the pale of possibility and reality and, as the Wolf Man himself said, "farfetched."

### Therapeutic Alliance or Misalliance?

Various authors have commented on the failure of Freud to form and maintain a therapeutic alliance with Pankejiff (Langs 1980b, Magid 1992, Meissner 1977, Offenkrantz and Tobin 1973). Offenkrantz and Tobin (1973) point out the special place of the

Wolf Man as an object of Freud's research and how this probably created problems for establishing and maintaining an effective therapeutic alliance.

Langs (1980b) presents convincing evidence for his formulations concerning the misalliance between Freud and the Wolf Man. The multitude of deviations from acceptable technique and the disruptive extensions of the boundaries of the patient-analyst relationship promoted a seductive atmosphere, a submissive and passive stance in the Wolf Man, together with an unconscious image of Freud as seductive, masculine, and powerful. According to Langs (1980b), Freud's deviations (e.g., setting an irrevocable termination date, asking for a gift on termination, extra-analytic contacts, pressures brought on the patient to support Freud's reconstructions, and so on) created a misalliance.

Langs (1980b) said,

> By pressuring the Wolf Man into a passive feminine position which intensified his castration anxieties and undoubtedly his fears of annihilation . . . Freud aggravated the Wolf Man's anxieties and conflicts in this area and thereby inadvertently contributed to the delusional symptomatology. [p. 380]

A psychoanalytic treatment based on the establishment of a therapeutic alliance is one founded on a process of collaboration and a respect for the boundaries and autonomy of the patient. It is not possible to form or to maintain an effective therapeutic alliance with patients where the analyst repeatedly uses covert methods of interpersonal control or other methods of indoctrination.

The use of any forcible technical device to control a patient's ideas, feelings, or behaviors, or to overcome his resistance to change, tends to produce a misalliance rather than a therapeutic alliance. Also, such controlling interventions often provoke an overt or covert power struggle between the analysand and analyst.

Freud and other clinicians who use such controlling interventions fail to appreciate that in order to work with patients without trying to control them, the practitioner must have confidence in their patients' capacities for spontaneous maturation and autonomous development. In viewing the patient as the "passive" partner and the analyst as the "active" partner in the analytic situation, Freud (1918) did not adequately respect the Wolf Man's autonomy or value the importance of creating a context for establishing and maintaining a therapeutic alliance based on the active collaboration of equal partners.

The problems in establishing a therapeutic alliance with the Wolf Man, according to Meissner (1977), stemmed from the serious nature of the Wolf Man's psychiatric disorders. Among those who have studied the Wolf Man case and the voluminous literature about it, there is agreement for the view that he suffered from severe psychopathology for almost all of his life and that he had psychotic episodes (Blum 1974, Brunswick 1928, Langs 1980b, Magid 1992, Mahoney 1984). Blum (1974) demonstrates that the Wolf Man's childhood disturbance was a "severe borderline disturbance" (p. 348) and that he had an "adult borderline personality" (p. 348). In Blum's view, the Wolf Man's psychotic states in adult life were regressive revivals of his psychosis in early childhood.

Meissner (1977) argues about the impossibility of forming a therapeutic alliance with patients such as the Wolf Man who come to analysis with such primitive needs and wishes. He opines:

> Freud spontaneously stepped into the role of such an idealized and powerful object by his manner of approaching the patient and the way he assumed the power of deciding on the Wolf Man's visits to his mistress . . . the narcissistic need for sustaining the inner integrity of the grandiose self was answered subsequent to the analysis with Freud by his becoming Freud's special and famous patient. Thus any attempt on the part of his analyst to gain a foothold on the plane of alliance was frustrated by the overwhelming dimensions and the power of the Wolf Man's rather primitive and archaic narcissistic transference. [p. 69]

In my view, Meissner (1977) is overly protective of Freud's conduct of the analysis. After all, Freud was not compelled to step "into the role of such an idealized and powerful object" (Meissner 1977, p. 69). The Wolf Man's compliance and masochistic submissiveness were matched by and dovetailed with the domineering and authoritarian tendencies in Freud's personality. (For studies on the authoritarian aspects of Freud's personality see Holt 1992).

A truly analytic process of mutual discovery based on a therapeutic alliance with Pankejiff was neither initiated nor established by Freud. From the beginning of the analysis and continuing throughout the treatment and afterward, Freud stepped into and enacted in various ways (such as the use of covert methods of interpersonal control) the role set up for him by the Wolf Man as the all-powerful omniscient and omnipotent object.

By his use of covert methods of interpersonal control and other indoctrination methods, Freud made a substantial and ongoing contribution to the misalliance and the pathological, symbiotic quality of his interactions with Pankejiff.

The psychoanalytic literature on the treatment of the more severely disturbed patients, together with my experiences as a therapist and supervisor, convinces me it is possible though difficult to form a therapeutic alliance with such patients and to successfully treat them using psychoanalytic methods. My opinion in this regard is somewhat at variance with analysts such as Zetzel (1958) and Meissner (1977), who hold that severely disturbed are unable to form a therapeutic alliance.

Zetzel (1958) linked the capacity to form a therapeutic alliance with the patient's capacity to form mature object relations. She and others assume that in order to form a workable therapeutic alliance there must be a sufficiently mature sector of the patient's personality for him to perceive the analyst as a separate person and to separate transference feelings from perceptions of the analyst as a unique and separate individual.

Zetzel (1958) and others have presented an ideal or model of the conditions considered important for forming and maintaining a therapeutic alliance. Analysts can strive for attaining these conditions while at the same time recognizing there are situations in which either the patient's and/or the clinician's abilities for living up to this ideal are temporarily impaired.

Though I am cognizant of the immense difficulties and deep developmental fixations standing in the way of forming and maintaining a therapeutic alliance with severely disturbed patients, my experience indicates it can be done. Moreover, my faith in my patients' capacities for forming more mature relationships based on mutuality and my hopeful expectations[1] of their abilities to grow in these respects can be and are often powerful facilitators of such constructive changes. Frequently there is an element of a self-fulfilling prophecy about our beliefs and attitudes concerning what patients are capable or not capable of doing (Dorpat and Miller 1992).

In other words, clinicians foster personality development when they treat patients as if they were capable of both forming mature relationships and maintaining a therapeutic alliance. On the other hand, they foster a misalliance and stultifying compliance when they attempt to control and direct their patients by using, as Freud did with the Wolf Man, covert methods of interpersonal control and other indoctrination methods.

Unfortunately, what took place in Freud's interactions with the Wolf Man is not uncommon. Many other practitioners would also, as Freud did, under the impact of the Wolf Man's passivity, seemingly intractable "resistance," and masochistic provocations, start to use directive methods.

## SUMMARY

This chapter presents an overview of Freud's analysis of the Wolf Man from an interactional point of view. As a result of Freud's use of various covert methods of interpersonal control such as the fixed

---

1. By my phrase *hopeful expectations* I refer to a silent attitude of the therapist and not to any explicit communications made to the patient. A therapist's respect and caring, hopeful attitude for a patient should almost always be conveyed indirectly through one's attitude and nonverbal communication rather than by explicit and direct verbal messages.

time limit on the length of his analysis, the Wolf Man gave in and provided material Freud could use to support his theories and reconstructions such as the primal scene interpretation of the nightmare about wolves.

By his repeated use of covert methods of interpersonal control and other directive methods, Freud fostered a misalliance with the Wolf Man and prevented the formation of a therapeutic alliance. In his interactions with the Wolf Man, Freud enacted a transference/countertransference complex organized and activated by the Wolf Man's need for an idealized omnipotent and powerful person. To maintain his relationship with Freud and to gratify his selfobject needs, the Wolf Man unconsciously complied with the pressures imposed on him by Freud's use of indoctrination methods.

7

---

# What Did Dora Want? The Abuse of Power in Freud's Analysis of Dora

In this study on Dora's analysis with Freud (1905), my major focus is on how Freud treated and related to Dora, as well as the unconscious dynamics of their interaction and its effects on Dora. Dora has become the most frequently re-examined and re-interpreted psychoanalytic case study. There exists a general agreement among both psychoanalysts and nonpsychoanalysts that Freud's paper on Dora is a literary masterpiece about a therapeutic failure.

My major criticism of Freud's way of treating Dora is that he was repeatedly and highly controlling of her and that he used gaslighting and other indoctrination methods to pressure Dora into accepting his interpretations about her unconscious desires and complexes. Though this issue of Freud's actions in controlling and dominating Dora is not given much attention in the psychoanalytic literature, it has been noted by a considerable number of nonpsychoanalytic writers.

After providing a critical review of the relevant literature, I shall present my study of Dora using an interactional perspective to illuminate what took place in her analysis with Freud. I have not attempted a comprehensive or exhaustive review of the literature on the Dora case; this has been done by Jennings (1986), Decker (1991), Lakoff and Coyne (1993), and Ornstein (1993).

## REVIEW OF LITERATURE

The family therapist, Maddi (1974), was one of the first of many to see Freud's article on Dora as a documentation of victimization of the powerless by her more powerful milieu. Maddi regards "Freud's approach as both unethical and unesthetic," and he concludes:

> As I read Freud's account of Dora, I find a beleaguered, overwhelmed youngster caught in a fantastic web of corruption constructed by all the important adults in her life . . . [Freud] accepts [the adults'] attribution of the sexual problem to Dora herself, and sets about convincing her of her guilt with all the manipulative weaponry of psychoanalysis. [p. 99]

In addition to offering his own self-psychological perspective, Paul Ornstein (1993) performs an exemplary task of presenting a balanced and carefully reasoned assessment not only of Freud's original paper, but also of the many articles and books about Dora and her brief analysis with Freud. While Ornstein acknowledges Freud's monumental contributions and his outstanding literary talents, he systematically exposes the harmful ways Freud treated Dora. The picture emerging from Ornstein's study, and also from most other recent writings on Dora's analysis with Freud, is one in which an unempathic and authoritarian Freud repeatedly attempts to impose his theories on Dora.

Ornstein presents a convincing argument for his notion that Freud did *not* understand Dora and furthermore Dora did not feel understood by Freud. Freud's overriding need to prove his theory right led him to insist on the validity of his interpretations, speculations, and inferences. In Ornstein's (1993) words, "He practically fought Dora's subjective experiences in order to establish the validity of his own (more experience-distant) dynamic-genetic explanation" (p. 67). He brought considerable pressure on Dora to induce her into accepting his interpretation and to obtain her agreement with his reconstructions.

According to Ornstein, Freud could not see or acknowledge how his theoretical assumptions and countertransference responses had adversely intruded on Dora's analysis. He asserted that he was reading Dora, when actually he was often only reading his own mind. A similar opinion comes from Kahane (1985), who put it this way, "What contemporary readings of Dora suggest is that . . . in constructing a narrative of Dora's desire [Freud] essentially represented his own" (p. 20).

According to Erikson (1962), Dora and Freud were in conflict as to what kind of truth they were searching for. Erikson (1962) said, "Dora was consumed with the historical truth as known to others, while her doctor insisted on the genetic truth behind her own symptoms" (p. 456).

In the context of discussing the adolescent's need for establishing the genetic truth, Erikson (1962) told about Dora's need to return to Freud for one consultation a year after she abruptly terminated her analysis to let him know she had succeeded in obtaining from Herr K. (the family friend who attempted to seduce Dora) his acknowledgment that the events had occurred as she described. This urgent need of adolescents to establish the actuality of events, according to Erikson, is related to their developmental concerns with fidelity and identity. In adolescents there is an overriding and imperative need for the consolidation and establishment of a stable, coherent sense of identity (Blos 1962, Erikson 1962).

According to Erikson, Dora's illness was an adaptive strategy —probably her only way of coping with the betrayals and seductions that constituted her environment.

The strongest case against Freud's handling of Dora's analysis has been made by individuals who have written from a feminist perspective: Daly (1978), Gallop (1982), Hertz (1983), Lakoff and Coyne (1993), Ramas (1980), and Sprengnether

(1985). Perhaps the most outspoken and harshest criticism comes from Crews (1993), who concluded that the Dora case "is one of the worst instances on record of sexist hectoring by a reputed healer" (p. 60).

In their opinion, Freud, as a male caught in Victorian patriarchal assumptions, misdiagnosed the patient. By legitimizing the treachery being carried on by her parents and by Herr K. and Frau K., Freud insured Dora's continued psychiatric illness. Also, in the opinion of recent critics, Freud brought aid and comfort to a social system that oppressed women and children for the aggrandizement of men.

Though Dora initially went to Freud unwillingly, for her he represented a final and desperate hope of establishing a relationship of trust and mutual respect with an adult. By betraying that hope in an authoritarian and bullying way, Lakoff and Coyne (1993) assert, Freud contributed toward her lifelong unhappiness and psychiatric symptoms.

Freud repeatedly overlooked or undervalued clear evidence that Dora and his other female patients were at the mercy, sexually and otherwise, of the male members of their families and that this exploitative relationship was at the heart of the psychiatric symptoms presented by so many of those women (Lakoff and Coyne 1993).

Lakoff and Coyne's (1993) book is, in my opinion, the most comprehensive and insightful study of Dora by any nonpsychoanalysts, and it successfully integrates the perspectives as well as the theoretical concepts of three different disciplines: psychotherapy, linguistics, and feminist studies. They use Freud's analysis of Dora as an example of the abuse of power by psychotherapists. They explore the nonreciprocity between Freud and Dora and demonstrate how the authoritarian Freud dehumanized his teenage patient by his badgering and his power ploys.

Dora's analysis with Freud in 1900 began after he had repudiated his seduction theory, a theory which held that one of the major causes of hysterical and other psychiatric symptoms was unconscious *memories* of sexual trauma. After he abandoned the seduction theory, he believed that unconscious repressed sexual *fantasies* (rather than unconscious memories) were the important proximal cause of psychiatric symptoms. Thereafter, first Freud and then for decades other psychoanalysts tended to minimize the significance of trauma and social and interpersonal relations in the psychogenesis of psychiatric disorders. What is most impressive about many of the articles written before 1975 by psychoanalysts about Dora's analysis is what I have called the "collective blindspot" most psychoanalysts have about reality factors and unconscious interactional dynamics which, together with preexisting intra-psychic elements, codetermine the patient's dynamics and symptoms (Dorpat and Miller 1992).

Fortunately, a few analysts have written about how Freud's exclusively intrapsychic emphasis led to distortion and error in the case of Dora, and they include Langs (1976b), Ornstein (1993), Stierlin (1976), and Erikson (1962).

In his introduction to the Dora case history, Rieff (1963) takes into account social and interpersonal factors when he concludes, "[Freud's] entire interpretation of the case . . . depends upon his limiting the case to Dora when, in fact, from the evidence he himself presents, it is the milieu in which she is constrained to live that is ill" (p. 10).

Decker (1991) and Ornstein (1993) also emphasize the important role of the increasingly anti-Semitic and antifeminist milieu in Vienna during Dora's life (before she emigrated to the United States) as important elements contributing to her psychopathology.

In Vienna, as well as in other parts of Central Europe in Dora's time, there was a general consensus that women were inferior and in Decker's (1991) words:

> . . . the anti-Semites insistently proclaimed that the proof of the Jews' deficiency lay in their exhibition of traits commonly associated with women. Thus did anti-feminism and anti-Semitism unite at the turn of the century. A young Jewish woman like Dora could be filled with more self-doubt, and even self-loathing, than a Jewish man. [p. 40]

## DORA'S ANALYSIS WITH FREUD—
## AN INTERACTIONAL PERSPECTIVE

In 1900, the 18-year-old Dora was brought to Freud for analytic treatment by her father, a former patient whom Freud had successfully treated for a Luetic infection. Dora suffered from a number of psychiatric symptoms, including dyspnea, headache, coughing spells, aphonia, and fatigue. Her analysis centered on the analysis of Dora's symptoms and two dreams. After only three months of interviews with Freud, Dora abruptly and without prior notice abandoned the treatment.

Several disturbing recent events led Dora's father to seek analytic treatment for Dora. Her parents had found a suicide note she had written. This, and her fainting after insisting that her father break off his affair with Frau K., induced her father to ask Freud to "try to bring her to reason." Though Dora's father had persistently lied about his sexual involvement with Frau K. to Dora, Freud, and others, he had actually been having an affair with Frau K. for several years.

The Ks were close friends of Dora's family, and Dora was especially intimate with Frau K., whom she idealized. Her idealization of Frau K. may have been enhanced by her unsatisfactory relationship with her mother. Dora looked down on her mother, whom Freud described as "foolish," "uncultivated," and suffering from a "housewife's psychosis" with the symptom of spending her days in compulsive cleaning of her house and its contents.

When Dora was 14 years old and again when she was 16, Herr K. made inappropriate sexual advances toward her, which she vociferously rejected. When she was 14, Herr K. suddenly kissed her in an explicitly sexual manner. Dora reacted with anger and disgust and abruptly left the room.

Dora wanted her father to terminate his affair with Frau K., and she was particularly enraged at him for almost literally handing her over to Herr K. with the hope that this would both squelch her protests as well as permit him to continue his affair with Frau K. undisturbed. When Dora complained to her father about his misconduct, he rebuffed her and sent her off to Freud to be cured, not just of her numerous symptoms, but also of her insubordination.

All four of the significant adults (Herr K., Frau K., and Dora's parents) in Dora's life were strongly committed to preserving a conventional appearance that each marriage was intact and that Dora's father and Frau K. had a merely platonic relationship, even while all four partners were aware that the contrary was true. All parties were conspiring to conceal what was going on and most of them (especially Dora's father) made demands upon Dora to maintain the mutual pretense. Dora then faced an overwhelmingly hostile and dishonest environment in the four significant adults in her life, who lied, pretended, malingered, and brought pressures upon her to collude with them in their deceit. All four showed little concern for her well-being and all attempted to use her for their own self-centered purposes.

Dora was determined to have her father stop his affair with Frau K. at all costs, and it was in this context that her symptoms escalated and her depression deepened to the point of writing a suicide note. A crucial moment for Dora's mental health came when she told her parents about Herr K.'s sexual advances and her father used a gaslighting tactic when he declared (with Dora's mother's tacit agreement) that she must have imagined the entire episode.

In light of what Dora told Freud, as well as his own accounts about Dora's father, Dora's criticisms of her father do not appear exaggerated or inaccurate. She had told Freud, "He was insincere, he had a strain of falseness in his character, he only thought of his own enjoyment, and he had a gift for seeing things in the light which suited him best" (Freud 1905, p. 34). Because of these character defects and her father's recent traumatic actions against her, Dora had experienced a severe and painful disappointment in her father where previously she had had an intense attachment to him. Freud repeatedly interpreted her reproaches against her father as defensively motivated to defend against her unconscious self-reproaches. Yet Freud never tells of dealing with this negative aspect of her feelings toward her father, but instead emphasized only the positive oedipal attachment with its supposed origins much earlier in her life.

## Freud's Gaslighting of Dora

Note the similarity between the gaslighting tactic used by Dora's father in the above vignette and the manner in which Freud treated her in the following interaction. Dora once insisted to Freud that the most important adults in her life had not only used her for their own ends, but then had also denied using her. When Dora protested such treatment to Freud, he interpreted it as a resistance by means of which she could avoid admitting the truth about her loving feelings for Herr K. Here, as in many other times in Dora's analysis, Freud discounted and/or repudiated Dora's subjective reality, her feelings, percepts, and judgments. His repeated and blunt interpretations of what he believed were Dora's unconscious sexual wishes were frequently used to brush aside and reject Dora's conscious experience. Such gaslighting interventions were probably the most common and effective tactics he employed for gaining control over Dora and her psychic functions.

Dora wanted Freud to intervene with her father and induce him to break off the affair with Frau K., and she hoped that Freud would at the least acknowledge that her judgments, invalidated as they were by the adults in her life, were nonetheless correct. Freud did neither, and by his repeated negative and critical judgments of her thoughts and feelings, he provided further invalidation of Dora's position. (For more on this point see Erikson 1962 and Langs 1976b.)

From the first, Freud took an adversarial position with his patient. His hostility and suspiciousness was communicated directly to her and must have influenced her feelings about him. Freud rejected her perceptions and ideas and prevented her from having a collaborative role in the construction of her narrative. Along with her father, Freud dismissed her ideas as "fantasies." In short, with Freud Dora could neither say nor do anything right; nothing about her met with Freud's approval.

Freud overpowered Dora by the anger of his communications with her. The explicit expression of anger, traditionally reserved for men and not women, is an effective way for men to reinforce power over others. Reports of his dialogues with his male patients suggest that Freud used this tactic more with women than men. Lakoff and Coyne (1993) note, "He [Freud] argues, he browbeats, he shames, he lectures; he doesn't explain, or illustrate, or explore" (p. 24).

Guided by his bias against real life interactions, Freud tried to impose on Dora his theory about the central importance of repressed sexual fantasies in the etiology of her neurotic symptoms. He attempted to convince her that because of her repressed latent homosexuality, her fantasies of oral sex and pregnancy, her memories of childhood masturbation and the primal scene, that she was to blame for the current miserable situation into which she in actuality had been plunged by her parents and the Ks.

Freud's repeated and blunt use of sexual interpretations and words for sexual organs had a marked effect on the power relations between himself and Dora. To be able to surprise and startle someone by the use of such shocking language is to impose power both over the content of the discourse and over the hearer. To allow such disturbing intrusions to pass unimpeded (as Dora did with Freud, though not with Herr K.) is to implicitly acknowledge the dominance of the intruder (Lakoff and Coyne 1993).

In his article on Dora, Freud (1905) attempted to defend himself against anticipated criticisms of his blunt and repeated use of sexual terms by rationalizing that this was normal medical practice and furthermore that Dora had already heard such ideas and terms.

His rationalizations for speaking to an adolescent in this startling way do not withstand close scrutiny. Most nonpsychoanalytic writers and a sizable number of psychoanalytic writers on the Dora case agree that Freud's repeated abrupt and intrusive sexual interpretations were hurtful and disturbing to her. Specialists in child and adolescent psychoanalysis indicate that such blunt sexual interpretations and terms are especially contraindicated in the analytic treatment of adolescent patients (Jennings 1986, Scharfman 1980).

Freud's repeatedly directing the analytic dialogue to sexual matters was one more way he asserted and kept control over Dora and the analytic situation. This criticism of Freud's unsparing use of intrusive sexual terms and sexual interpretations is valid regardless of whether or not Freud had prurient intent, whether or not it was normal medical practice, or whether or not Dora had heard it all already (Lakoff and Coyne 1993).

Among psychoanalysts who have written about the Dora case, there is some consensus for the view that Freud's premature and confrontational interpretations of unconscious sexual wishes contributed to Dora's erotization of the transference and probably also to her flight from the analysis (Jennings 1986).

Freud's account of the analysis of Dora is often much concerned with various pressures he brought to bear on her to convince her that she was unconsciously in love with Herr K. and with her "resistances" to those pressures. For example, he suggested that her angry and repeated recriminations against her father for carrying out an affair with Frau K. unconsciously defended against similar unconscious recriminations against herself for her loving and sexual feelings for Herr K.

After one of his many efforts to persuade and pressure Dora to admit her love for Herr K., Freud said, "She admitted that she might have been in love with Herr K. at B____, but declared that *since the [seduction] scene at the lake it had all been over*" (pp. 37–38, italics added).

Ornstein (1993, pp. 71–73) presents convincing arguments for the hypothesis that Dora's intense positive attachment to Herr K. prior to the time he attempted to seduce her when she was 16 was not one of romantic or sexual love, but stemming from an intense idealized much-needed stand-in for her father; in other words, a selfobject.

Freud (1905) persisted in making deep interpretations of Dora's romantic love and sexual desire for Herr K. in the absence of any convincing evidence of such feelings for Herr K. Few, if any, of the many arguments and interpretations Freud made about Dora's *unconscious* love for Herr K. are convincing and some are most implausible (Esterson 1993). Freud's notion that Dora was unconsciously in love with Herr K. was based on his speculations and assumptions that such were her unconscious feelings.

Freud, in my opinion, misinterpreted Dora's disgust and anger at Herr K.'s improper advances when she was 14 and again when she was 16 as "hysterical" and pathological. My opinion is similar to that of Scharfman (1980) who opined that Herr K.'s seductive advances were most probably experienced by Dora as being "like her father as someone interested in women primarily as sexual objects" (p. 53).

Freud (1905) writes:

> The behaviour of this child of fourteen was intensely and completely hysterical. I should without questions consider a person hysterical in whom an occasion for sexual excitement elicited feelings that were predominantly or exclusively unpleasurable. [p. 28]

In my opinion, it is highly questionable that one would expect a *pleasurable* sexual response in a 14-year-old girl who was sexually approached by an older man who was one of her father's best friends. (For similar views, see Erikson 1962, Esterson 1993, Ornstein 1993, and Scharfman 1980).

### Interpretations Used as a Way of Gaslighting

When Dora was sixteen, the K.'s maid (governess) confided to her that Herr K. had previous extramarital involvements, and just two days before Herr K. had propositioned Dora, the maid told Dora that Herr K. had seduced her and then lost interest in her. Herr K.

had used the same words ("I get nothing out of my wife") in his sexual advances toward Dora as he had previously used while pursuing the maid.

After Dora had told Freud how offended and outraged she had felt about Herr K.'s attempt to seduce her, Freud (1905) made the following gaslighting intervention in which he first attacks her judgment about what happened and how she felt about it and then proceeds with his interpretation of her supposedly unconscious sexual desires for Herr K. Freud (1905) states:

> It was not that you were offended at his suggestion; you were activated by jealousy and revenge. At the time when the governess was telling you her story you were still able to make use of your gift for putting on one side everything that is not agreeable to your feelings. But at the moment when Herr K. used the words 'I get nothing out of my wife'—which were the same words he had used to the governess—fresh emotions were aroused in you and tipped the balance. [p. 106]

Most probably, in my opinion and that of others who have studied this case, Dora recognized that Herr K. wished to exploit her as he had previously used and then discarded the K.'s maid. Instead of discussing this issue and Dora's other negative feelings for Herr K., Freud attempted to convince Dora that her reaction of anger at the time of the attempted seduction by Herr K. occurred because of her jealousy of Herr K.'s attention to the maid, and in doing so he invalidates Dora's own experience and judgments about the disturbing event. Scharfman (1980) argues convincingly for the proposition that Dora was deeply disillusioned and disappointed, first by her father's dishonesty and unethical behavior and later by Herr K.'s attempts to use her as he had previously used the maid and other women.

In the face of her repeated protests against Herr K. and his unwanted advances to her, Freud persistently attempted to discount her aversive attitudes and to discuss them as defenses against unconscious sexual and loving desires for Herr K.

Dora had attacks of coughing and aphonia, and in response to Freud's questioning, she said these attacks lasted from three to six weeks. When he inquired about the length of Herr K.'s absences, she replied that he was gone for three to six weeks. On this shaky foundation, Freud (1905) speculated about a causal connection between what he considered her unconscious love for Herr K. and her symptoms. "Her illness was therefore a documentation of her love for K. . . ." (p. 39).

Similarly, Freud made the inference of a causally efficacious unconscious fantasy of pregnancy in Dora on the unlikely basis that she had appendicitis-like abdominal pains nine months after Herr K. had attempted to seduce her. Though the evidence Freud cites for his hypothesis that her unconscious fantasy wishes for being pregnant caused appendicitis-like pains is skimpy at best, he presents this unlikely explanation for her symptoms as a fact, again both in his interpretations to Dora and later in his 1905 paper about her.

His repeated and attacking use of defense interpretations was a kind of gaslighting used against her judgments and perceptions. Another example of this controlling and demeaning tactic was his interpretation to Dora that her loving interest in the two children of the K.'s was a defense against her sexual love for Herr K. Freud (1905) wrote, "Her preoccupation with his children was evidently a cloak for something else that Dora was anxious to hide from herself and from other people" (p. 37).

Freud not only failed to be empathic or to validate Dora's understandable feelings of being betrayed and exploited by the most important men in her life (i.e., her father and Herr K.), but he also defended both of them, telling Dora that she really knew how much they loved her.

What matters most is that Freud withheld any sympathy, compassion, or empathy, and assailed Dora's fragile self-esteem at every turn. The deeply troubled and beleaguered Dora needed understanding and attunement with her perceptions and judgments and not the kinds of repeated repudiations of her judgments and experiences that came from Freud.

In view of the upper middle-class Jewish background of the participants at the turn of the century, the unethical and exploitative actions of the Ks and Dora's parents were neither socially acceptable nor customary. Though Freud himself had such a background, he did not discuss the unacceptable nature of their actions or their damaging effects on Dora (Marcus 1975).

If we remember that Dora's father had turned her over to Herr K. as a kind of implicit bribe to maintain his relationship with Frau K., we can recognize a striking parallel between that situation and the interactions occurring between Freud, Dora, and Dora's father at the time of her initial contact with Freud. Just as Dora's father had exploited his daughter to keep Herr K. from interfering with his affair with Frau K., he later attempted to use Freud as an accomplice to prevent Dora from criticizing and disrupting his illicit relations with Frau K. According to Freud (1905), Dora's father wanted Freud "to talk Dora out of her belief that there was something more than a friendship between him and Frau K." (p. 109).

Though not grossly immoral or dishonest, Freud's behavior to Dora was sufficiently similar in several ways to the abusive and hurtful actions of the important men in her life (her father and Herr K.) that Dora was never able to differentiate Freud from either her father or Herr K. Freud failed to observe that his own behavior toward Dora reinforced Dora's conviction that he was untrustworthy, hostile to women, and exploitative like her father and Herr K. (See Glenn 1980 and Scharfman 1980 for more on this point.)

Dora's original traumatic disappointment in her father was repeated first in her disturbing interactions with Herr K. and later by Freud by his use of the controlling and shaming methods described in this chapter.

In my criticism of Freud for using gaslighting tactics and other indoctrination methods, I do not mean to imply that he was either *consciously* or *unconsciously* attempting to attack or impair Dora's psychic functioning or her precarious self-esteem. Most mental health professionals who use gaslighting and other indoctrination methods are unaware of the abusive and psychicly damaging effects of such controlling interventions. I am not claiming that Freud's use of indoctrination methods arose out of unconscious motives to be hurtful to Dora. One would require much more evidence to either rule in or rule out such an inference. I do know, however, that Freud grew up in a culture where males learned to speak to women, children, and other individuals considered to be socially inferior in ways that communicated the speaker's superiority and dominance.

I doubt that Freud's use of indoctrination methods was substantially different than the ways other men of his status and in his culture talked with women or others they considered to be in a lower status. Most probably, Freud, like the majority of men both in his time as well as in our time, was unaware that he was communicating with women and others he considered to be of a lower status in ways which were abusive and psychically damaging to them.

### Shaming as a Method of Indoctrination

In addition to gaslighting and other tactics for controlling and dominating I have previously described, Freud used shaming— probably one of the most powerful as well as the most common tactics humans use for controlling and intimidating other individuals. Freud attempted to shame Dora into submission by the way in which he discussed Dora's alleged homosexuality and her masturbation. Freud's attribution to Dora of homosexual desires for Frau K. was a questionable and dubious inference he made on the basis of Dora's strong attachment to Frau K. There is no solid evidence from Freud's article on Dora or from other accounts of her life that she had either conscious or unconscious homosexual desires for Frau K. or for anyone else, for that matter.

Though Freud did *not* view homosexuality or masturbation as sinful or evil, he *did* view them as manifestations of psychiatric illness. (For more on Freud's use of shaming as a method of control, see Lakoff and Coyne 1993.)

## What Did Dora Want?

Freud concluded his famous case study with the confession, "I do not know what kind of help she wanted from me" (p. 122). The misunderstanding and misalliance (Langs 1976b) between Freud and Dora arose in part because they were talking past each other and at cross purposes. What Dora wanted was not what Freud wanted and vice versa. What Freud wanted was a scientific confirmation and acceptance by the scientific community of his new theories of infantile sexuality, unconscious fantasies, the oedipus complex, and female sexuality in the pathogenesis of hysteria, as well as in normal development (Decker 1991, Kahane 1985, Langs 1976b, Ornstein 1993). One reason Freud did not know what Dora wanted was because in his passionate pursuit of evidence to prove his theories, he failed to listen to much of what she said that was discordant with his hypotheses.

Thanks to today's greater store of psychoanalytic knowledge and to the many psychoanalysts and others who have written about Dora, we now have some better ideas both about what Dora wanted from Freud and what she did not receive from him. What Dora wanted from Freud was the affirmation of the validity of her perceptions and experiences and what Ornstein (1993) calls "the legitimization of her struggle to free herself from the impact of her noxious milieu" (p. 38).

Freud (1905) was puzzled by Dora's passionate repudiation of the idea "that she had merely fancied" (p. 46) Herr K.'s attempts to seduce her. Freud was "puzzled" by Dora's emotional disturbance when both her father and Herr K., with the complicity of their wives, repudiated and attacked Dora's perceptions of what Herr K. had done to her and her father's affair with Frau K., because he did not understand how important, even vital, it was for Dora to have her experiences and perceptions validated rather than attacked. As Erikson (1962) stated, Freud did not appreciate how much Dora was seeking the historical truth about her life. Freud did not understand that Dora's emotional disturbance came about in part because she was the victim of a severe and destructive form of gaslighting committed repeatedly by her parents and to a lesser degree by himself.

Freud's observation that Dora was "anxiously trying to make sure whether I was being quite straightforward with her" (p. 118) should have alerted him that issues of trust, fidelity, and integrity had an urgent priority over any explorations of the early childhood origins of her libidinal development.


## DISCUSSION

My purpose here is to briefly discuss some of the different elements which acting together brought about Freud's abuse of power in his relations with Dora. In my opinion, Freud's use of gaslighting and other indoctrination methods stemmed in part from authoritarian traits in Freud's personality. Analysts and others have written about how these proclivities were manifested in his interpersonal relationships with others and especially his patients (Holt 1992).

The potential, but not necessarily the actuality, of the therapist's abuse of his position is greater when the therapist is a male and the patient is female. This comes about because of the higher status usually accorded to males in Western societies. (For more discussion about this topic see Lakoff and Coyne 1993.)

In addition to the above factors, I believe there are other unique features of the psychoanalytic situation that sometimes facilitate the therapist's abuse of power. The nature of the therapeutic relationship and the different roles and responsibilities of the two members of the dyad tend to impose an imbalace of power in which patients are actually to a varying degree in a subordinate position.

There is some, but not much, truth to the claim made by Lakoff and Coyne (1993) that interpretation itself facilitates and exacerbates the power imbalance between psychotherapists and their patients. The emotional effects of interpretations on patients is highly variable and depends (among many other factors) on the nature of the conscious and unconscious communications made by the therapist. Though I think Lakoff and Coyne exaggerate the role of interpretations in creating a power imbalance, I do believe there is something about interpretations concerning unconscious contents or defenses against unconscious contents that is inherently more or less destabilizing to the smooth and automatic ego functioning of patients. In contrast to interpretations about unconscious content, interventions designed to validate, affirm, soothe, mirror, or indicate affective attunement tend to be, at least temporarily, stabilizing and integrating.

## A NOTE ON THE AWARENESS OF
## THE ABUSE OF POWER

I disagree with the assertion made by Lakoff and Coyne (1993) that the abuse of power by psychotherapists is "difficult to discern" (p. 13). Also, they are somewhat mistaken in writing that the abuse of power and untherapeutic manipulation will often "not be perceptible to patients or even to knowledgeable observers" (p. 73). My clinical experience in doing, teaching, and supervising psychoanalytic treatment, plus my study of this topic, convinces me that the occurrence of verbal abuse and untherapeutic manipulation by therapists is *not* difficult to discern by patients, therapists, or observers who do not have a need to deny this type of verbal abuse in themselves or others.

Patients who are subjected to gaslighting and other indoctrination methods may defensively deny this kind of treatment in order to protect their relationship with their therapist. Such patients are more likely to acknowledge and discuss the verbal abuse after their analysis or therapy has been terminated. Even patients who consciously deny being treated in this controlling way may unconsciously detect their therapists' use of abusive communications and represent the abusiveness in primary process derivatives. (For more discussion and clinical illustrations about patients whose primary process derivatives indicate they have *unconsciously* judged their therapists to be hurtful or controlling, see Dorpat 1991a and Dorpat and Miller 1992.)

The type of abuse of power in psychotherapeutic work committed by Freud and many of his contemporaries continues today, not much differently than in Freud's time. The use of gaslighting and other methods for controlling and dominating patients can and frequently does occur in any kind of psychotherapy. The problems of power imbalance in the case of Dora are not solely those of Freud's technique in 1900, or of psychoanalytic treatment today, but of any psychotherapeutic procedures. My examination of Dora's analysis concurs with the opinion of Lakoff and Coyne (1993), who said, "Dora is best read as a cautionary tale about the abuse of power in present-day psychotherapy" (p. 6).

## CONCLUDING COMMENTS

My review of Dora and the extensive literature about her concurs with opinions presented by Decker (1991), Ornstein (1993), Lakoff and Coyne (1993), and many others that Freud's treatment of Dora was harmful to her.

Writing from an historical perspective, Decker (1991) presents a well-informed and balanced presentation of the elements contributing to Dora's illness and the effects of Freud's treatment on Dora. She writes:

> Nevertheless the psychoanalysis did Dora permanent harm. Freud compounded her father's betrayal by his unconscious exploitation of her. . . . Freud's sexual intrusion, although again unconscious, mimicked only too well Mr. K.'s and her father's. To whatever extent Dora came to believe that the adult world was manipulative and scheming before she got onto Freud's couch, the analysis helped to solidify her view. [p. 199]

According to the analyst Felix Deutsch (1957), who saw her in two consultative sessions in 1922, and others such as Decker

(1991) and Ornstein (1993), Dora continued to suffer from the same array of psychiatric symptoms for which she originally saw Freud. Those who have studied Dora's life following her analysis with Freud tend to agree that she remained an emotional cripple for the remainder of her life.

In my opinion, Freud was most damaging to Dora in his use of gaslighting and other indoctrination methods in which he attacked, criticized, and shamed her for her perceptions, judgments, and attitudes. In this way, he created a misalliance rather than a therapeutic alliance with Dora, and he disrupted her abilities for using her own psychic resources for mastering her conflicts and traumatic experiences. His harmful interventions damaged her already low self-esteem, and impaired her abilities for trusting others, especially men.

# 8

## The Two Analyses of Mr Z—Revisited

Kohut's (1979) paper "The Two Analyses of Mr Z" has become a psychoanalytic classic in the relatively short time since its publication. The aim of this chapter is to provide a fresh look at this well-known, controversial paper and to present some different interpretations about the two analyses.

Kohut (1979) wrote "The Two Analyses of Mr Z" to show the differences between the classical theory Kohut said he used in Mr Z's first analysis and the self psychology approach he developed after he had completed Mr Z's first analysis and which he used for the second analysis of Mr Z. Kohut attributed the poor to mediocre results in the first analysis and the very substantial gains made in the second analysis to changes he had made in psychoanalytic clinical theory.

Though all who have reviewed Kohut's 1979 paper agree there were far more important therapeutic gains in the second over the first analysis, not all of them concur with Kohut's explanation for the different results obtained in the two analyses. This chapter presents an alternative hypothesis for explaining the much greater treatment progress in the second analysis of

Mr Z.[1] I do not dispute Kohut's claim that his self psychology theory ultimately led to a different and superior approach to patients such as Mr Z, but I doubt this was either the sole or

---

1. The interpretations I present do not go far beyond what Kohut wrote in "The Two Analyses of Mr Z." The absence of much clinical data or quotations of specific interactions precludes efforts to confirm or disconfirm novel interpretations of the two analyses. Several persons who knew Kohut both before and after he started the self psychology movement suggest that the paucity of clinical data in Kohut's article stems from Kohut's reluctance to reveal what actually occurred in the two analyses. They propose that Mr Z might really be Kohut himself. His account of the first analysis of Mr Z, they suggest, is a disguised story of his analysis with Ruth Eissler, a classical analyst, and his account of the second analysis portrays his self-analysis during the mid- to late 1960s.

In support of this hypothesis are the following observations:

1. There is marked similarity between his description of Z's narcissistic personality disorder and what some believe were Kohut's own narcissistic problems and deficits;
2. Some of the historical facts given about Mr Z match certain events and facts in Kohut's life. During Kohut's early childhood, his father was away serving in the Austrian Army in World War I. Kohut's mother, like Z's mother, was said to be an emotionally disturbed woman;
3. Another observation supporting this interpretation is that there is very little clinical data such as quotations of what either Z or Kohut said in his article. Does the lack of clinical data in his 1979 article mean that Kohut didn't have any clinical data or process notes because he *was* Z? Was Kohut reluctant to make up clinical data and give quotations because this would have stretched the already extended boundaries of what was permissible and ethical in disguising case material for a scientific paper?
4. A final reason I am skeptical of Kohut's claim that he was the classical analyst of Z in the first analysis of Mr Z is that I doubt from what I have learned from my own interactions with him plus what others have told me about Kohut that he was as harsh, rigid, unempathic, and even inhumane as he portrayed himself to be during the time of Mr Z's first analysis. In this way, I suggest, he protected his analyst, Ruth Eissler, from his own and others' criticisms.

The editor of Kohut's correspondence, Cocks (1994), indicates that both Kohut's wife and his son (Tom) believe that Mr Z was Heinz Kohut himself. They believe this because of the striking similarities between the biographical details about the so-called Mr Z and with what they both know about Kohut's life.

the most important cause of the changes made in Kohut's technique as well as the superior therapeutic gains made in the second analysis of Mr Z.

I plan to demonstrate that what was wrong with the first analysis of Mr Z was not so much the classical theory Kohut espoused but rather the way in which he conducted the analysis. A careful scrutiny of Kohut's (1979) paper, plus a critical review of the extensive literature about the two analyses of Mr Z, provides an understanding of the effects of some antianalytic deviations from accepted technique used by Kohut in the first analysis but not in the second analysis. In my opinion, the most harmful deviations were the harsh "pressures" he brought to bear on Mr Z to relinquish his narcissistic demands and rages at Kohut.

Most analysts disagree with Kohut's (1979, 1984) claim that he carried out the first analysis of Mr Z in conformity with the theories, principles, and accepted practices of classical psychoanalysis. Some writers sharply criticize Kohut's analytic technique in the first analysis, and they include Ostow (1979), Goldberg (1980), Rangell (1981), Peterfreund (1983), Gedo (1986), Muller (1989), and others. The second analysis was conducted during the years he was immersed in writing what many consider his masterpiece, *The Analysis of the Self* (published in 1971).

## THE FIRST ANALYSIS OF MR Z— AN OVERVIEW AND CRITIQUE

When Mr Z first came to analysis as a graduate student in his mid-twenties, he was living with his mother. His father, a wealthy businessman, had died four years previously. Mr Z felt he was socially isolated and unable to form relationships with girls. His addictive masturbation was accompanied by vivid masochistic fantasies in which he submissively performed menial tasks in the service of domineering women.

When he was about 3½ years old, his father became seriously ill and was hospitalized for several months. During the hospitalization, his father fell in love with a nurse who took care of him, and after his recovery he decided to not return home but to live with his nurse. When Mr Z was about 5 years old his father left the nurse and returned home. The parents' marriage was an unhappy one thereafter.

In the following passage, Kohut (1979) reveals the critical and confrontational stance he took in the first analysis toward the patient's rages and "narcissistic demands."

> The theme that was most conspicuous during the first year of the analysis was that of a regressive mother transference, particularly as it was associated with the patient's narcissism, i.e., as we then saw it, with his *unrealistic, deluded grandiosity* and his demands that the psychoanalytic situation should reinstate the position of exclusive control, of being admired and catered to by a doting mother who—*a reconstruction with which I confronted* the patient many times—had, in the absence of siblings who would have constituted pre-oedipal rivals and, during a crucial period of his childhood, in the absence of a father who would have been the oedipal rival, devoted her total attention to the patient. For a long time the patient opposed these interpretations with intense resistances. He blew up in rages against me, time after time—indeed the picture he presented during the first year and a half of the analysis was dominated by his rage. These attacks arose either in response to my interpretations concerning his *narcissistic demands* and his *arrogant feelings* of 'entitlement' or because of such unavoidable frustrations as weekend interruptions, occasional irregularities in the schedule, or, especially, my vacations. [p. 5, italics added]

Note Kohut's harsh value judgments about the patient's rages and narcissistic demands. This passage does not indicate much empathy for the patient's state-of-mind or even the traditional analytic attitude of neutrality. Sentences such as "a reconstruction with which I *confronted* the patient many times" suggest a harshness, disapproval, and arbitrary quality to the persistent pressures

Kohut was bringing to bear on the patient to conform with what Kohut wanted of him.

With remarkable candor, Kohut admits exerting strong pressures on the patient to accept his convictions.

> . . . I consistently, and with increasing firmness, rejected the reactivation of his narcissistic attitudes, expectations, and demands during the last years of the analysis by telling the patient that they were resistances against the confrontation of deeper and more intense fears connected with masculine assertiveness and competition with men. The patient seemed indeed to respond favourably to this consistent and forcefully pursued attitude on my part: the narcissistic features receded, the patient's demands and expectations became more realistic. . . ." [p. 8]

Kohut's statements such as the one about rejecting "with increasing firmness" the reactivation of the patient's narcissistic attitudes and demands tells also of the pressures Kohut was using to stop the patient from continuing to express these demands and angry protests. Though Kohut asserts that both his theory and his practice were "classical," he is mistaken in believing that his interventions regarding the "patient's narcissistic demands" were acceptable classical psychoanalytic technique. These repeated coercive interventions went far beyond mere suggestions; instead they were powerful projective identifications carried out to instill fear, guilt, and above all shame in the patient in order to coerce the patient into abandoning or suppressing his "narcissistic demands."

Others who have criticized Kohut for putting excessive pressures on Mr Z in the first analysis to relinquish his narcissistic demands include Ostow (1979), Peterfreund (1983), Muller (1989), and Gedo (1986). Muller (1989), for example, concludes that Kohut in the first analysis of Mr Z abandoned his analytic stance and with some success attempted to coerce Mr Z into complying with his ideas.

## WHY DID THE PATIENT CALM DOWN?

In this section, I would like to answer the question of what caused the patient to become more calm during the latter part of the second year of his first analysis and to discuss this from an interactional perspective. After about a year and a half of the analysis dominated by the patient's rages, the patient "rather abruptly became much calmer and his insistent assertion that his anger was justified because I did not understand him lessened conspicuously" (p. 5). When Kohut remarked approvingly on the change and made the following barbed interpretation to the patient, "the working through of his own narcissistic delusions was now bearing fruit, the patient rejected this explanation, but in a friendly and calm manner" (p. 5).

Mr Z said that the change had taken place not primarily because of change in himself but because of something Kohut had done. Kohut had introduced one of his interpretations concerning Mr Z's insatiable narcissistic demands with the empathic comment, "Of course, it hurts when one is not given what one assumes to be one's due." Kohut states he did not understand the significance of the above remark at the time. He believed that the patient was giving up his narcissistic demands and that his rages and depressions had diminished "because of the cumulative effects of the working-through processes concerning his narcissism" (p. 5). Kohut disagreed with Mr Z's view of Kohut's empathic comment, and he felt that it was innocuous and insignificant.

Kohut, at this stage, was not aware of how this temporary shift in his listening and attitude toward the patient had influenced the patient's responses. In fact, he believed that Mr Z's "improvements" came from his systematic defense analysis and his repeated confrontations with the "childish" and "delusional" quality of the patient's "narcissistic demands." During the first analysis of Mr Z, Kohut believed that these sorts of interventions (informed, he thought, by the classical theory) had led to the working through of the resistances to eventual emergence of the Oedipus complex in the transference.

Note the demeaning and patronizing quality in Kohut's interpretation: "I remarked approvingly on the change and said that the working through of his own narcissistic delusions was now bearing fruit . . ." (p. 5). A subtle kind of indoctrination took place in Mr Z's first analysis, one in which the patient was rewarded for behaviors approved by the analyst and shamed and reproached for behaviors rejected by the analyst. Describing the patient's behavior as narcissistic "delusions" is clearly defamatory and shaming.

The patient calmed down after Kohut's empathic comment ("Of course, it hurts when one is not given . . .") because it showed compassion and empathy for the patient's position. Probably Kohut's comment engendered hope in the patient that Kohut would ease off his relentless and repeated critical and confrontational interventions regarding the patient's narcissistic demands.

The whole complex of psychic defects, unconscious conflicts, disturbed feelings, and ideas covered by the umbrella term "narcissistic demands" was suppressed by Mr Z in the latter part of his first analysis, and in the following section we shall learn why he suppressed this highly disturbing complex.

### The Unresolved Transference in the First Analysis

Kohut admits that the unresolved transference in the first analysis was the patient's tie to his mother. This bond to the increasingly bizarre mother was enacted by both the patient and the analyst inasmuch as the patient complied with and accepted the analyst's convictions as he had previously with his mother. To maintain his relationship with Kohut and to conform with Kohut's demands, Mr Z suppressed his "narcissistic demands" in much the same way as he had previously done with his mother.

After the first analysis ended, Kohut belatedly and sadly concluded that some of what he had at first considered as therapeutic changes in the first analysis were merely temporary and cosmetic changes made by the patient in compliance with the pressures Kohut used on him to conform with Kohut's expectations.

Kohut (1979) wrote,

> . . . my theoretical convictions, the convictions of a classical analyst who saw the material that the patient presented in terms of infantile drives and of conflicts about them, and of agencies of a mental apparatus either clashing or co-operating with each other, had become for the patient a replica of the mother's hidden psychosis, of a distorted outlook on the world to which he had adjusted in childhood, which he had accepted as reality—an attitude of compliance and acceptance that he had now reinstated with regard to me and to the seemingly unshakable convictions that I held.
>
> . . . Within the analytic setting, the patient complied with my convictions by presenting me with oedipal issues. [p. 16]

I find this candid and revealing account highly plausible and convincing. What Kohut (1979) reported about the patient complying with him by presenting oedipal issues occurs, I suspect, far more frequently in analyses than many psychoanalysts want to recognize or admit. Along with Peterfreund (1983), I too could tell about cases where oedipal issues were presented by patients because the analysands either recognized there were issues of particular interest to the analyst or they were subtly indoctrinated by the analyst through various covert methods of interpersonal control to produce them (as Mr Z did in his first analysis).

Kohut states that the improvement resulting from the first analysis must therefore be considered a transference success. Kohut writes,

> Outside the analytic setting, he acceded to my expectations by suppressing his symptoms (the masochistic fantasies) and by changing his behaviour, which now took on the appearance of normality as defined by the maturity morality to which I then subscribed (he moved from narcissism to object love, i.e. he began to date girls). [p. 16]

## The Termination Phase of the First Analysis

In the termination phase of the first analysis, Kohut mistakenly believed that the patient was successfully working through his core oedipal conflicts. Kohut tells of how an important dream late in the analysis indicated to Kohut that they had reached oedipal issues.

> In this dream—his associations pointed clearly to the time when the father rejoined the family—*he was in a house, at the inner side of a door which was a crack open. Outside was the father, loaded with giftwrapped packages, wanting to enter. The patient was intensely frightened and attempted to close the door in order to keep the father out.* [p. 8, italics are Kohut's]

In his interpretation of the above dream, Kohut again used the same shopworn standard formulas and clichés such as "castration fears" and "fears of competition with father" he had used in discussions of other clinical material in the first analysis. This dream was taken up again during the termination of the second analysis when, as I shall discuss later, it received a different interpretation.

According to Kohut, both he and the patient knew preconsciously, though both failed to acknowledge and confront a consistent disturbing feature of the termination phase. Kohut (1979) wrote, "What was wrong was, to state it bluntly, that the whole terminal phase, in stark contrast to the striking contents that we transacted, was, with the exception of one area, emotionally shallow and unexciting . . ." (p. 9).

## THE SECOND ANALYSIS OF MR Z

Four-and-a-half years after the first analysis ended, Mr Z contacted Kohut again for treatment. He was unmarried, living alone, and worried about his social isolation. However, like his emotional state at the end of his first analysis, the relationships in which Mr Z was engaged were emotionally and sexually shallow and unsatisfying. He revealed the return of his compulsive masturbation accompanied by sadomasochistic fantasies. About one-and-a-half years before he had returned for the second analysis his mother had developed an incapsulated paranoid psychosis.

In the second analysis, Kohut learned that the first analysis had not achieved a cure of Mr Z's masochistic propensities via structural change, but now they had shifted to his work and life in general.

Much of the second analysis involved a reinterpretation of different topics and themes such as the patient's sadomasochistic fantasies and his primal scene experiences. In the second analysis, the sadomasochistic masturbation fantasies were understood as a desperate attempt to obtain at least some sort of pleasure, which Kohut called "the joyless pleasure of the defeated self" (p. 17), through self-stimulation. According to Kohut, Mr Z's masturbation was not viewed as drive-motivated but an effort to temporarily obtain the reassurance of being alive.

### The Working Through of the Mirror Transference

The patient developed a mirror transference in which he again (as he had in the first analysis) became self-centered, demanding and inclined to rage whenever the analyst was out of tune with his emotional state. In the second analysis, the full unfolding of the mirror transference allowed the patient to break the patient's pathological tie to his mother. Kohut (1979) stated "[Mr Z's] most significant psychological achievement in analysis was breaking the deep merger ties with his mother" (p. 25). A new and enriched image of the mother, a detailed reconstruction of her psychopathology, and its impact on Mr Z's development emerged and was worked through on the basis of memories and reconstructions that previously were defended against. These led to the discovery and mobilization of the profound "depression and hopelessness that the mother's attitude evoked in him" (p. 5) which remained relatively untouched in the first analysis.

Kohut (1979) makes the following comment about Mr Z's mother, ". . . the mother held intense, unshakable convictions that were translated into attitudes and actions which emotionally enslaved those around her and stifled their independent existence" (p. 13).

Note how similar Kohut's attitude and mode of relating to the patient in the first analysis was to the way his mother had treated him. Kohut, like Mr Z's mother, had "unshakable convictions," most notably his intensely negative and rejecting opinions about Mr Z's "narcissistic demands." Also, Kohut's use of various covert methods of interpersonal control repeated similar, though probably more coercive, methods of interpersonal control Mr Z's mother used on him throughout his life. In writing about Mr Z's transference to him of his compliant attitude in the first analysis, Kohut said, "[Mr Z showed] an attitude of compliance and acceptance that he had now reinstated with regard to me and to the seemingly unshakable convictions that I held" (p. 16).

In the first analysis, Kohut interpreted the patient's sadomasochistic masturbation fantasies in terms of his standard and stereotyped formulas concerning oedipal conflicts, castration anxiety and the like. During the first analysis, he was not aware of either the actual nature of the pathological bond between Mr Z and his mother or how their relationship was symbolized in the patient's erotic fantasies.

Kohut wrote the following about Mr Z's masturbation fantasies:

> In the fantasies which occurred invariably from age 5 to age 11 he imagined himself a slave, being bought and sold by women and for the use of women, like cattle, like an object that had no initiative, no will of its own. He was ordered about, treated with great strictness, had to take care of his mistress' excrements and urine—indeed, in one specific, often repeated fantasy, the woman urinated into his mouth, i.e., she forced him to serve her as an inanimate vessel such as a toilet bowl. [p. 6]

In a previous publication I explained how the master-slave erotic fantasies (similar to those of Mr Z) and the sadomasochistic perversion of a borderline patient replicated his actual traumatizing childhood interactions with his sadistic mother (Dorpat 1989b). Sexually perverse fantasies and actions are often sexualized enactments of childhood traumatic relationships. Thus, Mr Z's recurrent masturbating fantasy of serving as a toilet bowl-like receptacle for the excretions of women was a metaphor representing his actual traumatic relations with his mother. One of the selfobject functions he provided for her was to slavishly serve as a container for the disavowed parts of herself.

Ornstein (1981) astutely summarizes the central therapeutic changes in the second analysis in this way:

> . . . the working through of the archaic merger with the mother, against repeated and often intense unconscious resistances, ultimately also encompassed the successful analytic resolution of Mr Z's massive adaptive compliance in the first analysis, his childhood masturbation and masochistic fantasies, and the discovery of the meaning of his primal scene experiences. The working through of these elements in his psychopathology led to noticeable increase in Mr Z's vitality, buoyancy and hopefulness, gradually leading to the more direct expression and revival of the old repressed yearnings for the strong and powerful father in the idealizing transference. [p. 369]

## Kohut's Changed Attitude toward Narcissism

During the time between the two analyses, Kohut changed his concepts about narcissistic behavior. In Mr Z's first analysis he had viewed it as defensive, and he had "increasingly taken a stand against it" (p. 12).

Before the second analysis, Kohut had, in his words, "relinquished the health- and maturity-morality that had formerly motivated me. . ." (p 12). Kohut's rejection of health- and maturity-morality permitted him in the second analysis to "more genuinely than before, to set aside any goal-directed therapeutic ambitions" (p. 12).

In the second analysis, he no longer evaluated the patient's rage and disagreement as resistance. Instead he saw the patient "as desperately—and often hopelessly—struggling to disentangle itself from the noxious selfobject, to delimit itself, to grow, to become independent" (p. 12).

Kohut's "setting aside of goal-directed ambitions" was an important attitudinal change that was not directly related to his new classical theory or entailed by it. Unbridled therapeutic zeal, the setting of goals for patients, and manipulating patients through shame induction and other covert methods of interpersonal control to "relinquish" narcissistic demands are all opposed to basic psychoanalytic principles of treatment whether classical or of some other school.

Even in the second analysis, Kohut did not entirely give up his use of stereotyped approaches and his tendency to impose his ideas on the patient without first testing them by clinical evidence. One day, in the second analysis, the patient reported a simple dream, ". . . a starkly outlined image of the mother, standing with her back turned toward him . . ." (p. 19), a dream that filled the patient with anxiety. Again, as he had done so often before, Kohut used his favorite cliché, castration anxiety, in the following interpretation:

> When I suggested the horror of castration, of the sight of the missing external genital, of fantasies of blood and mutilation which children form by combining the sight of the menstrual blood and of the vulva, the patient brushed these suggestions aside. [p. 20]

What follows in his account tells us something about the change in Kohut's technique between the two analyses. Unlike his approach in the first analysis, he does not view the patient's disagreement as a sign of resistance and a signal for him to manipulate the patient to accept his views. Kohut writes:

> While he agreed that the imagery of mutilation, castration, and
> blood was related to the unnamed horror, he was sure that this
> was not the essential source of the fear. Although he himself
> was never able to formulate his fear in a concrete way, when I
> suggested that the mother may not have lost her penis but her
> face, he did not object but responded with prolonged silence
> from which he emerged in a noticeably more relaxed mood.
> [p. 20]

Though Kohut did not obtain much confirmatory material
from the patient to validate his interpretation about the faceless
mother, his empathic interpretation was certainly more attuned to
the current preconscious concerns of the patient about his delusional mother than the original interpretation about castration. The
image of the faceless mother could have represented the mother's
loss of identity in her psychosis. My point here is not so much
whether Kohut's interpretation was correct or empathicly attuned
to the patient, but rather that Kohut in the second analysis showed
much more respect for the patient's opinions and sharply reduced
using the covert methods of interpersonal control he had used in
the first analysis to pressure the patient into complying with his
views.

### The Termination Phase of the Second Analysis

According to Kohut, the actual onset of the terminal phase in the
second analysis was marked by the patient's returning to the analogous movement of the previous analysis when he had reported a
dream about his father returning home with a load of gift pack-
ages. Kohut wrote:

> The new meaning of the dream as elucidated by the patient
> via his associations, to put his message into my words, was not
> a portrayal of a child's aggressive impulse against the adult male
> accompanied by castration fear, but of the mental state of a boy
> who had been all-too-long without a father. . . . [p. 23]

The revised interpretation of this dream was that the return of the father in Mr Z's childhood was traumatic because of the child's overwhelming need for the father. In the second analysis, there was little to support Kohut's original interpretation of the dream representing an oedipal conflict. Probably the original interpretation was derived deductively from classical clinical theory and not inductively from clinical data. Shortly after the new and more authentic meanings of the dream were worked through, the analysis was terminated. One sign of the establishment of a therapeutic alliance between Mr Z and Kohut in the second analysis was the fact that Mr Z initiated and formulated the new meaning of the dream.

## AN INTERACTIONAL FORMULATION ON THE TWO ANALYSES OF MR Z

Using Winnicott's concepts about the false self and the true self, one can view Mr Z's relationship with Kohut as one that shifted from the support of the false self in the first analysis to the successful elucidation and partial dissolution of the false self in the second analysis concomitantly with the gradual emergence of the true or real self which had been previously hidden behind the defensive screen of the false self.

The patient's false self was based on a tie of compliance to his dominating mother, and during his childhood it was gradually constructed out of the patient's interactions with her. This compliant (i.e., false) self was first formed and later maintained because his mother did not tolerate expressions of independence and autonomy, and because she fostered the development of a compliant and fundamentally inauthentic false self. A defensive function was served by the false self inasmuch as it concealed and preserved from external trauma a hidden and only partially developed true, authentic, and real self.

Through the use of various covert methods of interpersonal control, Kohut in the first analysis replicated the kind of relationship Mr Z had experienced with his mother, and Mr Z complied with the pressures and demands Kohut placed on him in a manner similar to the way he had defensively submitted to his mother's coercive control over him.

The false self was the embodiment and representation of the mother's expectations, demands, and desires for her only child, Mr Z. In a sense, then, Mr Z, first as a child and later as a young adult, served as a selfobject for the mother. His false self served an important function in supporting her fragile self-cohesion and self-esteem. The false self was the price the patient had to pay to preserve his pathological relationship with his mother, Dr. Kohut and others, and to safeguard what small benefits and care he received from those deeply unsatisfying and, for the most part, demeaning relationships.

## The Emergence of the True Self in the Second Analysis

Behind the false self there existed a true self based on an early childhood idealization of the father. The second analysis enabled the patient's true self to emerge and develop past its childhood fixation. The gradual emergence and development of the true self in the second analysis stirred up intense separation anxiety and separation guilt. To detach himself from his mother meant he had to face his childhood fears of abandonment and loss. From a young child's perspective, such a loss is frightening and even catastrophic.

In the second analysis, Mr Z's anxiety-laden expressions of sexuality, rage, assertiveness, and exhibitionism together with the associated sense of his being an active agent responsible for what he expressed allowed Mr Z with Kohut's assistance to integrate and consolidate his true self. Kohut's changed attitude and approach in the second analysis allowed Mr Z to understand that it was not dangerous or wrong for him to separate from his psychotic mother. Because of Kohut's skillful interpretive work and his radically altered attitude toward Mr Z's "narcissistic demands," Mr Z learned that neither his mother nor he would be injured or destroyed by his long-delayed steps toward a life separate from his mother's tyrannical control.

According to Meyerson's (1981) account of the second analysis, ". . . Kohut was, in a fatherly way, implicitly encouraging the analysand to realize his potential for independence and to become more of an active agent responsible for his feelings and his actions" (p. 183).

## CLINICAL THEORY OR THEORY OF TECHNIQUE AND PROCESS

Kohut, along with many other analysts, believes there is a direct relationship between one's clinical theory and how one practices psychoanalysis. One's technique, what one does, according to this view, follows directly from one's clinical theory.

Kohut claimed (mainly erroneously, I believe) that the change in his clinical theory accounts for the improved therapeutic results obtained in the second analysis of Mr Z. In my view, the improved therapeutic results came about more from changes in his theories (conscious or preconscious) concerning technique and process than in his clinical theory.

How analysts carry out an analysis and how they relate and communicate with their patients is much more determined by whatever conscious or preconscious psychoanalytic theories of technique they espouse than whatever clinical theory they follow. Any and all psychoanalytic schools or clinical theories can form the basis of indoctrination or stereotyped approach.

The term clinical theory refers to the concepts used by psychoanalytic clinicians to order, understand, describe, and explain clinical findings and data, and it includes such concepts as conflict, defense, psychic development, unconscious processes, and the like. A theory of the therapeutic process refers, first, to the patient-therapist interaction, to the ways psychoanalysts investigate and understand their patients' communications and actions. Secondly, it refers to what psychoanalysts do with their patients, to the ways they relate to their patients, to the kinds of interactions analysts hope will lead to a therapeutic outcome. A theory of the therapeutic process includes such concepts as resistance, transference, the therapeutic alliance, interpretation, free association, working through, and so on.

The major and primary error in the first analysis of Mr Z was not in Kohut's use of classical theory, but in the practice, in how Kohut conducted the analysis. In response to some who criticized him for the harsh pressures he brought to bear on Mr Z in the later stages of the first analysis, Kohut (1984) wrote, "Many other analysts—including some of my most highly respected colleagues —would have reacted with the same firmness that characterized my stand toward Mr Z in the later phases of his analysis" (p. 88). Though I agree that his use of such "firmness" and "pressures" was common among analysts at the time of Mr Z's first analysis, there were also many analysts who viewed such methods as unacceptable deviations of psychoanalytic technique.

## CONCLUDING COMMENTS

Although Kohut's changed technique from the first to the second analysis was accompanied by major shifts in his clinical theory, the actual account of the two analyses shows a change from a dogmatic imposition of the analyst's ideas to a more respectful attitude toward understanding and interpreting the patient's experience.

In my opinion, the greater progress and growth of the patient in the second analysis stemmed from Kohut's changed attitude and method. From being authoritarian and directive, he changed to being more empathic and non-directive, his approach shifted from a stereotyped one toward a heuristic approach (Peterfreund 1983). In the second analysis he began to pay much more attention to the interactions between Mr Z and himself.

Because few of these beneficial changes in his attitude or technique are explicitly formulated in his clinical self psychology theory or entailed by that theory, it is problematic whether the modifications in clinical theory made by Kohut were either necessary or sufficient causes for his improved technique or superior analytic results.

Kohut overemphasizes the importance of clinical theory in determining psychoanalytic technique. That is to say, there are many other analysts who see themselves as classical analysts who would not have used the covert methods of interpersonal control used by Kohut, and as Peterfreund (1983) points out, there are some classical analysts who do not follow (as Kohut did) a stereotyped approach.

First Kohut and later other self psychologists have introduced important changes in both the clinical theory and in the practice of psychoanalysis. Because these new and improved practices and techniques are relatively independent of the clinical theory of self psychology, there is much to gain by studying these new techniques with the aim of developing a revised and contemporary theory of the psychoanalytic process and technique.

# 9

*Some Comparisons between*
*What Occurs in Cults and in*
*Psychoanalytic Treatment Carried Out*
*with Indoctrination Methods*

Cults provide a natural experiment for studying the interactions between cult leaders and followers, as well as for investigations on the psychological effects of using indoctrination and mind-control methods. In addition to religious cults, there are many other kinds of cults (Langone 1993a, Singer 1995).

In this chapter I have three major aims. The first is to provide an overview of some indoctrination and interactional processes taking place in religious, political, psychotherapy, and the many other types of cults. My second aim is to present a brief description of a relatively unknown kind of cult—psychotherapy cults. In the last and longest part of this chapter, my purpose is to present a comparative analysis of the similarities and differences between cults and what took place in the treatment of the eleven patients presented previously in earlier chapters who were treated by indoctrination methods.

## AN OVERVIEW OF INDOCTRINATION, BRAINWASHING AND MIND CONTROL METHODS USED IN CULTS

In addition to using covert methods of interpersonal control on their followers, cult leaders use a number of other mind-control, brainwashing and thought-reform techniques. Also, cults offer at least the illusion, if not the fact, of a number of highly prized positive rewards for obedience, including acceptance and fellowship, as well as the security accrued from membership in a cohesive group organized around a charismatic leader.

According to Singer (1995), the tactics of thought-reform used in cults are organized to (1) destabilize the follower's sense of self, (2) get the follower to drastically reinterpret his life's history and radically alter his worldview; induce the victim to accept the cult leader's new version of reality and causality, and (3) develop in the follower a dependence on the cult and thereby turn the follower into a deployable agent of the cult.

Probably the most powerful and intimidating methods used by cult leaders are various types of gaslighting. Cults grow and thrive to the extent that they succeed in destroying their followers' confidence in themselves and in their followers' own belief systems (Singer 1995). This destructive process provides the foundation for the cult leader's ability to then control the lives of his followers, to gain acceptance of the leader's belief system, and to insure the followers' obedience to the leader's directives.

Although some mind-control and brainwashing methods utilize exotic technologies such as hypnosis, drugs, physiological methods, and intrusive assaults on the brain, most methods of mind control and thought reform used in cults are more mundane and do not differ from the methods commonly used by many individuals in everyday life (Varela 1971). Individuals using indoctrination and mind-control methods rely on exploiting fundamental human needs in order to elicit compliance and conformity to what they want from others.

While some individuals who use mind-control, indoctrina-tion, or brainwashing methods are "compliance professionals" working within institutional settings such as cults as well as in governmental, religious, military, or business contexts, many oth-ers are intuitive or informal persuaders who regularly use "rule of thumb" home-remedy-type compliance tactics and heuristics for personal gain and control over others, especially their relatives, friends, and associates (Cialdini 1993).

Zimbardo and Andersen (1993) tell how cult leaders and oth-ers exert mind-control over followers:

> While total obedience to cult leaders can result in dramatic instances of mind control, lesser forms of control rely on the same basic principles: the manipulation of motives, the cre-ation of social rewards, and the meting out of social punish-ments, such as unacceptance, ridicule and rejection. [p. 105]

The major components for the effective use of mind control and of covert methods of interpersonal control exist in the most mundane aspects of human psychic and social functioning: the intense need to be bonded to other people, the persistent power of group norms, the force of social rewards such as a compliment, a smile, or a reassuring gentle pat on the back.

The process of mind control and indoctrination in cults most often occurs unconsciously. Most individuals do not know at the time that the thought-reform process is occurring or how much their thinking, feeling, and behavior is being influenced by oth-ers (Bowers 1984, Nisbett and Wilson 1977, Singer 1995).

Only by understanding our own vulnerabilities and the per-sistent but mistaken tendency to believe that our inner traits are more powerful than situational forces can we come to understand that there are indeed potent situational forces working on our minds. With this awareness of the operation of the fundamental attribution error (overestimating dispositional power while under-standing situational power) we can avoid unwanted forms of mind control and indoctrination by exercising our freedom to choose what we will think, feel, and do. (For more about the fundamental attribution error, see Dorpat and Miller 1992 and Nisbett and Ross 1980.)


## PSYCHOTHERAPY CULTS

In Chapter 2, I discussed the psychoanalytic psychotherapy of Bill by Dr. T. and how Bill unwittingly became inducted into a psychotherapy cult in which the charismatic cult leader (the psychiatrist, Dr. T.) drew around him a group of admiring mental health professionals including Bill's wife and some other patients he was supposedly treating with psychoanalytic psychotherapy. Both professional and personal boundaries were repeatedly transgressed by Dr. T. in his relationships with the cult members, and he was ultimately convicted of sexually abusing a number of his patients who were at the same time cult followers.

Temerlin and Temerlin (1982), in the first report on psychotherapy cults, studied five "bizarre" groups which were formed when five psychotherapists and psychoanalysts simultaneously served as friends, lovers, relatives, employers, colleagues, and teachers, all to their patients who were themselves health professionals. The idealization of the practitioner by the group members and the social structure involving the intermeshing of so many different and sometimes incompatible roles had a downright incestuous quality and was similar to what often occurs in many religious and political cults.

The psychotherapy cults studied by Temerlin and Temerlin (1982) varied from fifteen to seventy-five mental health professionals who were held together by their idealization of a shared therapist and the activities which they conducted jointly: workshops, seminars, courses, businesses, professional ventures, and social life.

The clinicians who established these cults included two psychoanalysts (physicians who were members of the American Psychoanalytic Association), two clinical psychologists (Ph.D's) and one Ph.D. who called himself a psychoanalyst. All five were charismatic, authoritarian, and dominating men with narcissistic features and a tendency to paranoid reactions.

The Temerlins studied the psychotherapy cults and cult dynamics by treating in psychotherapy seventeen former cult members, by interviews with other psychotherapists who had treated former psychotherapy cult members, and by attending workshops and seminars conducted by cult leaders.

The breakdown of professional and personal boundaries was severe and the Temerlins (1982) write, "None of these therapists maintained clean, fee-for-service relationships with patients. They took their patients into their homes, personal and business affairs, classrooms and hearts. Four had married patients, and one lived with an ex-patient. They were rarely seen except in the company of patients . . ." (p. 133).

Though psychotherapy cult members tend to have a temporary decrease in psychiatric symptoms when they join the cults, the long-term effect on their personality functioning and development is very negative (Singer 1995, Temerlin and Temerlin 1982). The Temerlins emphasize the enduring destructive psychological effects of cult memberships: "Cult membership perverted psychotherapy from an ego-building process of individuation into 'an infantilizing and destructive religion, which these patients could no more leave than most people can leave the religion of their youth" (p. 139). The Temerlins conclude that psychotherapy cult membership is an iatrogenically determined seriously pathological effect of psychotherapy.

Though membership in a cult is not common in mental health professionals, a cult mentality exists in many psychotherapists and psychoanalysts who accept uncritically the teachings of an idealized therapist, who ignore other approaches, and who treat all patients in the same ways (Temerlin and Temerlin 1982).

Hochman (1984) describes the development of a psychotherapy cult in a now defunct school of psychotherapy. The Center for Feeling Therapy was the locus of this school of psychotherapy, and it was established in 1974 by dissident therapists from

Janov's Primal Institute in Los Angeles. Founders of the Center established a "therapeutic community" where patients took up residence for extended periods until the Center abruptly closed its doors in 1980.

Hochman's clinical vignettes vividly illustrate his thesis that the Center for Feeling Therapy used some of the same indoctrination, mind-control, and brainwashing techniques as are used in other kinds of cults.

An important gaslighting approach involving the induction of shame and humiliation was extensively used by the cult leaders at the Center for Feeling Therapy. The actual purpose of the leaders in using this shame-evoking approach was to gain dominance over the minds and lives of the psychotherapy cult followers. However, they rationalized the use of this emotionally destructive indoctrination method as necessary for the leaders to remove their followers' defenses in order for the followers to reach their feelings.

This first step in destroying or impairing the subjects' confidence in themselves, in their belief systems, and in their mental capacities was followed by a stage in which the abused followers submitted themselves to the directives and controls of the cult leaders, many of whom were at the same time their personal therapists.

My clinical experience with treating and studying psychotherapy cult victims supports conclusions reached by the Temerlins (1982), Hochman (1984), and Singer (1995) about the immensely destructive and long-lasting pathologic effects of the abusive treatment endured in psychotherapy cults.


## CULTS COMPARED WITH PATIENTS TREATED BY INDOCTRINATION METHODS

Here my purpose is to compare the interactional process occurring in cults with what occurred in the eleven cases previously presented who were treated with indoctrination methods. The same or similar destructive interactional processes can and too often do occur in psychotherapy situations as occur in cults. Brainwashing, mind control, and indoctrination methods can be used in two-person relationships (such as the therapist-patient dyad) just as they are used with disturbing effectiveness in cults.

From my studies on religious, psychotherapy, and political cults, including the treatment of former cult followers and a review of the relevant literature, I constructed a list of six major characteristics of cults to use for comparing cults with the eleven cases discussed in this book.

The six characteristics of cults are:

1. Cult leaders are charismatic, authoritarian, and dominating individuals.
2. Followers join the cult when they are emotionally disturbed and/or in transition between developmental states; i.e., when identity and security needs are the greatest.
3. The followers idealize the cult leaders. Both the leader and followers consider the leader to be the supreme authority.
4. The cult leaders suppress the followers' disagreement or opposition.
5. Followers become totally involved in the cult, which often controls every aspect of their personal life, including sex, social relationships, diet, dress, work, and the like.
6. Cults tend to have long-lasting traumatic and destructive psychological effects on followers, who gradually lose their autonomy and their capacity for critical thinking.

Next I examined the prevalence of these six characteristics in the treatment of the eleven cases. Finally, I used the list of six characteristics to compare what took place in the eleven cases with what occurs in cults.

The eleven cases can be divided into two groups: the first group (patients treated by Drs. A., T., and X.) include patients who were most severely and harmfully affected by the use of indoctrination and brainwashing methods; the second group were the remaining other eight patients where the effects of the indoctrination methods were mild to moderate in severity.

The first group was most similar to cults in the following four major ways: (1) the personality profiles of Drs. A., T., and X. were most similar to the typical personality traits of cult leaders which I discuss below, (2) the severe psychopathological effects on the patients treated by Drs. A., T., and X. were similar to psychological effects cults have on their followers, (3) the mind-control methods (especially gaslighting) used by Drs. A., T., and X. were similar to those used in cults, and (4) the mind-control process and the nature of the interactions going on between Drs. A., T., and X. and their patients was similar to the interactional processes that occur between cult leaders and followers. Other similarities between cults and the treatments provided by Drs. A., T., and X. were the following characteristics of cults: the enactment of the followers' idealization of the cult leader, the cult leader's suppression of opposition, and the cult leader's control of the followers both during the treatment sessions and in their everyday lives.

In what follows, I shall discuss in turn each of the six characteristics of cults and compare what took place in the treatment of eleven patients treated by indoctrination methods with what typically occurs in cults.

### *Characteristic 1*—Cult Leaders Are Charismatic, Authoritarian and Dominating Individuals.

There is a general consensus among those who have studied cults for the prominence of these three personality traits in cult leaders (Langone 1993, Lifton 1979, Singer 1995). All of the cult leaders I have known or read about possessed these traits in abundance. Because most often two and sometimes all three of these traits were present and usually prominent in the ten clinicians who used indoctrination methods, I believe these same three traits are probably often associated with psychotherapists and analysts who use methods of indoctrination.

In their comparison between psychotherapy and religious cults, Temerlin and Temerlin (1982) mention the above three traits (charismatic, authoritarian, dominating) as typical of the leaders in both religious and psychotherapy cults, and in addition they describe three other decidedly pathological traits (narcissism, grandiosity, and paranoid features) which they believe (correctly in my opinion) are also prominent among cult leaders. Though these three more pathological traits were marked in Drs. A., T., and X., they were variably present or not at all apparent in the remaining seven clinicians in the present study.

### Characteristic 2—FOLLOWERS JOIN THE CULT WHEN THEY ARE EMOTIONALLY DISTURBED AND/OR IN TRANSITION BETWEEN DEVELOPMENTAL STAGES; I.E., WHEN IDENTITY AND SECURITY NEEDS ARE THE GREATEST.

Among individuals who have investigated cults there is a consensus for the view that individuals who join cults are emotionally disturbed and/or are involved in some kind of existential or developmental crisis at the time they join the cult (Langone 1993a). Their emotional distress provides one of the motivations for joining cults as well as for submitting to the cult leader's control over their lives.

The above is also true, of course, of psychotherapy patients and of the eleven patients treated by indoctrination methods, though the severity of their disorders varied a great deal.

The emotional distress in persons who join cults or who seek psychiatric or psychoanalytic therapy makes them especially vulnerable to the affective appeals and manipulations of charismatic, authoritarian, and dominating leaders or psychotherapists.

### Characteristic 3—THE FOLLOWERS' IDEALIZE THE CULT LEADERS. BOTH THE LEADER AND FOLLOWERS CONSIDER THE LEADER TO BE THE SUPREME AUTHORITY.

The enactment of the idealization is one of the central interactional dynamics of cults. Idealization serves the defensive function for both leaders and followers of denying the abusive and exploitive ways in which the followers are being treated by cult leaders.

Similarly, in the eleven indoctrination cases, the patients' idealization of their therapists was enacted by both parties and often throughout their treatment. That is to say, the patients attributed to their therapists idealized qualities such as power (even at times omnipotence), wisdom, omniscience, moral superiority, and the like, and the majority of clinicians in this study subtly encouraged and often enacted the idealization.

In the treatment situation, the conscious or unconscious communications of these eleven indoctrination patients indicating their desire for an idealized leader was often congruent with and matched by complementary communications from the therapist in which he or she tacitly, if not explicitly, communicated the idea he or she would fulfill and gratify these desires for an idealized object.

Both parties contributed to an enactment of a primitive and pathological symbiotic mode of relating in which the patient inhibits and suspends his or her critical and self-assertive functions.

The ten clinicians in the present study often acted as if they were the supreme authority over various issues and problems in the lives of their patients. One frequent way in which they did this was to behave as if they had a privileged and unique access to the unconscious contents and motives in the minds of their patients. (This attitude is one of the nine stereotyped approaches first described by Peterfreund (1983) and which I have summarized and listed in Chapter 11.)

## Characteristic 4—The Cult Leaders Suppress the Followers' Disagreement or Opposition.

Cult leaders discourage the rational thought of followers, and they use both covert and overt methods of interpersonal control and other thought-reform methods to stifle disagreement and enforce compliance with the cult leader. Followers are manipulated by a variety of unethical and psychically powerful methods to not only renounce their own belief systems but also to stifle any opposition to the cult leader. Cult members are systematically and subtly

coerced and directed into accepting the leader's ideas and practices as valid, true, and superior to all others.

Cult followers are gradually shaped and controlled by these
techniques to become what Hoffer (1951) called *The True Believer*.
Cult followers are ignored, punished, or threatened for their opposition to cult leaders and rewarded for their obedience and compliance with the leader. Gaslighting and techniques for publicly
shaming errant followers are powerful methods for enforcing obedience to the cult's rules and compliance with the cult leader.

The practice in cults of discouraging and even punishing followers for their disagreement is basically similar to the stereotyped
approach in which clinicians treat their patients' disagreement
as a sign of resistance (Peterfreund 1983). All of the ten clinicians
in the present study, to a varying degree, tended to stifle their
patients' disagreement and some of them rationalized their suppression of disagreement as interpreting the resistance.

The three clinicians (Drs. A., T., and X.) who had personality
traits (charismatic, authoritarian, dominating, narcissistic, grandiose, and paranoid) most similar to cult leaders were also the ones
who tended to use the most forceful and coercive methods for sti-
fling opposition and disagreement.

*Characteristic 5*—Followers Become Totally Involved in the
Cult, Which Often Controls Every Aspect of Their Personal
Life, Including Sex, Social Relationships, Diet, Dress, Work, and
the Like.

The cult leader's control over the lives of followers is one of the
defining features of cults (Langone 1993a, Singer 1995). Cults
make extensive use of unethically manipulative mind-control and
brainwashing methods to accomplish the leaders' goals of dominating the lives of the followers. Cults are totalitarian societies, and
they use many of the same thought-reform methods as are used in
totalitarian nations such as Nazi Germany under Hitler and the
USSR under Stalin's rule.

The cult leaders' domination of followers in cults and in totalitarian nations is not limited to the regulation of the followers' overt actions and observable behaviors. Indeed the leaders' principle focus is on controlling the inner world of emotions and thinking of the cult members. Most cult leaders, like the dictators of totalitarian nations, are not satisfied with regulating the outward behaviors of their followers. They want to possess and dominate the souls and minds of their victims.

All ten clinicians in the present study were to a varying degree similar to cult leaders in their use of covert methods of interpersonal control and other indoctrination methods to influence and control the mentation and affectivity of their patients *during* their analytic and therapy sessions. However, only three of them (Drs. A., T., and X.) regularly attempted to control their patients' lives outside of the therapeutic situation.

There were, however, occasional times when some of the other seven clinicians (in addition to Drs. A., T., and X.) also intruded into the outside lives of their patients and attempted to control their extraanalytic behavior. For example, Bak used threats and directives in his forceful efforts to regulate Richard's behaviors outside of the analytic sessions (Bloom 1991). Freud sometimes actively intervened in the Wolf Man's extraanalytic activities. These interventions included not permitting the Wolf Man to marry until he completed his analysis, advising him to not become a painter, advising him to not return to Russia in 1919, and when the analysis was about to end, asking the Wolf Man to give him a gift. (For more on these intrusions on the Wolf Man's life, see Langs 1980b and Mahoney 1984.)

*Characteristic 6*—CULTS TEND TO HAVE LONG-LASTING TRAUMATIC AND DESTRUCTIVE PSYCHOLOGICAL EFFECTS ON FOLLOWERS, WHO GRADUALLY LOSE THEIR AUTONOMY AND THEIR CAPACITY FOR CRITICAL THINKING.

In their comprehensive and documented reviews of studies of cults and cult followers, both while they are in the cults and afterwards, Langone (1993b) and Singer (1995) discuss the many destructive effects of cults. A majority of cult members show a need for professional help for moderately to severe psychiatric disturbances caused by the cult experience (Langone 1993b, p. 36). Some of the effects include anxiety, depression, loneliness, slipping into altered states of consciousness, guilt, shame, cognitive imprisonments, and a host of other psychological disturbances. According to Langone (1993), recovery from cult membership takes about three years.

During the time they are in the cult and for variable time after they leave cults, members tend to show marked pathological changes in personality functioning and in the ways they think and communicate.[1] These pathological changes have been described by Adorno and colleagues (1950), Hoffer (1951), Lifton (1961), Fromm (1941), Langone (1993b) and Singer (1995).

Cult followers escape personal responsibility and uncertainty by their masochistic and submissive merger with the cult leaders. Fromm (1941) has described the psychopathology and loss of autonomy of persons who join totalitarian movements. His description applies also to cult members and to a variable degree to the eleven patients in the present study. As a result of brainwashing and indoctrination methods, cult followers deny complexity and ambiguity and substitute a black and white, rigid organization of experience. Cults instruct and indoctrinate their followers to think in dichotomies, stereotypes, and clichés. Followers form a pathologically dependent and submissive relationship with the cult leader, and their submissive attitude toward their leaders brings many of them to lose, or to at least suspend, their individuality, flexibility, and critical thinking.

---

1. The serious and prolonged emotional and mental disturbances of followers of cults caused by the chronic and cumulative trauma of cult membership has led to the development in the United States of an informal subspecialty of mental health professional who study and treat the psychiatric casualties of cults. They have a journal, *Cultic Studies*, and an extensive literature has accumulated about the various kinds of cults, as well as about cult survivors and victims.

Another frequent psychiatric syndrome noted by Singer (1995) and others is the formation of a psuedopersonality in cult followers during the time they are in the cults and for a variable time afterwards. Singer's (1995) description of this condition matches the one described by Winnicott (1960) as the false self. For more on the false self, see Chapters 1 and 4 and Dorpat 1994a.

Another clinical finding common to cult leaders and followers as well as to the ten clinicians and eleven patients in the present study is a defensive denial and/or ignorance about the damaging methods being used as well as their effects (Langone 1993b, Singer 1995). In unconscious compliance with the cult leaders or clinicians who use indoctrination methods, both the cult followers and the patients of such authoritarian clinicians often tend to deny both the destructive significance of the indoctrination methods being used as well as their psychopathologic effects.

One explanation for the fact that cult followers are almost always unaware of being controlled, abused, and exploited has been advanced by Galanti (1993), who says that mind-control techniques used in cults "are not easily recognized because they are the techniques utilized by all cultures—directly and indirectly—to socialize children and acculturate immigrants" (p. 101). The relevant literature on this topic, plus my own experience in evaluating and treating both cult victims and patients who have been treated by therapists who use indoctrination methods, indicates that their denial about the trauma, abuse, and/or the oppressive control they have suffered often lasts for years after the abuse.

These findings should come as no surprise for those who are familiar with the long-term effects of psychic trauma, which leaves in its wake two kinds of repetitive pathological behaviors. The first is the repetition of the trauma itself in dreams, symptoms, enactments, and the like, and the second class of replications are the specific modes of denial also for the most part formed out of the victims' interactions with their victimizers. Families in which there is physical, sexual, or verbal abuse most often unconsciously collude with their abusers in denying the relevant personal meanings of the abusive practices. For example, one incest victim's father described his abusive sexual acts with the daughter as expressions of his "love" for her. For decades afterward and not until she entered psychoanalytic treatment, she used the wholly false notion of her father's incestuous acts being "loving" to conceal their true meanings, especially their destructiveness. (For more on the shared denial involving both victims and victimizers, see Dorpat 1985 and King and Dorpat 1992.)

In both cults and in psychotherapy contexts where the therapist uses indoctrination methods, the cult leader or psychotherapist consciously or unconsciously communicates (sometimes simultaneously) *both* the *abusive* message plus messages which *conceal* or distort the abusive message. Recall what I wrote in Chapter 1 about a kind of verbal abuse described by Elgin (1980) in which an apparently benign communication conceals as it were an abusive communication which Elgin calls a *presupposition*.

The psychic traumas suffered by cult followers and by patients of clinicians who use indoctrination methods continue to fester and thrive in the lives of ex-followers and ex-patients, both in their replications of their traumatic experiences but also in the false ideas, rationalizations, denials, and cover-up stories that followers and patients have internalized from their interactions with their cult leaders or authoritarian therapists.

The working through of their denials about their traumatic and abusive experiences in therapy as well as in cults is a necessary part of their recovery process. The traumatic nature of these abusive experiences cannot be fully understood, articulated, integrated, and assimilated until the denial defenses which prevent the subject from talking about and understanding the traumatic experience are identified and worked through.

# 10

# Psychoanalytic and Management Approaches: A Comparative Analysis

In this chapter, I aim to use two case studies to discuss and to illustrate the differences between psychoanalytic treatment methods and psychiatric management approaches and methods.[1] Though the case studies are about the treatment of two schizophrenic patients, what I have to write about the differences between psychoanalytic and management methods applies also to the therapy of other psychiatric disorders. Interactional and object relations perspectives will be used to compare the two modes of treatment and to illuminate patient-analyst interactions (Dorpat and Miller 1992). The first case, Mr. A., was treated predominantly with psychoanalytic methods; and the second case, Mrs. B., was and still is being treated by management methods of treatment.

---

1. My use of the term *management methods* includes indoctrination methods as well as other types of psychological, social, and biological manipulative methods, for example, psychotropic medications.

## PSYCHOANALYTIC TREATMENT OF MR. A.

Mr. A. was a tall and very thin young, unemployed, single man who, on his first interview, explained to me that he had been recently discharged from a Veterans Administration Hospital. He wanted to know if I used "psychoanalysis for the treatment of schizophrenic disorders." I replied that I did, and began seeing him in psychoanalytic therapy—a treatment lasting over nine years with a usual frequency of three interviews a week.

Initially he had several psychotic and paranoid symptoms, including the delusion that his parents were not his real parents. For several years of his analytic treatment, he rigidly maintained the fixed idea that he had been born on Mars of nonhuman parents and that he was transported to Earth, as Jesus Christ had been, to fulfill some special mission for mankind.

### Present Illness and Past History

The patient was raised mainly by his mother and two older brothers in various cities on the West Coast of the United States. His mother divorced his father when the patient was 5, and later divorced two other husbands. Mr. A. graduated from high school and shortly thereafter joined the Army.

His illness began, I believe, when he was 16 and developed what he later called "an overall sense of fear of people and things" associated with feelings of unreality about himself (depersonalization) and others (derealization). In treatment sessions he remembered that, as an adolescent, he experienced people as "unreal" and how he would manage to touch or to bump into nearby individuals in order to test his feelings about whether they were real and substantial.

He did not receive psychiatric treatment until he had a psychotic breakdown and was hospitalized at age 28. For a period of about two-and-one-half years prior to his initial interview with me, he had spent most of the time in V.A. psychiatric hospitals, where he was treated with phenothiazine psychotropics and group psychotherapy.

## Parameters and Management Methods

Though the major treatment method used throughout the therapy was interpretation, it was necessary initially to employ, for varying periods of time, several nonanalytic parameters and management methods. Others who have written on the concomitant use of psychoanalytic and management methods include Boyer and Giovacchini (1967), Eissler (1953), and Searles (1965). Eissler (1953), in my opinion, is correct in his recommendation that parameters in psychoanalysis should be kept to a minimum and that they should be discarded when there is no longer any pressing need for them.

Management methods and parameters used in the therapy of Mr. A. included: (1) several brief (two or three days) hospitalizations during suicidal crises, (2) art therapy, (3) the use of the sitting-up position rather than the couch, and (4) phenothiazine drugs. The employment of these nonanalytic parameters was discontinued when there was no longer any need for them; and during the final years of his analytic treatment, no parameters or management methods were used other than the sitting-up position.

## Art Therapy

By the term *art therapy*, I refer to my encouragement of Mr. A.'s painting in oils and my analytic work with him in interpreting his paintings. During the early years of his treatment with me, he sometimes would bring one or more of his paintings to his sessions to show me what he had painted and to free associate to the symbolic presentations in the paintings. In the analytic hours, we successfully used the paintings in much the same way as dreams are used for free association and interpretation of unconscious dynamics.

## Couch or Sitting-up Position?

My clinical experience indicates that schizophrenic and border-line patients can use the couch if they and the analyst can maintain a viable therapeutic alliance and emotional contact without the need for face-to-face contact. It was my judgment that Mr. A. probably could not maintain affective contact with me when I was outside of his visual field, and because of this he sat opposite me in a chair whose axis was at right angles to my chair. This position of the two chairs allowed him easily to look directly at or away from the analyst.

## Psychotropic Medications

When I first saw the patient, he was on a high dosage of chlorpromazine, and he complained of the sleepiness and "dopey" feeling caused by the drug. I discontinued the chlorpromazine and substituted trifluoperazine, a tranquilizer which did not make him feel drowsy nor interfere with his abilities for working and driving. Later, when I believed he could regulate the drug dosage levels himself, I wrote orders for drugs on a take-as-needed (prn) basis. In my view, many schizophrenic patients who are recovering and who are not grossly out of touch with reality can regulate their own prn dosage of phenothiazine and certain other psychotropic medications. This policy worked well with Mr. A., and as his mental functioning improved, he took progressively fewer tranquilizers until he no longer needed them to calm himself.

## Environmental Support

Adequate management therapy for schizophrenic inpatients and outpatients should optimally include a sustaining environment that not only meets physical needs such as shelter but also satisfies vital needs for humane care and friendship. A supportive environment was not available to Mr. A. when I first saw him, and he lived in shabby boarding houses where he shared his meals with other boarders. Early in his therapy, he had no friends or relatives immediately available to him, and his entire income consisted of government checks for his service-connected psychiatric illness. With these funds he supported himself and his therapy until he obtained employment in the fourth year of his treatment.

## Mr. A.'s Outer-Space Delusion

In what follows, my aim is to reconstruct some of the underlying and unconscious dynamic and genetic foundations of the patient's delusion that he came from outer space and that he was sent to Earth on a special mission. Though he was vague about his parentage in outer space, he did indicate that his parents were not human. Later I learned that his idea of nonhuman parentage had both negative and positive meanings. The alleged nonhuman property of his parents at times meant for him that they were *divine* and at other times that they were *subhuman!*

He seemed to have an unshakable belief in his delusion, and early on I learned how counterproductive it was to either directly confront or to interpret the unreality of his false ideas. One day late in the third year of his treatment, he sheepishly confessed to me that he no longer believed that he came from Mars. He said he knew that he had really been born from his mother's womb. He paused, waiting for my response; and when I remained silent he became intensely angry at his mother. He recounted several instances of his mother's rejections of him, and he spoke of how much he wished he had different parents.

## Alienation Symptoms in Schizophrenia

In order to provide background information for understanding the psychogenesis of his delusional ideas, I shall explain the dynamic relationships between his *alienation* (depersonalization and derealization) symptoms that appeared early in his illness, and the later formation of his outer-space delusion. As noted earlier, Mr. A.'s alienation symptoms began when he was 16, when both human and nonhuman objects began to seem to him as though they were unreal.

First Federn (1952) and later others describe alienation symptoms as frequently being the initial symptoms of a schizophrenic illness. They are viewed as a manifestation of a destructive psychic process including some regressive dissolution of the patient's ties to reality. Alienation symptoms should be distinguished from *restitutional* symptoms, such as delusions and hallucinations, which are defensive substitutes for the portions of the patient's ties to reality that have been subjectively destroyed in the alienation symptoms. In my opinion, alienation symptoms are the products of an almost complete breakdown in the schizophrenic patient's vital relations to himself and others, and they stem from a primitive denial of overwhelmingly painful relations with other humans. This denial is at the same time a defense against further fragmentation and psychic dissolution.

I do not mean to imply that all persons with alienation symptoms are psychotic or will become psychotic. What I do emphasize is that such symptoms and feeling states often, if not always, occur in the early stages of the schizophrenic process, and that they pave the way for the later formation of restitutional symptoms. Mr. A. unconsciously defended himself against actual or anticipated painful relations with human objects by disavowing their human actuality, and the derivatives of this defensive strategy were expressed in his outer-space delusion.

The underlying unconscious content in depersonalization—"This isn't happening to me"—contains a denial, as does the defensive content in derealization—"All of this isn't real. It is just a harmless dream, a make-believe" (Arlow 1966).

Unconscious object relations conflicts in which the typical need-fear dilemma of schizophrenic patients played a prominent part provided the motive force for Mr. A.'s denial of human reality and the resultant derealization symptom (Burnham et al. 1969, Dorpat 1976). Burnham and associates (1969) and others have shown how the schizophrenic is caught in a painful dilemma between a need for human objects and a fear of the same objects.

## Identification with the Aggressor

At the deepest level, his turning away from and rejection of reality stemmed in part from a hostile identification with the rejections he had sustained from his own parents. This included the familiar dynamic of unconsciously turning traumatically helpless and passive experiences into active, aggressive ones in which the victim of some trauma unconsciously attempts to master trauma and helplessness by becoming the victimizer rather than the victim. He unconsciously rejected the real world in a way that replicated how he had felt rejected.

## The Introject of a Rejecting Mother

The patient's memories about his mother's rejections, and my interpretive reconstructions of his childhood relations with her as involving his attempts to deal with her rejecting behavior, were indirectly supported by the patient's accounts during his therapy of his futile attempts both in the present and in the past to make contact with her. During the time I saw him, his mother rebuffed or ignored his repeated efforts to correspond or speak with her. Also, early in his treatment, I had one interview with an older brother of the patient who confirmed my hypothesis about the repeated rejections Mr. A. had sustained early in his life from his mother.

## Defensive Preoccupation with Physical Space and Physical Objects

An important feature of schizophrenic illness is a circumscribed defect in abstraction ability, and this was manifested in this patient by his inability to think abstractly about his conflictual human interactions. His obsessive and delusional concerns with psychical space (as in his outer-space delusion) and physical objects were concretizations of his conflicts over human objects—conflicts he defensively avoided thinking about and conceptualizing. A critical and transformative aspect of his therapy sessions was avowing and conceptualizing what he had previously disavowed and therefore failed to think about consciously and make a part of his representational world.

The patient's unconscious anxieties and conflicts over his relations with human objects and the psychological space that separates representations of human objects were unconsciously displaced onto physical object and actual physical space. In other words, the patient's delusional ideas abut being from "outer space" and about the nonsubstantial quality of physical objects were derivatives of his unconscious conflicts concerning past and present object relations.

Early in his psychosis he became very fearful of the physical space that surrounded him and of the "terrifying" human and nonhuman objects that filled the space around him. From his perspective, all sorts of frightening things happened in this awesome space that separated people and physical things. He vividly described the destructive and menacing objects that could fill "space," and they included "fires," "bullets," "fists fly," "knives are thrown," "cars, trains, and planes travel fast!"

When Mr. A. first became ill during adolescence, he developed the quasi-delusion that material objects were nonsolid to the extent that he could pass through them, and many times he tried to walk through things such as trees and walls. Each time he did this he was, of course, rudely shocked and dismayed when he could not pass through them or, in his words, "immerse" himself in the objects. His wish to "immerse" himself in objects stemmed from a basic and urgent need to reestablish a healthy symbiotic union and a connection with real persons and things. With the analyst, he gradually established a constructive and mainly normal symbiosis in which he could at times of stress "immerse" himself. Searles (1965) writes about the need for schizophrenic patients to establish a constructive symbiotic relationship with their therapists, and he conceptualizes a symbiotic stage as one of the early phases of psychoanalytic treatment of such patients.

## Trees as Transitional Objects

During treatment, his feelings and attitudes toward physical objects gradually changed. Early in his psychosis, he attempted to walk through trees or to "immerse" himself in them. Later, at times of intense turmoil, he physically embraced trees, and he reported feeling at least momentary relief and comfort from the solid presence of the trees he had been clinging to. Trees were used as accepting and solid transitional objects. Above all, they were *real* and something he could hold on to when he felt as if he would fragment and lose any contact with himself or others. Physical objects substituted for the human objects who had rejected him and whom he, in turn, had defensively abandoned.

As treatment continued, objects became more solid, more substantial, and he told of how he began to perceive and appreciate physical objects as "not only solid, but also non-mobile." During the latter stages of his treatment, he gained insight into why he had previously been so defensively preoccupied with physical space and concrete objects. In the beginnings of his long illness, he had rejected the efforts of others to communicate with him, and he had displaced his anxious concerns with human objects to nonhuman objects. Looking back at an earlier time of his illness, he reflects, "I chose physical objects instead of people."

At first he confused and conflated the literal meaning of physical space with the metaphorical meaning of "space," the psychological space or boundaries individuals require for distinguishing between self and object representations. Recovery from his psychosis was manifested by his increasing ability to understand and to use the metaphorical meanings of words having to do with human relations. Bateson (1972), among others, has discussed the schizophrenic's confusion about the literal and metaphorical meanings of words.

Toward the end of his treatment, he gave me an unpublished paper he had written, entitled "Concerning the Unrealized Importance of Space Between People," wherein he summarized the changes he had made in his ideas about space during his analytic treatment.

As treatment continued, objects became solid to me, not only solid but non-mobile. Perhaps, since I felt untied emotionally to my world, I wanted objects to be united (misery likes company, in this case I chose objects which can't hurt like people can). Improving seemed to mean a recognition of unity within objects, a uniting friendliness of non-human elements, a step toward a greater goal. As time went on, I was learning to see objects at peace. Then human came into the scene. I suppose people would and should enter for they are a higher order than the inanimate, but more important, because in the beginning of my illness, I rejected the attempt in trying to communicate with them further and chose objects instead. Even now as improvement continues, people moving about in space disturbs me, but at an ever decreasing rate. . . . Relatively soon, more will happen as space will permit those powerful abstract things known as "words" to come forth—from me—through space—to the other.

In sum, through psychoanalytic treatment, Mr. A. gradually developed a more loving and accepting attitude toward physical space and the psychological "space" that exists between persons, and he began to recognize that the space existing between individuals need not prevent human communication and relatedness. In fact, he discovered how those "powerful abstract things known as 'words,'" that pass through space from one person to another, could serve for communicating and relating to others.

### The Schizophrenic's Loss of Reality

Because of his unconscious object relations conflicts and psychic defects that arose out of his early interactions with his parents and later with other persons, the patient actively rejected relating and communicating with his fellow human beings. The withdrawal from reality in schizophrenia is not simply a passive shrinking away from human contact. Rather, it is an active and motivated destructive process in which the schizophrenic, because of his profound fear and hatred of other humans, subjectively destroys whatever links himself to others (Bion 1959b).

The psychotic not only hates his object world, but also hates and attempts to inhibit or to deny any emotion (with the exception, in some, of hate itself) that links the self with others. Emotions are indicators of relations and bonds to human objects that are not self and are outside the omnipotent control of the self. Schizophrenics often turn away from and disavow affects such as affection, envy, jealousy, sexual desire, and love because they are the immediate manifestations and evidences of the individual's relations with human objects. Mr. A.'s hatred and fear of human objects was defended against and also symbolically represented in the symptoms of derealization and depersonalization. His restitutional outer-space delusion constituted a reparative attempt to replace in the external world what had been destroyed within his mind.

## The "Return" of the Denied in Delusion

Mr. A's alienation symptoms included a denial of his relations and emotions concerning present and past human object relations. What was denied "returned" in a derivative form in his frightening preoccupations, anxieties, and delusions about physical space and physical (nonhuman) objects. The portion of reality denied by the psychotic "returns," as it were, in the form of a projection, a delusional idea. Waelder (1951) coined the phrase "return of the denied," and he explains this dynamic in the formation of paranoid ideas and delusions. As an example of "return" of the denied, he tells of a toddler who denied wetting his bed by blaming the deed on his teddy bear. What the child denied (i.e., responsibility for wetting his bed) he then projected onto his teddy bear.

This basic differentiating mechanism which either facilitates or blocks access to the reality of truth about human reality has been studied by Bion (1962) using the concept of minus-K phenomena and in France by Lacan (1956), who has chosen the term *foreclosure* to designate this mechanism. The unconscious object relations conflicts the patients would not or could not symbolize and maintain in his self and object representations returned in his delusional ideas about physical space and physical objects. What he destroyed internally through the denial of reality and consequent failure to sustain veridical representations of actual human and nonhuman objects reappeared in his outer-space delusion.

## Attacks on Linking

As I explained in an earlier publication, the dynamic underlying denial reactions is a destructive process in which the denier attacks and destroys whatever disturbs him (Dorpat 1985). These attacks, or what Bion (1959b) has called "attacks on linking," prevent the denier from forming realistic representations of something that disturbs him and his relation to it. Denial thus includes a destruction of meaning and a failure to represent, to put into words, whatever is disturbing to the denier. The object relations conflicts and anxieties denied by Mr. A "returned" in his delusion of coming from outer space of nonhuman parentage.

## Disavowal of Sexuality

Mr. A.'s outer-space delusion reinforced his denial of his parents' and his own sexuality and defended against unconscious conflicts and traumas arising from both preoedipal and oedipal levels of libidinal development. The wholly false notion of coming from nonhuman beings on Mars denied his physical and sexual origin from his parents and substituted more perfect, asexual, and celestial parents for his actual father and mother. His delusion of coming from outer-space nonhuman parents expressed the abandonment and rejection he had suffered in his childhood relations with his parents. The outer-space delusion symbolized in a disguised fashion the absence of warm, affectionate bonds with his parents. His idea of being sent from Mars to Earth on a special mission derived from wishes for a noble or even divine birth—wishes defensively constructed to compensate for his deep feelings of low self-esteem, inadequacy, and lovelessness.

## The Working Through of the Delusion

After he gave up the outer-space delusion, I wondered what had occurred to induce him to abandon it. Gradually I realized that the analysis had dealt with the major elements, the disavowed conflicts and traumas which had unconsciously provided both the contents and the motives for his delusion.

I believe, but I cannot prove, that the most important element in his recovery was dealing analytically with his fear of rejection and his history of maternal rejection. One way this was accomplished was by having him sit up where he could assuage his fear of rejection by seeing my facial expression. Searles (1984) writes on the importance to some patients of monitoring the emotional reactions of their therapists by viewing their facial expressions. Though with many therapy dyads face-to-face contact is a disruptive distraction and a potential resistance for one or both parties, with this patient the face-to-face position was not an impediment or strain for either party. At most times, the patient could see or hear my interest and concern for him, and I believe he was able to use my mainly benevolent attitudes as a holding environment and safe place he could employ for his self-understanding and growth.

## Avowal and Disavowal

Just as Mr. A.'s *disavowal* of conflicts, wishes, and emotions was crucial in the formation of his delusion, so was his *avowal* of previously disavowed wishes and feelings of utmost importance in the working through of his delusion. Through the repeated scrutiny, verbalization, and interpretation of his transference reactions in the analysis, he could gradually avow his personal history, including his unhappy childhood. The outer-space delusion had prevented him from understanding and accepting his personal history by its disavowal of his biological, social, and family origins.

By avowing instead of disavowing himself, his history, and his emotions, he slowly formed a more cohesive and stable sense of self, one that was separate from but still related to his fellow human beings. Interpretations about his preoccupations concerning first physical space and later psychological space assisted him in strengthening his boundaries between self and object representations.

### Outcome of Psychoanalytic Treatment

The patient made fairly steady progress in the important areas of his life during the time I saw him and afterwards. His speech and thought became more rational and coherent, and when I last saw him there was no evidence of paranoid thinking or thought disorder. He established new friendships and his interpersonal relations with close relatives and others became immensely more gratifying.

About four years after treatment began, Mr. A. obtained and held a job in a factory. The development of sublimations can be therapeutic as well as pleasurable, and Mr. A.'s enthusiastic participation in hobbies such as oil painting played a major role in his recovery. Another manifestation of both recovery and psychic development was a vast improvement in his sense of humor. I recall with particular delight an hour when he informed me that he had been able to tease and be teased by his fellow workers. Formerly he would become withdrawn and paranoid when others teased him, and he had exclusively focused his attention on the hostility expressed in teasing. What he had not previously recognized was how teasing and kidding are forms of playing and include, in addition to expressions of hostility, equally important feelings of affection and playfulness. In the past he was all too ready to detect and respond in a paranoid and suspicious way to the hostile feelings and ideas expressed in teasing. The recovery of or improvement in an individual's sense of humor is one of the major indications of the dissolution of a psychosis. Mental health requires some capacity for play, as well as reasonably intact abilities for loving and working.

Toward the end of his therapy with me, he became seriously involved with a young woman whom he later married. Years later, I received announcements of the births of two children, a boy and a girl.

## MRS. B.—A CASE STUDY

We turn now to a case summary of Mrs. B.'s treatment, and to a comparison of analytic and management modes of treatment.

Mrs. B. is a 67-year-old married woman, the mother of one child; she first began treatment with me thirty-five years ago and I have seen her irregularly since then. Interview frequency has ranged from four to fifty visits a year. Though in the fifteen years before she first came to see me she had numerous psychiatric hospitalizations in both private and public hospitals for treatment of her schizophrenic illness, she has not required hospitalization during the time I have treated her. She lives with her husband, a retired businessman, and maintains a fairly active social life with relatives and in her neighborhood Protestant church.

On her last psychiatric hospitalization over thirty-five years ago, she reported fears of losing her mind, inability to concentrate, and generalized feelings of intense anxiety and tension. She had ideas of self-deprecation and unworthiness, and she was suspicious and withdrawn. Mrs. B. was given a short course of electroconvulsive therapy, and she was started on Thioridazine 100 mg. qid, a dosage that was maintained until about nine years ago.

The patient was born in a large Southern city in the United

States, and her father died when she was six years old. She had her first psychiatric hospitalization for schizophrenia shortly after she left home at age 18 to attend college. Later she married and had one daughter.

Throughout the time I have seen Mrs. B., I have used a number of management and supportive treatment methods. Even when I attempted early in her treatment to use psychoanalytic methods such as interpretations, I noted that the patient would misconstrue my interpretations as directives on how she should think, feel, or conduct herself. For various reasons, including the patient's motivation, as well as my own countertransference, my efforts in the first two years of her treatment to gradually eliminate management methods and to use a psychoanalytic method were not successful.

## Self-Regulation of Tranquilizing Drugs

As I noted earlier, some psychotic and borderline patients can regulate their own use of tranquilizer drugs. My repeated efforts to enhance Mrs. B.'s autonomy by encouraging her to take fewer Thioridazine tablets were to no avail, and she rigidly maintained the four times a day schedule. Her fears of dyscontrol and psychosis supported her psychological dependence on high dosage levels. Finally, in 1984, I abandoned my attempts to have her regulate or vary the frequency of taking the Thioridazine, and I reduced the tablet size from 100 mg. to 50 mg. tablets. Then, for the first time in over 25 years, she ingested a substantially lower dosage and she did so without any relapse or adverse effects.

## The Introject of an Engulfing Mother

The major pathological introject associated with what I have conceived as her core pathology was the patient's conscious and unconscious representations of an *engulfing* mother. From early childhood, she has felt helpless and overwhelmed by her mother and her mother's inordinate and intrusive demands upon her. This engulfing representation of her mother was a concretized symbol of her interactions with her mother. Repeated and detailed reviews in her therapy hours proved beyond question that her mother, in the present as in the past, was not only inattentive to the patient's legitimate needs for privacy and individuality but persistently demanding of the patient's attention. The patient's phobia about driving an auto protected her for at least a decade from her mother's demand to be chauffeured about town.

## Improvement Following Death of a Parent

After her mother died, the patient's phone calls for crises or emergency interviews markedly decreased. From a symptomatic point of view, the patient improved considerably, and she no longer had the extremely stressful episodes of panic, insomnia, and disorganization precipitated in the past by gross kinds of intrusions and demands placed upon her by her mother. Though the literature contains many accounts of psychiatric and psychosomatic illnesses evoked by object loss, I am not aware of reports of patients who improved, as this patient did, after the death of a parent. It is humbling for me to realize that the death of the patient's mother probably has had a greater therapeutic benefit for Mrs. B. than have my supposedly therapeutic ministrations.

The patient's denials of her mother's destructiveness posed a serious adaptive problem and treatment resistance, because she either did not or could not maintain a realistic image of her mother or develop ways to protect herself from her mother's gross intrusions and imperious demands.

Her many years of management therapy could be characterized as a series of crisis-oriented and crisis management interventions, and the following vignette is typical of the many crisis situations in which I provided various supportive interventions. At times of crisis, she appeared near a relapse into psychosis, and archaic primary process elements would begin appearing in her speech. She had severe insomnia, and she would become terrified about the prospect of becoming psychotic and being hospitalized.

### Unconscious Mayhem in a Sunday School Class!

One Sunday in a church Bible class taught by the patient, the patient's mother again behaved in an outrageous and provocative fashion by arguing and interrupting her daughter, ridiculing what she said. The patient became distraught and was barely able to contain her emotional turbulence and disorganizing anxiety during the remainder of the Bible class session. The next day she called me, and, as I had done frequently before, I arranged to see her the same day. She gave a vivid account of her traumatic encounter with her mother on the previous day, and she presented herself to me as helpless to protect herself. She spoke again of her old fears of losing control and having to go to the state hospital. In addition to the interpersonal conflict with her mother, the patient was most anxious about an unconscious conflict in which wishes to destroy her mother were countered by somewhat conscious superego demands to be dutiful and compliant. Her rigid superego forbade her to do anything to displease her mother, and she childishly considered it her Christian and filial duty to do and to be what her mother wanted of her. Mrs. B. wanted to quit the Sunday school teaching to avoid further stress with her mother, but she was loath to quit because her teaching was viewed by herself and others as a valuable and much-admired activity.

In my most authoritarian manner, I tried to persuade her to set limits on her mother's destructive behavior, and I urged her to tell her mother that what she had done in the Bible class was outrageous and harmful. Going on, I said, "Tell your mother this, 'If you ever disrupt my Bible class again, George [the patient's husband] and I will not drive you to church again.' That should stop her!" I added firmly.

Wiping her eyes and sobbing, she agreed to talk with her mother and to set limits on her mother's behavior. To support her resolve to confront her mother and to continue teaching the Bible class, I arranged to see her again later that week and again during the week following her next Sunday's Bible class session.

In the following session, I was chagrined to discover just how she had used my psychiatric authority to thwart her intimidating mother. The patient told me that she had said the following to her mother. "Dr. Dorpat told me that you shouldn't mess up by Bible class again. The doctor said I'm not supposed to drive you to church if you ever do that again!"

On this occasion as on so many other similar ones, she needed to use an external authority to back up and justify the expression of her basic psychological needs. In the third visit in this crisis sequence, she calmly and dutifully reported that her mother was now "behaving herself" in the Bible class and that because she (the patient) was again in control of herself, she did not require further interviews with me.

### Short-Range Versus Long-Range Effects of Management Methods

From a short-range perspective, my directives were therapeutic, and they helped Mrs. B. to prevent another traumatic encounter with her mother. The patient's anxieties and fears supported her idealization of my directives, and they allowed her to use what I had prescribed for her to do with her mother as a countervailing force against the repetitive intimidations of her engulfing mother. From a long-range point of view, my directive interventions were not therapeutic. The best evidence of this was the fact that the patient did not learn new ways of communicating or relating or to avoid becoming embroiled in similar turbulent encounters with her mother in other contexts.

In short, the mother continued being intrusive and demanding (except in the Bible class) and the patient continued being unable either to protect herself or to say "no" to her mother's persistent manipulations.

## An Object Relations Perspective on Management: Patient–Therapist Interactions

At times when I used directive and indoctrination methods I would become uncomfortably aware of how much I was behaving like the powerful engulfing mother from whom I was trying to protect the patient. In other words, I was exerting upon the patient a kind of moral and interpersonal power and control not unlike that of the patient's mother from whom she unconsciously wished to escape. In her interactions with me, Mrs. B. repeated the same kinds of pathological symbiotic relations and servile compliant attitudes she had developed in early childhood and later extended to other relationships.

As the vignette above illustrates, I frequently acted out with her the roles and psychic functions the patient projected onto me, and I behaved with her *as if* I knew what she should think and do. At times of acute stress, I temporarily co-opted her ego and superego functions that she was only too ready to surrender to me.

Her fear of losing control of her mind, coupled with her idealization of my psychiatric knowledge and powers, provided the leverage through which I could exert an impressive degree of influence on how she behaved with me and, at times, with others such as her mother. At times of crisis, I related to her as if I had some unique authority and moral power that could in some unspoken and magical way show her the true pathway to mental health. During these disturbing episodes I was, in a sense, unconsciously engaged in an unacknowledged struggle with her engulfing mother introject, as well as her actual mother, for power and influence over the patient's life. Perhaps at such times the therapist embodied for her the image of her powerful father, who died when she was 6 years old.

In pathological symbiotic relations (such as the relations the patient had with both her mother and her psychiatrist), each party shapes, choreographs, and to some degree controls the responses of the other. For example, in master–slave interactions, the slave as well as the master unconsciously molds and to some extent controls the affective reactions of the other.

By her repetitive protestations of helplessness, by her whining refusals to protect herself, and by her threats of going crazy again the patient put unremitting pressures upon her therapist and at times others to immediately take care of her. The patient's plaintive tone of voice and pathetic sobbing when she felt overwhelmed were powerful nonverbal communications for provoking me into acting out the role of the authoritarian psychiatrist and omnipotent protector.

In the vignette just presented, each party unconsciously contributed to the other's mode of interaction. The therapist's directiveness partly evoked and reinforced the patient's compliant communications, and the patient's urgent appeals for direction contributed to the therapist's controlling prescriptions about how the patient should deal with her engulfing mother.

In pathological symbiotic interactions, the conscious and mainly unconscious communications of one party tend to evoke *complementary* responses in the other party. Thus the sadist, for example, will often unconsciously provoke masochistic responses in the masochist (and *vice versa*). In such interactions, the "sadist" disavows his or her own masochistic attitudes and affects and then manipulates a designated "masochist" to behave masochistically. Then the "masochist" often may, in turn, disavow his or her own sadism and unconsciously provoke the "sadist" into playing the sadistic role.

What I previously described as mutual projective identification and what Langs (1978a) calls a "Type B field" are important dynamic aspects of the kind of interaction depicted in the above vignette (Dorpat 1985). The repetition compulsion is a powerful driving force in such interactions, and individuals who extensively use projective identification may endlessly enact in their current interpersonal relations pathological and archaic object relations in which disavowed and often poorly developed parts of the self are projected on to their representations of other persons.

## The Analysis of Countertransference

Because the patient's transferences were enacted rather than talked about or interpreted in the management therapy, it is not possible to write much about their genesis or meanings. In such situations, it is frequently more enlightening to use countertransference analysis to unearth clues about the crucial intrapersonal and interactional dynamics occurring in the therapy dyad. As time went on, I gradually became aware of disturbing countertransference responses to the patient, and my self-analysis yielded some insights into the nature of my interactions with the patient. Once I impatiently scolded her and lectured to her when she called pleading for sleeping pills. Another time during an interview with her, I had some unusual feelings of disgust about her and I silently imagined how I might summarily eject her from my office. These uncomfortable feelings came in response to her whining demands, her response to again feeling overwhelmed by her mother's encroachments; and she in turn, in an unconsciously hostile identification with her mother introject, was placing unreasonable pressures upon me to protect her.

My increasingly disturbing reactions of impatience and irritability with the patient called for some self-analysis and working through. One contribution to my emotional reactions was, of course, the patient's evocative behavior. Most individuals, I suppose, would have been bothered if not actually angered by her whining demands and her exaggerated helplessness. But this explanation does not account for much of my countertransference, because similar provocative behavior in other patients does not trouble me as much or as often.

Another clue I used in my attempts to unravel and understand my countertransference reactions was the fact that I had not felt negative emotions abut Mrs. B. early in her treatment. Then I had shown much patience and sympathy for one who appeared to have so much trust in and childlike admiration for me. Also, delivering authoritarian pronouncements and moral directives was much more ego-syntonic and consistent with my attitudes toward psychiatric treatment thirty-five years ago than it is now.

The painful truth became clear to me as I recognized that my troublesome impatience with Mrs. B. came about because I had been unconsciously holding her responsible for my use of management methods I no longer believed in or used (except for emergencies). When I had first begun seeing Mrs. B. my practice was in transition from the predominant use of management methods acquired in my psychiatric residency to the development of non-manipulative psychoanalytic methods of treatment.

## COMPARISON OF TREATMENT RESULTS IN PSYCHOANALYTIC AND MANAGEMENT TREATMENT

In this section I propose to evaluate and compare the treatment results of Mr. A., treated predominantly by psychoanalytic modes of treatment, with those of Mrs. B., treated by conventional methods of management and supportive psychotherapy. Both patients achieved symptomatic improvement and were able to avoid psychotic relapses and psychiatric hospitalization. Unlike Mrs. B., Mr. A. was able to make important structural changes in his personality. He slowly internalized important aspects of the analyst-analysand interaction including the analyst's holding environment. From a basically paranoid orientation in which he looked on the whole of his earthly existence as hostile, forbidding and persecutory, he was able to change to an orientation in which he could view others as helpful, protective, and caring. He used psychoanalytic therapy to work through and resolve some of the basic psychic causes of his schizophrenic disorder and his maladaptive ways of relating to himself and others.

According to conventional and contemporary standards of psychiatric treatment and management, the treatment of Mrs. B. was successful. From a superficial point of view, she has functioned fairly well in her role of housewife, and she has been able to participate with some pleasure to herself and others in family, social, and church gatherings. On the positive side of the ledger, my psychological and psychopharmaceutical interventions have relieved many highly disturbing crisis situations and probably helped her to avoid a psychotic relapse and institutionalization.

On the negative side of the ledger are the following conclusions reached after both an analysis of my countertransference and a careful review of the many years of Mrs. B.'s management therapy. During thirty-five years of psychiatric management therapy, I have observed no underlying therapeutic personality changes nor improved understanding of herself or others. Her pathological symbiotic modes of communicating and relating to others that arose out of childhood parent–child relations have been generalized and extended to all of her relationships, including the one with her psychiatrist. The therapist's directive interventions are a type of projective identification, and they have facilitated the maintenance of her pathological symbiotic relations.

The extended use of management approaches such as advice, education, limit-setting, and indoctrination methods has contributed to, or at the very least reinforced, her pathological symbiotic relations, one of the central causes of her immature personality structure and her schizophrenic illness. Moreover, the prolonged employment of management methods has placed the short-term and superficial benefits of symptom relief ahead of the long-term character changes that can accrue from nonmanipulative psychoanalytic methods of treatment.

Mrs. B. did not attain any of the goals or products of successful psychoanalytic treatment such as insight, psychic development, or positive freedom. The future prospect is for more of the same. Because of the nature of her dependency on management psychotherapy and tranquilizing drugs, it seems improbable that she will terminate therapy with me until one or the other of us dies. Management modes of therapy tend to bring about interminable treatment, because the conflicts and relations that are transferred onto the therapist are mutually enacted rather than analyzed and surmounted.

In short, psychoanalytic treatment assisted Mr. A. to recover from his psychiatric illness and to attain higher levels of personality development. Although management methods did give Mrs. B. temporary symptom relief, they did not assist her in recovering from her psychiatric illness. A negative aspect of her treatment was the fact that the type of interactions she had with her therapist supported and reinforced her infantile and pathological modes of relating to others.

## A COMPARISON OF THE GOALS AND METHODS IN PSYCHOANALYTIC TREATMENT AND MANAGEMENT APPROACHES

Let us now briefly outline the major differences in goals, methods, and values between psychoanalytic treatment in which indoctrination methods are *not* used and management approaches. The fundamental difference is that the psychoanalytic approach is basically non-directive and *nonmanipulative*, and it assists the patient to obtain higher levels of psychic development and insight through understanding and interpretation. The various management modes of treatment include a variety of biological, social, and psychological kinds of interventions for *manipulating* the patient in order to alleviate psychic distress, relieve symptoms, and reduce social deviance. The covert methods of interpersonal control and other types of indoctrination methods I have discussed in other chapters are management methods.

Many of the techniques used in supportive psychotherapy or in psychoanalytic treatment contaminated by the use of indoctrination methods such as advice-giving, limit-setting, education, reassurance, directives, confrontation, and the like readily serve as vehicles for projective identification and for manipulating the patient to think, feel, and behave in some way designed by the therapist. Sometimes, as in the case vignette presented earlier, such directive methods may bring about symptom relief and other short-term therapeutic goals. However, the patient pays a high price for the short-term benefits of management interventions, because manipulative methods of treatment tend to maintain and strengthen pathological symbiotic relationships and all that those relations imply in terms of diminished positive freedom, individuality, and personal autonomy. Pathological introjects are often strengthened and reinforced as a result of the therapist's employment of projective identification in the so-called supportive types of psychotherapeutic interventions.

In such interactions there is an implicit trade-off in which the patient's need for maintaining the stability and security of pathological symbiotic relations is gratified at the cost of at least temporarily sacrificing opportunities for attaining whole object relations and achieving other long-range goals of insight, psychic development, and positive freedom.

The overriding value informing and guiding tactics for using management methods is the alleviation of unpleasurable emotions in the patient and/or those close to the patient, such as relatives and mental health workers. Psychoanalytic methods imply different values and concepts about what constitutes mental health as well as mental illness. It places a higher value on the long-range curative goals of insight and psychic development than on the short-range goals of reducing psychic pain and symptoms.

## A CRITIQUE OF THE MENTAL HEALTH SYSTEM

The management methods used with Mrs. B. are, with some exceptions, the same general types of manipulative modes of treatment used by most mental health professionals (psychiatrists, psychologists, and social workers) and others today in their therapies of psychiatric patients. I do not mean to make a general and total repudiation of management modes of treatment, because such methods of treatment are often effective for meeting short-term treatment goals in emergency and crisis situations. My point is rather that the management methods of treatment are used excessively and inappropriately in ways that are destructive to the positive freedom and psychic development of patients.

The present system's commitment to management modes of therapy such as managed care programs neglects the treatment methods (best exemplified by the psychoanalytic method) of facilitating patients' working through of unconscious conflicts and attaining higher levels of personality development. In their exclusive promotion of management methods for the relief of symptoms, managed care companies are committing a cruel hoax on the American public.

My second criticism is a more serious and controversial one inasmuch as I claim that management approaches and indoctrination methods can cause psychological harm to patients, especially when they are continued past the period they may be required for some emergency or crisis situation. By their excessive use of management modes of treatment, mental health professionals may contribute toward the maintenance of their patients' psychiatric illnesses. This they unconsciously accomplish by the inappropriate and repetitive employment of manipulative techniques which co-opt their patients' ego and superego functions. These manipulative methods tend to stabilize and reinforce the pathological object relations underlying their patients' neurotic, characterological, and psychotic disorders.

# Part III

## Remedies
## and Correctives

# 11

## Steps toward a Non-Directive Approach in Psychoanalytic Treatment

In this final chapter, my goal is to articulate and discuss some basic principles for creating and maintaining a non-directive and egalitarian ambience in psychoanalytic treatment—one which is conducive to attaining the traditional goals of insight and personal growth. These principles also provide guidelines for the detection, prevention, and correction of antianalytic stereotyped approaches and the use of indoctrination methods.

Though this list of six heuristic principles is neither exhaustive nor comprehensive, I believe that following these principles will help prevent and correct problems and difficulties encountered by clinicians who follow stereotyped approaches and/or who use directive methods. Another reason for choosing these principles over others is that all of them, with the exception of number 5 (on the therapeutic alliance) are relatively new and unfamiliar to most individuals practicing psychoanalytic treatment.

## PRINCIPLE #1—USE HEURISTIC APPROACHES AND AVOID STEREOTYPED APPROACHES

This chapter expands on a point made by Peterfreund (1983) about how stereotyped approaches and strategies bring about a process of indoctrination, rather than a truly psychoanalytic process of discovery and psychic development. My study of psychoanalytic treatment cases in which covert methods of interpersonal control and other directive methods were used strongly supports Peterfreund's link between the use of stereotyped approaches and the formation of a process of indoctrination. All of the ten clinicians described in Part II who used directive methods also frequently, consciously or unconsciously, employed the stereotyped approaches and strategies first described by Peterfreund (1983) and summarized later in this section.

### *The Distinction between Clinical Theory and the Theory of the Psychoanalytic Process and Technique*

For the purposes of this chapter, it is important to emphasize the distinctions I made in Chapter 8 between psychoanalytic clinical theories and theories of process and technique. The focus of this chapter is on the psychoanalytic process and on psychoanalytic technique, and it is not on the psychoanalytic clinical theory. This entire book is designed as a contribution to the psychoanalytic theory regarding the psychoanalytic process and psychoanalytic technique and not, for the most part, to psychoanalytic clinical theory.

Theories of the therapeutic process include such concepts as transference, resistance, the therapeutic alliance, interpretation, free association, and the like. These concepts and theories refer to patient-therapist interactions, to the ways psychoanalysts investigate and understand their patients' utterances, to what clinicians do with their patients, and finally to the kinds of interventions which will have therapeutic results. Psychoanalytic clinical theories include such concepts as conflict, psychic development, psychic structures, unconscious processes, and so on. These concepts are useful for ordering, understanding, and describing clinical observations and findings.

Any and all psychoanalytic schools or clinical theories (e.g., Classical, Kleinian, Lacanian, self psychology, object relations, and so on) can form the basis of a stereotyped approach, and the principle characteristics of stereotyped approaches are the same regardless of the clinical theory on which they are based.

There are two classes of psychoanalytic practitioners: those who use stereotyped approaches and those who use heuristic approaches to conduct psychoanalytic treatment (Peterfreund 1983). Those who follow stereotyped approaches believe they possess some truths they aim to impart to their patients and to accomplish this they impose their ideas onto their patients.

The overriding goal of stereotyped approaches is to fit the case into the analyst's clinical theory that forms the basis for the clinician's initial formulations about the patient (Peterfreund 1983). A tendentious approach is taken in which the psychoanalytic process is viewed as one where the clinicians attempt to get patients to accept and understand the analyst's formulations.

In contrast to stereotyped approaches, the fundamental aim of heuristic approaches is to initiate and foster a process whereby patient and therapist work together to understand and discover as much as possible about the patient and his or her past and present interactions with others.

With those who use stereotyped approaches, there is no place for an analytic process in which either the analyst or the patient learns anything new or different than what the analyst's initial formulation leads him to look for, to expect, and to (sooner or later) find. As a result, stereotyped approaches have not progressed or changed in many years. As examples of prominent analysts who employ stereotyped approaches, Peterfreund mentions Arlow, Brenner, Greenacre, and Kohut in the first analysis of Mr. Z. Stereotyped workers such as the above find only the known and familiar. Peterfreund uses their case reports and writings to show their use of stereotyped approaches and strategies and how they repeat the same basic themes with only minor variations.

## Nine Characteristics of Stereotyped Approaches

What follows are my summaries of what Peterfreund (1983) calls the nine characteristics of stereotyped approaches.

1. The primary aim is to fit the case into the clinical theory that forms the basis for formulations made very early in the analysis.
2. A tendentious approach is taken in which the psychoanalytic process is viewed as an attempt to get the patient to understand the initial formulation.
3. The patient's objections to an interpretation tend not to be seen as having any intrinsic legitimacy, and the patient's failure to accept what the analyst says is viewed as resistance.
4. Stereotyped clinicians believe they possess an understanding of the "truth," and that they have a privileged awareness of the patient's "deep unconscious."
5. Stereotyped workers fail to validate their clinical hypotheses, and the issue of evidence is of little significance.
6. Those who work in a stereotyped manner tend to think and write, not in terms of the patient's experience, but in highly intellectualized jargon, in clichés based on a supposedly "true" clinical theory.
7. The patient is not allowed more than a minimal role in establishing the truth about what is going on in the present or may have happened in the past. Consequently, a therapeutic alliance is not established.
8. Although often thought of as Freudian, stereotyped approaches all too often abandon some of the basic tenets of classical thinking. Formulations are made about the unconscious meanings of dreams, for example, in the absence of the patient's associations.

9. Built into stereotyped approaches are many circular self-confirming hypotheses in which refutation has no place.

Peterfreund (1983) presents convincing arguments for his assertion that Kohut (1979), in the first analysis of Mr. Z., used predominantly stereotyped approaches instead of the more constructive and therapeutic heuristic approaches. Meanings are assumed rather than constructed or discovered by clinicians who use stereotyped approaches and indoctrination methods.

The basic clinical formulation Kohut used in the first analysis of Mr. Z. was that castration anxiety arising out of oedipal conflicts caused a defensive regression to narcissism. Kohut tried to fit Mr. Z.'s case to the above theoretical formulation and discounted or ignored evidence contrary to it. Kohut's basic clinical formulation during the first analysis of Mr. Z. was derived from a stereotyped strategy widely used until about 1975 and still promoted by some practitioners. This rigid approach is one in which it is assumed that all symptoms, as well as other manifestations of psychopathology, are caused by similar kinds of genital and oedipal conflicts. Starting to treat someone with specific stereotyped assumptions about the meanings of symptoms is totally unnecessary and far from an optimal approach (Peterfreund 1983). The optimal and heuristic approach is, instead, to gear one's thinking to the establishment of an investigative analytic process, a process that can lead to novel insights and discoveries.

The heuristic clinician's goal is to initiate and to foster a psychoanalytic process of discovery and renewed psychic development beginning with whatever the patient presents or communicates. The heuristic analyst has no specific content in mind as his goal. Webster (1957) defines heuristic as "helping to discover or learn." An analyst who uses heuristic approaches does not impose his ideas or values, rather he establishes an alliance with the patient in the interactional process of learning and constructing or reconstructing illuminating ideas about the patient's life.

## Doing Psychoanalytic Treatment Is Not Doing Science

Linked with the use of stereotyped approaches is the fallacy that carrying out psychoanalytic treatment is doing something scientific such as conducting an experiment. More or less unconsciously, many clinicians who use stereotyped approaches also are constrained in their interactions with their patients by adherence to the attitudes and methods of science.

Though psychoanalysis as a field of knowledge and investigation is a science, the practice of psychoanalysis is an art and not a scientific activity. Freud (1937b) was correct in saying, "Analysts are people who have learned to practice a particular *art* . . ." (p. 247, italics added).

A distressingly prevalent and damaging mistaken attitude about the practice of psychoanalysis is to view it as doing science, or doing something scientific or conducting an experiment. Frequently in the psychoanalytic literature terms, attitudes, and procedures appropriate for conducting some scientific activity such as an experiment, or maintaining an objective and neutral attitude are used to indicate the kinds of attitudes, methods, and procedures analysts should follow whilst carrying out psychoanalytic treatment.

I do not mean to imply that psychoanalysis is not a science, and I disagree with critics hostile to psychoanalysis who claim it is not. Although we may use scientific knowledge of a psychoanalytic kind or sometimes of other kinds in our conduct of an analysis, we are not doing science or carrying out an experiment while we are analyzing patients. Though conducting an analysis is an art, the data acquired from an analysis can be used for scientific investigations; the information contained in process notes, or from audio or video recordings can be used for the testing of hypotheses and other scientific purposes.

When we are doing psychoanalytic treatment we are not doing science any more than engineers are doing science when they are building a bridge, or surgeons when they are operating, or farmers when they are plowing. Farmers, surgeons, engineers, and psychoanalysts do, however, use knowledge from different sciences to inform their professional activities.

## THE SIGNIFICANCE OF THE
## INTERACTIONAL PERSPECTIVE

### PRINCIPLE #2
### EVERYTHING TAKING PLACE IN THE ANALYTIC SITUATION CAN AND OFTEN SHOULD BE MONITORED AND EVALUATED FROM AN INTERACTIONAL PERSPECTIVE AS WELL AS FROM AN INTRAPSYCHIC PERSPECTIVE.

Psychoanalysis is moving away from thinking about treatment simply as an exchange of words between patient and therapist. The theory of meaning analysis my associate Dr. Miller and I advanced in previous publications pays close attention to the conscious and unconscious intricate interplay of interactions through which the work gets done, and it focuses on the concept of interaction in psychoanalytic treatment (Dorpat and Miller 1992).

A fundamental principle of the interactional perspective is that both parties contribute by their actions and communications to everything that occurs in the analytic dyad. A second principle is that in the analytic situation a high priority should be given to monitoring and understanding patient-analyst interactions.

Every human action is an interaction. Everything we do is influenced by the other, whether we are conscious of being affected or not, and everything we do or say to another individual is partly regulated by desires to influence, whether we are aware of such intentions or not.

It is misleading to distinguish between interactive and non-interactive elements of the psychoanalytic situation. There is an interactional aspect in *everything we do or say* in psychotherapy as well as in interpersonal relations outside the therapy situation (Dorpat 1991a). It is not possible to *not* communicate, to *not* relate, to *not* interact with others. Even the mute psychotic who avoids eye contact is communicating something like the following: "I don't want to have anything to do with you" (Dorpat 1992).

In psychic development, what is internalized and becomes psychic structures are the individual's interactions with others. Interaction plays an integral part of the structure of the mind, and psychic structure in psychoanalytic treatment and elsewhere can be modified by new types of interactions because structure itself consists of internalized interactions represented in a particular way. In the psychoanalytic treatment situation, the essence of structural change comes when a newly represented interaction between the patient and significant other (most notably the analyst) modifies an original pathogenic interaction.

Spoken communication has a content aspect and a relational (i.e., interactional) aspect, and the relational aspect is mediated by the primary process system. The relational aspects of communication are primary process derivatives, and they include affects, tone of voice, nonverbal communication, imagery, metaphors, narratives, and the like.

Attention to what is going on interactionally between patient and analyst consciously and especially unconsciously is essential for detecting misalliances, enactments, and other derailments of the therapeutic process. It is vital for the analyst to monitor patient-analyst interactions in order to avoid the dangers of manipulation, intimidation, indoctrination, coercion, collusion, transference cure, and enactments. Attention to the subtleties and nuances of unconscious communication as well as other interactive factors is essential for maintaining the integrity of the analytic process with any kind of patient.

What I call the interactional perspective is very similar to what Stolorow and his associates (1994) call the intersubjective perspective and what Langs (1978a) and the Barangers (1966) conceptualize as the bipersonal field.

A central and defining feature of the interactional theory being presented here resides in not assigning any greater intrinsic validity to the analyst's perceptions, judgments, and views of reality than to the patient's. An important part of this theory is the stance that the analyst does not have any unique and special access to the patient's unconscious mentations. One of the stereotyped approaches described by Peterfreund (1983) was one in which clinicians believe they possess an understanding of the "truth," and that they have a privileged awareness of the patient's "deep unconscious."

The objectivist epistemology of classical psychoanalysis tends to support and facilitate an indoctrination process because it posits an objective external world, a true world to which the analyst is presumed to have privileged access (Stolorow et al. 1994). Corresponding to this latter stance, one goal of psychoanalytic treatment for many has been to assist the patient to correct distortions of reality and to bring the patient's judgments, perceptions, and attitudes into alignment with the analyst's conception of reality. This goal appears in the notion of helping to resolve parataxis distortions in the interpersonal therapy founded by Sullivan, in the idea of connecting transference distortions, and in the efforts to dissolve delusions by aiding psychotic patients to recover contact with "reality."

Because the traditional theories of affects, defense, transference, and resistance were constructed almost entirely from an intrapsychic point of view, we need to revise those theories to take into account interactional factors. Rather than viewing transference, affects, resistance, and defense as solely the products of the patient's isolated mind, psychoanalytic clinicians can now examine and interpret these phenomena as the interactional products of the intersubjective field and search for the contributions made by both parties in the therapeutic dyad.

The traditional and for the most part exclusively intrapsychic views on defense, transference, affect, and resistance are being challenged by those theorists who are organizing and conceptualizing clinical phenomena from relational and interactional points of view (Dorpat and Miller 1992, 1994, Stolorow et al. 1994).

The intrapsychic and interactional points of view are not antagonistic or mutually exclusive; both are necessary perspectives for a comprehensive understanding of what is occurring within the patient, as well as what is occurring between the two parties of the dyad.

Therapeutically effective psychoanalysis requires that the analyst frequently monitor the nature of the ongoing interactions between himself and the patient. The ten clinicians discussed in Part II who used indoctrination methods tended to view the analytic process almost exclusively from an intrapsychic point of view and with rare exceptions failed to use an interactional perspective for understanding what was occurring consciously and unconsciously in their relations with their patients.

Because they did not use an interactional perspective and did not validate their interventions, they were not able to evaluate feedback information from their patients about what effects their interventions had on their patients. Had they used an interactional perspective to first recognize what was going on in their interactions with their patients together with a method for validating their interventions, they could have been in a position to first, recognize their errors, and secondly, to correct them.

In the past, most psychoanalytically oriented therapists and analysts have had a collective blindspot for interactional elements in psychoanalytic psychotherapy and psychoanalysis (Dorpat and Miller 1992). Only in recent decades with the advent of various object relation theories, self psychology, and the communicative approach have a growing number of clinicians begun to overcome this blindspot.

An important aspect of using the interactional perspective is frequently monitoring the patient's primary process derivatives for valuable and specific information on how the patient is *unconsciously* evaluating and representing his or her interactions with the therapist (Dorpat 1991a, 1992, Dorpat and Miller 1992, 1994). During their analytic sessions, patients are constantly and unconsciously monitoring, analyzing, and representing their assessments of their relations with the analyst in primary process derivatives such as affects, narratives, images, metaphors, and nonverbal communications.

## An Interactional Perspective on Defense

In previous publications, I have discussed defenses and the interpretation of defenses from an interactional perspective (Dorpat
1983, 1985, 1987b, 1993d, 1994a, Dorpat and Miller 1992). Systematic and controlled research by Weiss and his associates (1986,
1993) supports an interactional approach to defenses. Their work
demonstrates that the interactions between a patient and analyst
are important determinants of a patient's defensive activity. Weiss
points out that defenses are given up when the ego feels it is safe
to do so, indicating that the lifting of defenses is under the unconscious control of the ego. When the individual unconsciously
judges the situation with the analyst to be a safe one, he lifts the
defenses and allows the emergence of contents previously defended
against.

Patients unconsciously test their analysts to judge whether the
analyst can endure and contain the revelation of the patient's anxi-
ety-provoking impulses. When the clinician is so judged to be a
safe person, the patient will lift his defenses and allow warded-off
impulses to emerge into consciousness. In this way, previously
unconscious impulses can then become conscious and subject to
ego regulation.

If we look back over the history of how different groups have
conceptualized and dealt with defenses, we see a continuum ranging from the attacking and shaming approach taken by the Center
for Feeling Therapy cult to the nonadversarial and non-directive
approach recommended by Gray (1994) and Weiss (1993). At the
Center for Feeling Therapy, the systematic attacks and ridicule of
their patients' defenses were called "busting." Their coercive and
unethical approach evoked shame in their patients, and it was
psychically damaging to many of them. On this continuum, the
traditional approach instituted by Freud stands somewhat in the
middle. As I have indicated previously in this volume, Freud had
an authoritarian approach in which he brought pressures to bear
on patients to give up their defenses and other resistances. See also

Gray (1994) and Schafer (1992) for more about Freud's authoritarian approach to his patients' defenses and resistances.

## An Interactional View of Affects

In previous decades many mental health professionals (including myself) were taught that emotions had exclusively endogenous origins stemming from one's unconscious fantasies and instinctual drives and isolated from social and interpersonal influences. In contrast, contemporary theorists view affects as emerging out of an individual's interactions between real people. Affects are signs telling about an individual's current and major transactions with the outside world. The more a patient's representations of self and other deny the reality of mutual influence on the vicissitudes of affective states, the closer the patient lives to the center of the narcissistic world (Spezzano 1993). Affects are the cor expression of the primary process system and its struggles to emerge into consciousness and the world (Dorpat and Miller 1992).

Later in this chapter I advance an interactional perspective on resistance and in a previous publication I discussed the concept of transference from an interactional point of view (Dorpat and Miller 1992).

## The Crucial Importance of Interventions Being Pro-Plan

A fundamental mistake made by therapists and analysts who follow stereotyped approaches and who use indoctrination methods is the clinician's attempt to impose his ideas onto the patient. To the best of my knowledge, there is only one psychoanalytic approach specifically designed to prevent the therapist from imposing his ideas on to the patient, and it is the Pro-Plan approach as formulated by Weiss (1993) and by Weiss et al. (1986).

In contrast to those clinicians who use pro-plan approaches, clinicians who use stereotyped approaches and directive methods set the agenda for the patient and tend to control the analytic dialogue. In analytic treatment guided by the pro-plan approach, the patient rather than the analyst sets the agenda. The pro-plan approach does not assume that any sort of knowledge or insights are necessary or helpful to the patient *unless* they meet the criteria for being pro-plan. Unlike stereotyped and indoctrination approaches, the pro-plan approach to interpretation and other interventions supports the therapeutic forces within the patient.

Weiss and associates have developed a distinct theory of psychoanalytic therapy which accords a central role to the patient's unconscious plan. The plan approach and the plan concept are founded on a new and distinct theory of therapy and psychopathology conceived by Weiss et al. (1986) which views the patient as autonomous and purposeful throughout treatment.

## PRINCIPLE #3
## PRO-PLAN INTERPRETATIONS AND OTHER INTERVENTIONS SUPPORT THE THERAPEUTIC PROCESS; ANTI-PLAN INTERVENTIONS IMPEDE THE THERAPEUTIC PROCESS.

Interpretations that assist the patient to disconfirm his pathogenic beliefs and meet his goals are called pro-plan interventions. Pro-plan interventions focus on what *the patient is trying* to accomplish rather than what the therapist believes the patient should be doing or what the therapist thinks the patient is resisting.

Formulating a patient's plan involves constructing four components: (1) a patient's goals (usually unconscious), (2) the patient's *pathogenic beliefs* (also most often unconscious) which serve as obstacles to achieving the goals, (3) the tests used by the patient for confirming or disconfirming the pathogenic beliefs in relation to the analyst, and (4) the insights the patient can use to disconfirm the pathogenic beliefs.

*What* should the clinician interpret? The answer according to the Weiss system is to interpret what is pro-plan, whatever illuminates the patient's efforts to disconfirm his pathogenic beliefs and to attain his goals. The clinician's task is to help the patient in accord with the patient's unconscious plans to disprove his pathogenic beliefs and to pursue his goals. Often the only insights helpful and therapeutic to patients are those which help the patient disconfirm his pathogenic beliefs and attain his goals.

Weiss and his associates propose that psychopathology stems from unconscious pathogenic beliefs of dangers if the patient were to pursue certain important goals. Unconscious pathogenic beliefs are irrational and they involve feelings of guilt, shame, and anxiety. These are mainly formed in childhood out of traumatic relationships with parents and others.

Weiss's theory of therapy and technique follows directly from his concept of psychopathology. According to Weiss, patients enter psychoanalytic treatment with an unconscious plan that is a flexible strategy for testing these pathogenic beliefs in relation to the therapist in the hope of disconfirming them and using the therapist's interpretations for acquiring insight into them. Weiss views psychoanalytic treatment as a process in which the patient works to disconfirm his pathogenic beliefs with the help of the clinician.

Patients are powerfully motivated to disconfirm these beliefs because they are maladaptive and grim, and they produce much mental pain. Weiss conceptualizes the therapist's basic task as being one of helping patients to disprove their pathogenic beliefs, particularly their *unconscious* pathogenic beliefs, and to help patients pursue the goals that have been blocked by these overwhelmingly disturbing ideas.

Since the analyst's task is to help the patient go where the patient wants to go, the analyst should in each session infer the patient's unconscious plans for overcoming the patient's pathogenic ideas as well as attaining his goals by helping the patient disconfirm his pathogenic ideas, pursue his goals, and carry out his unconscious plans for solving his problems. For example, he should help a patient who is struggling to overcome his fear of competition to understand and master it.

Weiss and his associates reformulate a type of transference reaction as *testing*. In treatment, the patient works actively to disconfirm pathogenic beliefs by testing the therapist. In testing, patients unconsciously repeat with the analyst traumatic relationships with the significants. In *transference testing*, the patient reenacts a key relationship from childhood with the patient viewing himself as a child and the analyst playing the role of a parent or significant other. In *passive into active testing*, the patient repeats a traumatic relationship but reverses the roles.

The Plan concept enables the clinician to address, on a case-specific basis, all pathogenic beliefs that are transfered to a variety of important relationships, including, but not only, the relationship with the clinician. Thus the real therapeutic power of the Plan concept derives directly from the fact the Plan includes all of the patient's major pathogenic transferences, rather than only those directed explicitly toward the relationship with the therapist (Fetter et al. 1994).

Weiss and his associates (1986) carried out formal research studies which provide strong support for their hypotheses about the patient's unconscious plan, about the patient's testing of the therapist, and of the patient's use of the therapist's interpretations.

The psychoanalytic practitioner who is guided by the heuristic approach of making pro-plan interpretations shows greater respect for the patient's capacity to spell out his or her goals as well as inhibitions and blocks to achieving those goals, and what the analyst should do and not do for the goals to be accomplished. Pro-plan approaches exclude coercive or controlling methods. I doubt if it is possible to make a pro-plan interpretation that is at the same time indoctrinating or controlling.

When clinicians consistently make antiplan interventions, patients most often fail to improve, become worse, or stop treatment.

In his discussion about the pro-plan approach, Rosbrow (1993) concludes, "The profound respect for the patient's unconscious creativity and intentionality implicit in the plan concept meets the patient's legitimate demands to be treated as an equal, not a pupil or sick person" (p. 530).

## TOWARD AN INTERACTIONAL CONCEPT
## OF RESISTANCE

The argument made in what follows is opposed to the classical psychoanalytic concept of resistance which views it wholly from an intrapsychic perspective and which holds the patient responsible for whatever interferes with the therapeutic process. I recommend an interactional perspective on resistance which looks to both analyst and patient and their interactions for understanding whatever is impeding the analytic process of insight and personal growth.

## PRINCIPLE #4
## THE PATIENT'S DISAGREEMENT OR NONACCEPTANCE OF THE ANALYST'S INTERPRETATIONS DOES NOT CONSTITUTE RESISTANCE. AN INTERACTIONAL PERSPECTIVE ON RESISTANCE CONSIDERS RESISTANCE TO BE THE PRODUCT OF BOTH PARTIES OF THE ANALYTIC DIALOGUE.

One of the stereotyped approaches discussed by Peterfreund (1983) is one in which the analyst views the patient's failure to understand the analyst or to accept what he says as resistance.

All of the analysts or psychotherapists of the eleven cases mentioned in Part II tended to follow this stereotyped approach. The three clinicians (Drs. A., T. and X.) who were most similar to cult leaders were especially forceful and, unfortunately, successful in eliminating any disagreement or opposition of their patients to what they wanted them to believe.

There probably is no idea more embedded in the traditional psychoanalytic concept of the analyst as the arbiter of the patient's reality than the Freudian notion of resistance. Some analysts have abandoned the usage of "resistance" because of its judgmental connotations (for examples, see Giovacchini 1979 and Schafer 1992).

Kohut (1979) frequently dealt with Mr. Z.'s angry oppositional comments and his disagreements as resistances in the first analysis of Mr. Z. When the patient in a friendly and calm manner disagreed with Kohut's interpretation (i.e., "the working through of his own narcissistic delusions was now bearing fruit" [p. 5]), Kohut considered the patient's disagreement as a form of resistance. Kohut (1979) writes,

> . . . I even considered pointing out to the patient that by denying the effectiveness of my interpretation he was putting up a last-ditch resistance against the full acceptance of the delusional nature of his narcissistic demands. [p. 5]

Kohut's planned but unspoken interpretation in the above quotation is one of several places where he equates the patient's disagreement and nonacceptance of his interpretations as resistance. I do not mean to imply that a patient who disagrees or opposes something the analyst says or does may not also be manifesting resistance. What I do assert is that the criteria for determining the presence of resistance should not include merely the fact of the patient's disagreement or nonacceptance.

Though some clinicians would not define resistance as the patient's disagreement with the analyst, they do in practice deal with their patients' disagreement or opposition to interpretations as if they were "resistances" and something to overcome.

First Freud and later some other psychoanalysts have had a militaristic or adversarial orientation in both their clinical and theoretical writings on resistance. As Schafer (1992) has shown, Freud viewed resistance as an active and relentless, albeit unconscious force against which the analyst had to wage war. By resistance Freud meant a negative force that both the analyst and the patient struggled against. Though some mainstream Freudian analysts maintain Freud's position, others have begun to question the traditional theory and to propose important revisions (Gray 1994). Schafer (1992) asserts that from the beginning of his clinical work, Freud was under the influence of a countertransference attitude that introduced an *adversarial* orientation into both his theoretical writings and his clinical work with resistance.

A close reading of Freud's papers on technique reveals remnants of the pre-analytic Freud, emphasizing the aim of combating and banishing resistance instead of just understanding it. Freud's militaristic view of resistance was, I suspect, inextricably linked with, and probably an integral aspect of, the unanalyzed authoritarian tendencies in his personality. (For an excellent study of Freud's authoritarian tendencies, see Holt 1992.)

Schafer (1992) argues that the whole concept of resistance does, in fact, reflect the widespread and collective hostile countertransference responses of analysts, beginning with Freud, to the patient's image cast upon the analyst via projective identification of an uncaring, ungrateful, and critical individual whose interventions are simply accusations of badness and noncompliance.

Those who have studied and reviewed Freud's writings on the techniques and approaches toward the analysis of resistance and/ or defense agree that he retained to the end vestiges of his early hypnotic techniques and relied on the transference of authority to the analyst to overcome resistance by suggestion (Gray 1994, Newsome 1994, Ritvo 1994). Gray (1994) tells how Freud's technique of analyzing resistance is often still used today. He criticizes it on the grounds that it ". . . compromised precise conflict analysis by *using* the transferred superego authoritarian power in order to *persuade* the patient to respond to interpretation" (p. 132).

Gray (1994) tells of how Freud's technique for dealing with resistance and defense preserved the "*authoritarian* element in hypnosis." Freud's technique for analyzing defense and resistance throughout his analytic career was, according to Gray, "an authoritative approach that relies heavily on suggestion to influence rather than on analysis of the resistance" (p. 39). In Gray's opinion, the clinician's task should be one of *analyzing* and not one of *overcoming* resistance.

Freud's aggressive approach to resistance was amplified and made an explicit part of the analysis of character defenses and character "armor" in the writings of W. Reich (1933).

Freud's concept of resistance was used to rationalize his countertransference and his use of indoctrination methods to combat the patient's failures to communicate or change in the ways Freud expected. Freud's countertransference-based attitudes toward resistance led him to blame his patients without critically examining himself or his method (Schafer 1992).

In the following passage, Freud (1898) reveals his adversarial view of resistance as well as one of the directive methods he used to "conquer" it:

> Having diagnosed a case of neurasthenic neurosis with certainty . . . we are in a position to translate the symptomatology into aetiology; and then we may *boldly demand* confirmation of our suspicions from the patient. We must not be led astray by initial denials. If we keep firmly to what we have inferred, *we shall in the end conquer every resistance by emphasing the unshakable nature of our convictions.* [p. 269, italics added]

Freud (1898), I infer, anticipated some criticism for his aggressive methods for removing resistances by adding later in the same passage the following defense of his approach:

> The idea that one might, by one's insistence, cause a patient who is psychically normal to accuse himself falsely of sexual misdemeanors—such an idea may safely be disregarded as an imaginary danger. [p. 269]

Let us explicate and analyze Freud's indoctrination tactic expressed as "conquer every resistance by emphasizing the unshakable nature of our convictions" (p. 269). Talking enthusiastically and/or firmly in a way that conveys the speaker's deep conviction, certitude, and unswerving confidence in what he is saying is a well-known method used by cult leaders as well as charismatic religious and political leaders to gain followers. According to Langone (1993b) and others who have studied cults, speaking in this way is an important aspect of the ways cult leaders communicate with their submissive followers.

In a U.S. naval officer training school for midshipmen during World War II, I recall our overconfident instructors loudly telling us to always speak in a loud, confident voice and in a manner that absolutely did not betray any doubt or uncertainty. Gedo (1986) tells of Kohut's way of speaking with an "excess of certitude" (p. 121) as one of the important features of Kohut's charismatic manner of making interpretations to his patients.

My repeated readings of Freud's writings and especially his case studies of analyses he conducted (e.g., Dora, the Rat Man, and the Wolf Man) agree with a judgment made by Esterson (1993), who opined that Freud "almost invariably treated opposition to his interpretations as expressions of resistance" (p. 226). Rieff (1959) eloquently describes Freud's response to Dora's "resistance" in this passage: "Dora expressed disbelief, Freud applauds his own persistence; he speaks of using facts against the patient and reports how he overwhelmed Dora with interpretations, pounding away at argument, until 'Dora disputed the facts no longer'" (p. 82).

Freud (1937b) had a pessimistic view about the possibility of changing many of the elements contributing to resistance because he considered them to be constitutional. An interactional point of view is more optimistic because, as Sumners (1994) points out, "The fact that resistance is an object relationship makes it interpretable as a need to attach in a particular way. The object relations paradigm approaches resistance by investigating the patient's need to form *this* type of relationship with the analyst, rather than viewing it as a constitutional given" (p. 368).

Treating a patient's disagreement to interpretations as resistance is an occupational hazard for some candidates in psychoanalytic training. Edward Glover (1952), who was at one time Director of Research at the London Institute of Psychoanalysis, tells how difficult it is for candidates in training to defend their scientific integrity against the practice and theory of some of their analysts, for "according to his analyst the candidate's objections to interpretation rate as resistances" (p. 403).

With indoctrination approaches, a precondition for success is that the patient agree that his own perceptions and judgments of the analyst are distorted or at the least of secondary importance. Failure on the part of the patient to agree that his perceptions of the analyst are distorted and thus to validate the analyst's views of himself and of the patient is treated as a resistance. Stolorow and his associates (1994, p. 108) warn of the harmful effects on the patient when the patient feels compelled by his need for the analyst and because of the pressures placed on him by the analyst to substitute the analyst's subjective view of reality for his own.

### A Contemporary and Interactional Concept of Resistance

Psychoanalysis urgently needs a modified, nonadversarial concept of resistance, a view that does not blame the patient or rationalize the use of charisma or coercive methods for overcoming resistance. In the past decade, an interactional and nonadversarial concept of resistance is evolving in which resistance is conceptualized as the product of both parties of the analytic dialogue. Resistance is no longer seen as arising solely from sources from within the patient, but rather as emanating from the intersubjective field and as such gaining important contributions from both the therapist and the patient.

Boesky (1990) describes the interactional nature of the phenomena of resistance and how it is a collaborative creation of both patient and analyst. In the following passage, Schwaber (1983) highlights an interactional perspective on resistance.

> The understanding of the resistance has shifted from being viewed a phenomenon arising from internal pressures within the patient, from which the analyst as a blank screen could stand apart and observe, to that in which *the specificity of the analyst's contribution was seen as intrinsic to its own nature* [p. 381, italics added]. (For more about interactional aspects of resistance, see Langs 1981.)

## THE USE OF INDOCTRINATION METHODS PREVENTS THE FORMATION OF THE THERAPEUTIC ALLIANCE

### PRINCIPLE #5
### THE PSYCHOANALYST SHOULD FOSTER THE DEVELOPMENT AND SAFEGUARD THE MAINTENANCE OF A THERAPEUTIC ALLIANCE WITH THE PATIENT.

According to Peterfreund (1983) the failure to foster development of a therapeutic alliance is one of the characteristics of analyses conducted according to stereotyped principles.

In the first analysis of Mr Z, Kohut did little to facilitate and support the formation of a therapeutic alliance. Instead of fostering a process of analyzing the patient's false self (which, as Winnicott 1960 noted, is based on compliance) and providing an interpersonal environment conducive to the emergence and growth of a true self, Kohut's use of covert methods of interpersonal control reinforced the maintenance of Mr Z's fundamentally inauthentic false self.

The heuristic strategy of the analyst's facilitating active, independent, analytic work on the part of the patient has long been understood to be desirable and sometimes essential to establishing the therapeutic alliance. The emphasis on the creation and maintenance of a therapeutic or working alliance by analysts such as Meissner (1977) and Zetzel (1958) has probably persuaded more clinicians to appreciate the therapeutic value of treating patients as active collaborators and equal partners. This more egalitarian stance contrasts sharply with the authoritarian position of many in the earlier generations of psychoanalysts in this country and Europe.

The failure to foster a therapeutic alliance was a constant feature at most times in the cases reported in Chapters 4, 5, 6, 7, and 8. The repeated use of methods of indoctrination with those patients prevented the development of an ambience of cooperation and mutual respect. My studies of Freud's analyses of the Wolf Man and Dora in Chapters 6 and 7 suggest that his authoritarian attitudes and the use of covert methods of interpersonal control in those cases precluded the establishment or maintenance of a therapeutic alliance.

It is not possible for a viable and stable therapeutic alliance to develop in psychoanalytic treatment in which there is repeated use of indoctrination methods. The intimidating power of gaslighting, for example, depends on the clinician's attacks, however much concealed or subtle they may be, on the patient's judgments and perceptions.

A humane and heuristic approach to psychoanalysis requires the analyst's acceptance of the patient's psychic reality. The importance of this stance was eloquently presented by Stolorow and Atwood (1992) in the following passage:

> It cannot be emphasized too strongly that the analyst's acceptance of the validity of the patient's perceptual reality in the ongoing delineation of intrapsychic experience is of inestimable importance in establishing the therapeutic alliance. Any threat to the validity of perceptual reality constitutes a deadly threat to the self and to the organization of experience itself. When the analyst insists that the patient's perception is a secondary phenomenon distorted by primary forces, this, more than any other single factor, ushers in the conflictual transference-countertransference spirals that are so commonly described as resistance to analysis or negative transferences. [p. 94]

## VALIDATION—A PRAGMATIC METHOD FOR EVALUATING INTERVENTIONS

### PRINCIPLE #6
**ALL OF THE ANALYST'S INTERVENTIONS SHOULD BE VALIDATED BY AN EXAMINATION OF THE PATIENT'S RESPONSES TO AN INTERVENTION INCLUDING ESPECIALLY THEIR PRIMARY PROCESS DERIVATIVES AND CHANGES IN THEIR MODE OF COMMUNICATING.**

The failure to validate and test clinical hypotheses is one of the stereotyped approaches described by Peterfreund (1983). According to Peterfreund (1983), for clinicians who use stereotyped approaches, "the issue of evidence is of little importance" (p. 53).

A non-directive and heuristic approach to psychoanalytic treatment requires validation, a methodology for evaluating patients' responses to the analyst's interventions. The evaluation of the patient's responses to an interpretation provides the information necessary for modifying the analyst's hypotheses contained in his interpretation and for recognizing and correcting errors and misattunements.

Though learning to carry out a method of validation is one of the most important tools necessary for doing psychoanalysis and psychoanalytic psychotherapy, it is almost entirely neglected in most training institutions. There is a widespread misconception that validation stops when the clinician intervenes or interprets. Many clinicians have the false belief they have silently validated their proposed interpretation by weighing the evidence for and against it *before* they have intervened. Few understand the simple truth that validation comes from examining how the patient responds to an interpretation or other intervention. I am not referring here to the patient's conscious disagreement or agreement, since neither is usually helpful for disconfirming or confirming an analyst's interpretation. Validation requires evaluating the patient's unconscious communication and is achieved by an examination of the patient's primary process derivatives such as stories, images, affects, and the like, *following* the clinician's intervention. A process of validation provides necessary feedback information for the clinician to know not only what is going on in his therapy sessions, but to understand the effect he or she is consciously or unconsciously having on his patients. Where validation is not carried out, psychoanalytic treatment tends to become stalemated or corrupted into a process of indoctrination.

No interpretation no matter how brilliant, empathic, timely, tactful, or whatever is any good unless it does something constructive for the patient. We cannot know whether any intervention has a healing or constructive effect until *after* the intervention is carried out. Then the analyst can perform the process of validation by checking the patient's primary process derivatives and other responses as information needed for validating the therapist's interventions with the patient.

The regular use of validation provides a systematic way for using feedback information from the patient to correct and modify the analyst's hypotheses, attitudes, and approaches to the patient. In this way the analyst becomes conscious of the effects his actions and communications have had on the patient. The validation system I am proposing is both practical and pragmatic, and it is a powerful method for detecting the effects of directive methods. This method of validation may be viewed as a technique helpful for preventing and correcting indoctrination and stereotyped approaches as well as other antianalytic interventions.

Indoctrination methods usually require or at the least facilitate compliant responses from the patient and such responses (e.g., in the Wolf Man's analysis by Freud and Mr Z's first analysis with Kohut) can be used to provide a spurious and circular self-confirming confirmation of the therapist's hypotheses about the patient. The heuristic approach using the method of validation proposed in this chapter provides for correction and refutation. As Peterfreund (1983) indicates, built into stereotyped approaches are many circular self-confirming hypotheses in which refutation has no place.

Throughout the first analysis of Mr Z, Kohut (probably unconsciously) continued to try to impose his ideas on the patient, apparently without recognizing the necessity for confirming or disconfirming his basic clinical formulation or the various subsidiary hypotheses derived from the basic formulation. In fairness to Kohut and others who have used stereotyped or indoctrination approaches, I do not think this criticism applies only to them. In fact, this persistent deficiency in psychoanalytic practice has been more or less endemic among all psychoanalytic practitioners from Freud until the present time (Langs 1978b). In their review of the literature, Ramzy and Shevrin (1976) expressed astonishment at the paucity of psychoanalytic studies on the issue of confirmation. Their bibliography cites only a dozen articles by psychoanalysts on this subject in a period of fifty years.

The patient's emotional and cognitive responses to an intervention provide the crucial information needed for evaluating what the intervention meant to the patient, as well as the value and accuracy of the analyst's interventions. Muslin and Gill (1978) caution us, "The test of the validity of a transference interpretation lies in the patient's response to the interpretation. If the interpretation has not been made, one cannot be sure of its validity" (p. 320).

In the validation process, the psychoanalytic therapist should listen to primary process derivatives, to the mode of communication, to changes in the mode of communication, and to the verbal content of the patient's responses. A sharp and sudden change to a Type C (affectless) communication or to emotionally disturbed responses frequently means that the intervention was not attuned to the patient's affective states and/or that the intervention disrupted a selfobject transference.

Heuristic methods for evaluating, testing, and validating specific clinical hypotheses about what is going on both within the patient and in the analyst's interactions with the patient should be an integral part of the working skills and habits of any professional who professes to do psychoanalytic therapy.

An essential tool in the analyst's armamentarium is the silent reflective process of evaluating, comparing, and contrasting different hypotheses and weighing the clinical evidence for and against particular hypotheses. The process does not stop when the clinician makes an interpretation; in fact, the critical and decisive information comes *after* the analyst intervenes.

Clinicians should not place much stock in their patients' initial conscious confirmation, agreement, or disagreement following an interpretation. Rather, it is incumbent upon the clinician to especially examine their patient's unconscious cognitive and affective responses. Does the interpretation elicit new memories or primary process derivatives confirmatory of the analyst's clinical hypothesis? Did the intervention lead to new insights and understandings for the patient?

The central pragmatic maxim for evaluation of the clinician's interventions can be expressed as, "By their fruits shall you know them." If the therapist's intervention yields understanding and self-cohesion for the patient, then it deserves serious consideration. Contrariwise, if any intervention evokes disruption of a selfobject transference, fragmentation of the self, or a Type C mode of communicative response, then the therapist should investigate how and why his interventions triggered such untoward responses.

A sudden shift in the patient's mode of communication following any intervention should be carefully evaluated to determine what psychic effects the therapist's interventions have had on the patient. In my study of questioning (reported in Chapter 3), I attempted to validate the effects of questioning on patients by listening to their primary process derivatives after their therapists had asked a question.

At first, I was dismayed and frustrated in my attempts to detect affective responses and other primary process derivatives in response to a clinician's questioning because such responses were usually markedly diminished. Later I recognized that the questioning by clinicians had frequently evoked an abrupt switch in the patient's mode of communication from an A or B mode to an affectless Type C mode of communicating. This discovery along with others led to my conclusion about the generally negative effects of questioning on the therapeutic process.

I do not mean to imply that directive methods always or only trigger a switch in the patient to a Type C mode; sometimes they change to one of the other more defensive modes such as the Type B (projective identification) mode or Type D (inauthentic) mode. Most importantly, patients will almost always change their mode of communication in response to an intervention containing a covert method of interpersonal control or other violation of the psychoanalytic frame. In my experience, it is rare for a patient who is predominantly a Type A communicator to continue communicating in the A mode in response to an intervention containing a covert method of interpersonal control message.

An abrupt change toward one of the B, C, or D modes of communication may also indicate a derailment of the analytic process through a disruption of a selfobject transference (i.e., mirror, idealizing, or twin-ship). A major strategy advanced by self psychology is monitoring the patient-analyst relationship by being sensitive to even minor and temporary disruptions or interruptions in selfobject bonds between analyst and patient. Once such a disruption has been identified through the validation process, the analyst and patient in a cooperative inquiry can discuss what the analyst said or did to disrupt the selfobject transference as well as what personal meanings the disruptive intervention had for the patient.

As Weiss (1993) indicates, the analyst may check on whether he is working in accordance with the patient's unconscious plans by observing the patient's reactions to his interpretations and other interventions. The clinician may assume that he is on the right track if the patient reacts to his interventions by moving toward his unconscious goals. A reduction in anxiety and increased insight are usually positive signs tending to validate the analyst's intervention. By the same token, the clinician may in most instances assume that he is off course if the patient reacts to his interpretations by becoming more anxious and defensive, less insightful, less confident in the analyst, or if the treatment becomes stalemated.

## CONCLUDING COMMENTS

Along with Lakoff and Coyne (1993) and others, I urge changes in psychoanalytic and psychotherapeutic technique in the direction of a more egalitarian relationship, and one which limits the potential for the therapist's abuse of his or her powers. Psychoanalysis needs more emphasis, such as is contained in Weiss's Pro-Plan approach, on helping patients achieve a greater degree of autonomy. As patients become more skillful and courageous in participating in the treatment process, they should be entrusted with greater responsibility and freedom for making their own interpretations and reconstructions as well as devising operative metaphors and narratives.

We need an ideal for psychoanalytic treatment which emphasizes a more fully democratic ambience and in which patient and therapist from the beginning understand the need for both to take responsibility for the discourse in order to facilitate the patient's insight and recovery. I hope this book helps the cause supported by many psychoanalysts and psychotherapists of advancing a less authoritarian and more egalitarian approach to psychoanalytic treatment.

# References

Adorno, T. W., Frenkel-Brunswick, E., Levinson, D. J., and Sanford, R. N. (1950). *The Authoritarian Personality*. New York: Harper.

Arlow, J. (1966). Depersonalization and derealization. In *Psychoanalysis: A General Psychology*, ed. R. M. Loewenstein, L. M. Newman, M. Schur, and A. J. Solnit, pp.456–478. New York: International Universities Press.

Bach, G. R., and Goldberg, H. (1974). *Creative Aggression*. New York: Doubleday.

Baranger, W., and Baranger, M. (1966). Insight in the analytic situation. In *Psychoanalysis in the Americas*, ed. R. E. Litman, pp. 56–72. New York: International Universities Press.

Barton, R., and Whitehead, T. A. (1960). The gaslight phenomenon. *Lancet* 1:1258–1260.

Bateson, G. (1972). *Steps to an Ecology of Mind*. New York: Ballantine.

Bateson, G., Jackson, D. D., Haley, J., and Weakland, J. (1956). Toward a theory of schizophrenia. *Behavioral Science* 1:251–269.

Benson, S. (1991). Why I quit practicing law. *Newsweek* November 4, p. 10.

Bion, W. R. (1959a). *Experiences in Groups*. New York: Basic Books.

——— (1959b). Attacks on linking. *International Journal of Psycho-Analysis* 40:308–315.

———— (1962). *Learning From Experience*. London: Heinemann.

———— (1985). *All My Sins Remembered: Another Part of a Life*. Abingdon, England: Fleetwood.

Bloom, V. (1991). The Case of Dr. Renee Richards. *Academy Forum* 35:11–12.

Blos, P. (1962). *On Adolescence*. New York: Free Press.

Blum, H. P. (1974). The borderline childhood of the Wolf Man. *Journal of the American Psychoanalytic Association* 22:721–742.

Boesky, D. (1989). The questions and curiosity of the psychoanalyst. *Journal of the American Psychoanalytic Association* 37:579–604.

———— (1990). The psychoanalytic process and its components. *Psychoanalytic Quarterly* 59:550–584.

Bowers, K. S. (1984). On being unconsciously influenced and informed. In *The Unconscious Reconsidered*, ed. K. S. Bowers and D. Meichenbaum. New York: Wiley.

Boyer, L. B. and Giovacchini, P. L. (1967). *Psychoanalytic Treatment of Schizophrenia and Characterological Disorders*. New York: Science House.

Brunswick, R. M. (1928). A supplement to Freud's "History of an Infantile Neurosis." In *The Wolf-Man by the Wolf Man*, ed. M. Gardner, pp. 263–307. New York: Basic Books, 1971.

Burnham, D., Gladstone, A. I., and Gibson, R. W. (1969). *Schizophrenia and the Need-Fear Dilemma*. New York: International Universities Press.

Busch, F. (1986). The occasional questions in psychoanalytic assessment. *International Review of Psychoanalysis* 13:453–462.

Calef, V., and Weinshel, E. M. (1981). Some clinical consequences of introjection: gaslighting. *Psychoanalytic Quarterly* 50:44–66.

Carter, J. (1989). *Nasty People*. New York: Dorset.

Cawthra, T. (1987). Imposed psychosis—a case variant of the gaslight phenomenon. *British Journal of Psychiatry* 150:553–556.

Chodorow, N. J. (1989). *Feminism and Psychoanalytic Theory*. New Haven: Yale University Press.

Cialdini, R. B. (1993). *Influence: Science and Practice*. New York: HarperCollins.

Cocks, G. (1994). *The Curve of Life—Correspondence of Heinz Kohut 1923–1981*. Chicago: University of Chicago Press.

Crews, F. (1993). The Unknown Freud. *New York Review of Books* XL:55–66.

Daly, M. (1978). *Gyn/Ecology*. Boston: Free Press.

Decker, H. S. (1991). *Freud, Dora, and Vienna 1900*. New York: Free Press.

Deutsch, F., and Murphy, W. F. (1955). *The Clinical Interview Vol. I & II*. New York: International Universities Press.

—— (1957). A footnote to Freud's "Fragment of an analysis of a case of hysteria." *Psychoanalytic Quarterly* 26:159–167.

Dewald, P. A. (1972). *The Psychoanalytic Process*. New York: Basic Books.

Dorpat, T. L. (1976). Structural conflict and object relations conflict. *Journal of the American Psychoanalytic Association* 24:855–874.

—— (1978–1979). Introjection and the idealizing transference. *Journal of Psychoanalytic Psychotherapy* 7:21–53.

—— (1983). Denial, defect, symptom formation—and construction. *Psychoanalytic Inquiry* 3:223–253.

—— (1984). The technique of questioning. In *Listening and Interpreting: The Challenge of the Work of Robert Langs*, ed. J. Raney, pp. 55–74. New York: Jason Aronson.

—— (1985). *Denial and Defense in the Therapeutic Situation*. New York: Jason Aronson.

—— (1987a). Positive freedom and psychoanalysis. *Dynamic Psychotherapy* 5:99–116.

—— (1987b). A new look at denial and defense. *The Annual of Psychotherapy* 15:23–47.

—— (1989a). Abusive practices in medical training. *King County Medical Society Bulletin* 68:20,26.

—— (1989b). An object relations perspective on masochism. In *Essential Papers on Character Neurosis and Treatment*, ed. R. F. Lax, pp. 204–228. New York: University Press.

—— (1991a). Primary process meaning analysis. *The Society for Psychoanalytic Psychotherapy Bulletin* 6:3–11.

—— (1991b). The primary process revisited. *The Society for Psychoanalytic Psychotherapy Bulletin* 6:5–22.

—— (1991c). On the use of questioning as a psychoanalytic technique. *Psychoanalysis and Psychotherapy* 9:106–113.

—— (1992). A note on the interactional perspective. *Psychoanalytic Psychotherapy Review* 3:13.

—— (1993a). On gaslighting: how to dominate others without their knowledge or consent. *Psychoanalytic Psychotherapy Review* 4:7–14.

—— (1993b). The double-whammy—a species of gaslighting. *Newsletter of the North West Alliance for Psychoanalytic Study* September:4–5.

———— (1993c). On gaslighting: the double whammy. *Psychoanalytic Psychotherapy Review* 4:7–14.

———— (1993d). The type C mode of communication—an interactional perspective. *The International Journal of Communicative Psychoanalysis and Psychotherapy* 8:47–54.

———— (1994a). On inauthentic communication and interactional modes of defense. *Psychoanalytic Psychotherapy Review* 5:25–35.

———— (1994b). Foreword to *Doing Supervision and Being Supervised* by R. Langs, pp. vii–xii. London: Karnac.

———— (1994c). On the double whammy and gaslighting. *Psychoanalysis and Psychotherapy* 11:91–96.

———— (1994d). Clinical comparisons between psychoanalytic and management approaches. *Psychoanalytic Psychotherapy Review* 5:91–104.

———— (1994e). The double-whammy—a species of gaslighting. *Psychoanalytic Psychotherapy Review* 5:130.

———— (in press-a). The Wolf Man's analysis—an interactional perspective. *The Psychoanalytic Review*.

———— (in press-b). An interactional perspective on Freud's analysis of Dora. *International Journal of Communicative Psychoanalysis* 10(1–2).

Dorpat, T. L., and Miller, M. L. (1992). *Clinical Interaction and the Analysis of Meaning: A New Psychoanalytic Theory*. Hillsdale, NJ: Analytic Press.

———— (1994). Primary process meaning analysis. *Contemporary Psychoanalysis* 30:201–212.

Eissler, K. R. (1953). The effect of the structure of the ego on psychoanalytic technique. *Journal of the American Psychoanalytic Association* 1:104–143.

Elgin, S. H. (1980). *The Gentle Art of Verbal Self Defense*. New York: Dorset.

Erikson, E. H. (1962). Reality and actuality. *Journal of the American Psychoanalytic Association* 10:451–474.

Esterson, A. (1993). *Seductive Mirages—An Exploration of the Work of Sigmund Freud*. Chicago: Open Court.

Evans, P. (1992). *The Verbally Abusive Relationship*. Holbrook, MA: Bob Adams, Inc.

Federn, P. (1952). *Ego Psychology and the Psychoses*. New York: Basic Books.

Feiner, A., and Levenson, E. (1968–1969). The compassionate sacrifice: an exploration of a metaphor. *The Psychoanalytic Review* 55:552–573.

Fetter, P. B., Bucci, W., Broitman, J., et al. (1994). How the plan relates to the concept of transference. *Psychotherapy Research* 4(1):58–72.

Fish, S. (1989). Withholding the missing portion: psychoanalysis and rhetoric. In *The Trial(s) of Psychoanalysis*, ed. F. Meltzer, pp. 183–211. Chicago: University of Chicago Press.

Flarsheim, A. (1972). Treatability. In *Tactics and Techniques in Psychoanalytic Therapy*, ed. P. Giovacchini, vol. I, pp. 113–131. New York: Jason Aronson.

Flax, J. (1990). *Thinking Fragments—Psychoanalysis, Feminism, and Postmodernism in the Contemporary West*. Berkeley: University of California Press.

Freud, S. (1898). Sexuality in the aetiology of the neuroses. *Standard Edition* 3:261–287.

——— (1905). Fragment of an analysis of a case of hysteria. *Standard Edition* 7:3–122.

——— (1918). From the history of an infantile neurosis. *Standard Edition* 17:7–122.

——— (1937a). Construction in analysis. *Standard Edition* 23:256–288.

——— (1937b). Analysis terminable and interminable. *Standard Edition* 23:216–255.

Fromm, E. (1941). *Escape from Freedom*. New York: Avon Books.

——— (1960). Foreword to *Summerhill—A Radical Approach to Child Rearing* by A. S. Neill. New York: Hart.

Galanti, G. (1993). Reflections on "Brainwashing." In *Recovery From Cults*, ed. M. D. Langone, pp. 85–103. New York: Norton.

Gallop, J. (1982). Keys to Dora. In *The Daughter's Seduction: Feminism and Psychoanalysis*, ed. J. Gallop, Chapter 9. Ithaca, NY: Cornell University Press.

Gardner, M., ed. (1971). *The Wolf-Man by the Wolf-Man*. New York: Basic Books.

Gass, G. Z., and Nichols, W. C. (1988). Gaslighting: a marital syndrome. *Contemporary Family Therapy* 10:3–16.

Gedo, J. (1986). *Conceptual Issues in Psychoanalysis*. Hillsdale, NJ: Analytic Press.

Giovacchini, P. (1979). *Treatment of Primitive Mental States*. New York: Aronson.

Glenn, J. (1980). Freud's adolescent patients: Katherina, Dora, and "the homosexual woman." In *Freud and His Patients*, ed. M. Kanzer and J. Glenn, pp. 23–47. New York: Jason Aronson.

Glover, E. (1952). Research methods in psychoanalysis. *International Journal of Psycho-Analysis* 33:404–409.

———— (1955). *The Technique of Psycho-analysis*. New York: International Universities Press.

Goldberg, A. (1980). Letter to the editor. *International Journal of Psycho-Analysis* 61:91–92.

Gray, P. (1994). *The Ego and Analysis of Defense*. Northvale, NJ: Jason Aronson.

Greenberg, J. (1991). *Oedipus and Beyond—A Clinical Theory*. Cambridge, MA: Harvard University Press.

Greenson, R. R. (1967). *The Technique and Practice of Psychoanalysis*. New York: International Universities Press.

Gruen, A. (1988). *The Betrayal of the Self: The Fear of Autonomy in Men and Women*. New York: Grove.

Haley, J. (1969). *The Power Tactics of Jesus Christ and Other Essays*. New York: Avon Books.

Hamilton, P. (1939). *Angel Street*. New York: Samuel French, 1942.

Hertz, N. (1983). Dora's secrets, Freud's techniques. *Diacritics* Spring, pp. 65–76.

Hirsch, I. (1993). Countertransference enactments and some causes related to external factors in the analytic life. *Psychoanalytic Dialogues* 3:343–366.

———— (1994). Countertransference, love and theoretical model. *Psychoanalytic Dialogues* 4:171–192.

Hochman, J. (1984). Iatrogenic symptoms associated with a therapy cult: examination of an extinct "New Psychotherapy" with respect to psychiatric deterioration and "Brainwashing". *Psychiatry* 47:366–377.

Hoffer, E. (1951). *The True Believer*. New York: Harper and Brothers.

Hollender, M. H. (1965). *The Practice of Psychoanalytic Psychotherapy*. New York: Grune & Stratton.

Holt, R. R. (1992). Freud's parental identifications as a source of some contradictions within psychoanalysis. In *Freud and the History of Psychoanalysis*, ed. T. Gelfano and J. Kerr, pp. 1–28. Hillsdale, NJ: Analytic Press.

Janis, I. (1982). *Groupthink*. Boston: Houghton Mifflin.

Jennings, J. L. (1986). The revival of "Dora": Advances in psychoanalytic theory and technique. *Journal of the American Psychoanalytic Association* 34:607–635.

Kahane, C. (1985). Why Dora now? (Introduction, Part 2.) In *In Dora's Case*, ed. C. Bernheimer and C. Kahane, pp. 19–32. New York: Columbia University Press.

Kanzer, M., and Glenn, J. (1980). Integrative memory. In *Freud and His Patients*, ed. M. Kanzer and J. Glenn, pp. 398–405. New York: Jason Aronson.

Kernberg, O. (1972). A critique of the Kleinian School. In *Tactics and Techniques in Psychoanalytic Therapies, Vol. I*, ed. P. Giovacchini, pp. 62–93. New York: Science House.

King, K. R., and Dorpat, T. L. (1992). Daddy's girl: an interactional perspective on the transference of defense in the psychoanalysis of a case of father–daughter incest. In *Psychoanalytic Perspectives on Women*, ed. E. Siegel, pp. 63–88. New York: Brunner/Mazel.

Klein, M. (1961). *Narrative of a Child Analysis*. London: Hogarth.

Kohut, H. (1971). *The Analysis of the Self*. New York: International Universities Press.

———— (1979). The two analyses of Mr Z. *International Journal of Psycho-Analysis* 60:3–27.

———— (1984). *How Does Analysis Cure?* Chicago: University of Chicago Press.

Lacan, J. (1956). Réponse au commentaire de J. Hyppolite sur la 'Verneinung'. In *Ecrits*, pp. 38–47. Paris: Seuil, 1966.

Laing, R. D. (1961). *Self and Others*. New York: Pantheon Books.

Lakoff, R. T., and Coyne, J. C. (1993). *Father Knows Best: The Use and Abuse of Power in Freud's Case of Dora*. New York: Teachers College Press.

Langone, M. D. (1993a). *Recovery From Cults*. New York: Norton.

———— (1993b). Helping cult victims: historical backgrounds. In *Recovery From Cults*, pp. 22–47. New York: Norton.

Langs, R. (1976a). *The Bipersonal Field*. New York: Jason Aronson.

———— (1976b). The misalliance in Freud's case histories. I. The case of Dora. *International Journal of Psychoanalytic Psychotherapy* 2:411–431.

———— (1978a). *The Listening Process*. New York: Jason Aronson.

———— (1978b). *Technique in Transition*. New York: Jason Aronson.

———— (1979a). *The Therapeutic Environment*. New York: Jason Aronson.

———— (1979b). *The Supervisory Experience*. New York: Jason Aronson.

———— (1980a). *Interactions: The Realm of Transference and Countertransference*. New York: Jason Aronson.

———— (1980b). The misalliance dimension in the case of the Wolf Man. In *Freud and His Patients*, ed. M. Kanzer and J. Glenn, pp. 372–385. New York: Jason Aronson.

———— (1980c). The misalliance dimension in the case of Dora. In *Freud* and His Patients, ed. M. Kanzer and J. Glenn, pp. 58–71. New York: Jason Aronson.

———— (1981). Resistances and Interventions. New York: Jason Aronson.

———— (1982a). Psychotherapy: A Basic Text. New York: Jason Aronson.

———— (1982b). The Psychotherapeutic Conspiracy. New York: Jason Aronson.

Lerner, H. G. (1992). The Dance of Deception: Pretending and Truth-Telling in Womens's Lives. New York: Harper Collins.

Lichtman, R. (1982). The Production of Desire: The Integration of Psychoanalysis and Marxist Theory. New York: Free Press.

Lifton, R. J. (1961). Thought Reform and the Psychology of Totalism: A Study of "Brainwashing". New York: Norton.

Linn, D. (1994). Freud in practice, 1907–1939, and the role of the analyst. An audio tape recording of a talk presented at the Annual Meeting of the American Academy of Psychoanalysis in Philadelphia, May. Audio Tape 13-935-94A.

Lomas, P. (1987). The Limits of Interpretation. Northvale, NJ: Jason Aronson.

Lund, C. A., and Gardiner, A. Q. (1977). The gaslight phenomenon—an institutional variant. British Journal of Psychiatry 131:533–534.

Mack Brunswick, R. (1928). A supplement to Freud's "History of an infantile neurosis." International Journal of Psycho-Analysis 9:439–476.

Maddi, S. (1974). The victimization of Dora. Psychology Today September, pp. 91–100.

Magid, B. (1992). Self psychology meets the wolf-man. Psychoanalysis and Psychotherapy 10:178–198.

Mahoney, P. (1984). Cries of the Wolf-Man. New York: International Universities Press.

Marcus, S. (1975). Freud and Dora: story, history, case-history. In Representations, pp. 67–94. New York: Random House.

Meissner, W. W. (1977). The Wolf Man and the paranoid. The Annual of Psychoanalysis 5:23–74.

Menninger, K. A., and Holzman, P. S. (1973). Theory of Psychoanalytic Technique, second edition. New York: Basic Books.

Meyerson, P. (1981). The nature of the transactions that occur in other than classical analysis. International Review of Psycho-Analysis 8:173–189.

Mitchell, S. (1993). Hope and Dread in Psychoanalysis. New York: Basic Books.

Modell, A. H. (1984). *Psychoanalysis in a New Context*. New York: International Universities Press.

Muller, J. P. (1989). Lacan and Kohut: from imaginary to symbiotic identification in the case of Mr. Z. In *Self Psychology—Comparisons and Contrasts*, ed. D. W. Detrich and S. P. Detrich, pp. 275–291. Hillsdale, NJ: Analytic Press.

Muslin, H., and Gill, M. (1978). Transference in the Dora case. *Journal of the American Psychoanalytic Association* 26:311–328.

Newsome, M. (1994). The legacy of hypnosis: Freud and subjectivity. In *Progress in Self Psychology*, ed. A. Goldberg, pp. 115–129. Hillsdale, NJ: Analytic Press.

Nisbett, R., and Ross, L. (1980). *Human Inference*. Englewood Cliffs, NJ: Prentice-Hall.

Nisbett, R., and Wilson, N. (1977). Telling more than we can know: verbal reports on mental process. *Psychology Review* 84: 231–259.

Nuetzel, J. (1993). Report on panel "Learning from unsuccessful cases." *Journal of the American Psychoanalytic Association* 41: 743–754.

Obholzer, K. (1982). *The Wolf-Man Sixty Years Later*. New York: Continuum.

Offenkrantz, W., and Tobin, A. (1973). Problems of the therapeutic alliance: Freud and the Wolf-Man. *International Journal of Psycho-Analysis* 54:75–78.

Ogden, T. (1982). *Projective Identification and Psychotherapeutic Technique*. New York: Jason Aronson.

Olinick, S. L. (1954). Some considerations on the use of questioning as a psychoanalytic technique. *Journal of the American Psychoanalytic Association* 2:57–66.

——— (1957). Questioning and pain, truth and negation. *Journal of the American Psychoanalytic Association* 5:302–304.

——— (1980). *The Psychotherapeutic Instrument*. New York: Jason Aronson.

Oremland, J. P. (1991). *Interpretation and Interaction—Psychoanalysis or Psychotherapy*. Hillsdale, NJ: Analytic Press.

Ornstein, P. (1981). The bipolar self and the psychoanalytic treatment process: clinical-theoretical considerations. *Journal of the American Psychoanalytic Association* 29:353–376.

——— (1993). Did Freud understand Dora? In *Freud's Case Studies: Self-Psychological Perspectives*, ed. B. Magid, pp. 31–85. Hillsdale, NJ: Analytic Press.

Ostow, M. (1979). Letter to the editor. *International Journal of Psycho-Analysis* 60:531–532.

Paul, I. H. (1989). *The Craft of Psychotherapy*. Northvale, NJ: Jason Aronson.

Peterfreund, E. (1983). *The Process of Psychoanalytic Therapy—Models and Strategies*. Hillsdale, NJ: Analytic Press.

Pulver, S. E. (1987). How theory shapes technique: perspectives on a clinical study. *Psychoanalytic Inquiry* 7: 147–165.

Ramas, M. (1980). Freud's Dora, Dora's hysteria: the negation of a woman's rebellion. *Feminist Studies* 6:472–510.

Ramzy, I., and Shevrin, H. (1976). The nature of the inference process in psychoanalytic interpretation: A critical review of the literature. *International Review of Psycho-Analysis* 57:151–160.

Rangell, L. (1981). From insight to change. *Journal of the American Psychoanalytic Association* 29:119–142.

Reich, W. (1933). *Character Analysis*. New York: Orgone Institute Press, 1945.

Reiss, D. (1981). *The Family's Construction of Reality*. Cambridge: Harvard University Press.

Richards, R. (1983). *Second Serve*. New York: Stein and Day.

Rieff, P. (1959). *Freud: The Mind of a Moralist*. London: Gollancz.

——— (1963). Introduction. In *Dora, An Analysis of a Case of Hysteria*, trans, J. Riviere. New York: Collier.

Ritvo, S. (1994). Preface to *The Ego and Analysis of Defense* by P. Gray. Northvale, NJ: Jason Aronson.

Ross, L., and Nisbett, R. E. (1991). *The Person and the Situation: Perspectives of Social Psychology*. New York: McGraw-Hill.

Rosbrow, T. (1993). Significance of the unconscious plan for psychoanalytic theory. *Psychoanalytic Psychology* 10:515–532.

Roustang, F. (1983). *Psychoanalysis Never Lets Go*. Baltimore: Johns Hopkins Press.

Sachs, D. M. (1991). Book review of *Panic: The Course of a Psychoanalysis* by T. Vanggaard. *International Journal of Psycho-Analysis* 72:748–750.

Schafer, R. (1992). The "Resistance" and Freud's countertransference. *The Association for Psychoanalytic Medicine Bulletin* 31:54–57.

Scharfman, M. A. (1980). Further reflections on Dora. In *Freud and His Patients*, ed. M. Kanzer and J. Glenn, pp. 48–57. New York: Jason Aronson.

Schwaber, E. (1983). Psychoanalytic listening and psychic reality. *International Review of Psycho-Analysis* 10: 379–392.

Searles, H. F. (1959). The effort to drive the other person crazy: an element in the aetiology and psychotherapy of schizophrenia. *British Journal of Medical Psychology* 32:1–13.

———— (1965). *Collected Papers on Schizophrenia and Related Subjects.* New York: International Universities Press.

———— (1975). The patient as therapist. In *Tactics and Techniques in Psychoanalytic Treatment—Countertransference Aspects*, ed. P. Giovacchini, pp. 95–151. New York: Jason Aronson.

———— (1984). The role of the analyst's facial expressions in psychoanalysis and psychoanalytic therapy. In *International Journal of Psychoanalytic Psychotherapy, Vol. 10*, ed. R. Langs, pp. 47–53. New York: Jason Aronson.

Silverman, M. (1987). Clinical material. *Psychoanalytic Inquiry* 7:147–165.

Singer, M. T. (1995). *Cults in Our Midst—The Hidden Meaning in Our Everyday Lives.* San Francisco: Jossey-Bass.

Sprengnether, M. (1985). Enforcing Oedipus: Freud and Dora. In *In Dora's Case*, ed. C. Bernheimer and C. Kahane, pp. 254–275. New York: Columbia University Press.

Spezzano, C. (1993). *Affect in Psychoanalysis: A Clinical Synthesis.* Hillsdale, NJ: Analytic Press.

Stierlin, H. (1976). The dynamics of owning and disowning. *Family Process* 15:277–288.

Stolorow, R. D., Brandchaft, B., and Atwood, G. E. (1987). *Psychoanalytic Treatment—An Intersubjective Approach.* Hillsdale, NJ: Analytic Press.

Stolorow, R. D., and Atwood, G. E. (1992). *Contexts of Being: The Intersubjective Foundations of Psychological Life.* Hillsdale, NJ: Analytic Press.

Stolorow, R., Atwood, G., and Brandchaft, B., eds., (1994). *The Intersubjective Perspective.* Northvale, NJ: Jason Aronson.

Sumners, F. (1994). *Object Relations and Psychopathology—A Comprehensive Text.* Hillsdale, NJ: Analytic Press.

Tannen, D. (1990). *You Just Don't Understand.* New York: William Morrow.

Temerlin, M. D., and Temerlin, J. W. (1982). Psychotherapy cults: an iatrogenic perversion. *Psychotherapy: Theory, Research & Practice* 19:131–141.

Terkel, S. (1967). *Division Street: America.* New York: Pantheon.

Van Fleet, J. K. (1983). *Twenty-five Steps to Power and Mastery Over People.* West Nyack, NY: Parker Publishing.

Vanggaard, T. (1989). *Panic: The Course of a Psychoanalysis.* New York: Norton.

Varela, J. (1971). *Psychological Solutions to Social Problems: An Introduction to Social Technology*. New York: Academic Press.

Videman, S. (1977). *Le Céleste et le Sublunaise*. Paris: Presses Universitaires de France.

Waelder, R. (1951). The structure of paranoid ideas. *International Journal of Psycho-Analysis* 32:167–177.

Weiss, J. (1993). *How Psychotherapy Works*. New York: Guilford.

Weiss, J., Sampson, H., and the Mount Zion Psychotherapy Research Group (1986). The psychoanalytic process: theory, clinical observation, and empirical research. New York: Guilford.

Winnicott, D. W. (1960). Ego distortion in terms of true and false self. In *The Maturational Processes and the Facilitating Environment*, pp. 140–152. New York: International Universities Press, 1965.

Zetzel, E. R. (1958). Therapeutic alliance in the analysis of hysteria. In *The Capacity for Emotional Growth*, pp. 182–196. New York: International Universities Press, 1970.

Zimbardo, P., and Andersen, S. (1993). Understanding mind control: exotic and mundane mental manipulations. In *Recovery From Cults*, ed. M. D. Langone, pp. 104–125. New York: Norton.

# Credits

The author gratefully acknowledges permission to quote material from the following sources:

"On Gaslighting: How to Dominate Others without Their Knowledge or Consent," by Theo. L. Dorpat, in *Psychoanalytic Psychotherapy Review* 4:7–14. Copyright © 1993 International Universities Press.

"The Double-Whammy—A Species of Gaslighting," by Theo. L. Dorpat, in *Psychoanalytic Psychotherapy Review* 5:130. Copyright © 1994 International Universities Press.

"Clinical Comparisons between Psychoanalytic and Management Approaches," by Theo. L. Dorpat, in *Psychoanalytic Psychotherapy Review* 5:91–104. Copyright © 1994 International Universities Press.

"The Technique of Questioning," in Listening and Interpreting: The Challenge of the Work of Robert Langs, edited by J. Raney, pp. 55–74. Copyright © 1984 Jason Aronson Inc.

"The Wolf Man's Analysis—An Interactional Perspective," by Theo. L. Dorpat, in press. *The Psychoanalytic Review*. Copyright © *The Psychoanalytic Review*.

# Index